Contents

Preface

CHERIoT Concepts 11

The RTOS Core 27

Getting started writing CHERIoT software 37

Contents

Contents

Preface

This is the first edition of the CHERIoT Programmers' Guide. This book is intended as a companion to the CHERIoT Platform. The latest draft is published on the CHERIoT web site[1]. The online version will include any errata from the first edition.

1. Acknowledgements

A few months ago, this book was less than half its current length. Completing this was supported by the UKRI Discribe Hub+, funded through the Economic and Social Research Council [ES/V003666/1].

The version that you are now reading has had some significant improvements in accuracy and structure thanks to some great feedback from technical reviewers Phil Day, Richard Edgar, Adam Finney, Hugo McNally. It was then copyedited by Amanda Robinson, who has done an excellent job in fixing my typos, missing words, baroque sentence structures and all of the places where I just forgot that sentences needed finishing. Any remaining errors, omissions, or poor explanations are my responsibility.

The cats on the cover represent safe, secure, compartmentalisation (what is safer or more secure than a cat in a box?). Each cat is in a separate, isolated, compartment, in the model for which CHERIoT was designed.

The cat photos were contributed by some wonderful people from the Fediverse. Starting at the top left, numbered left to right then top to bottom, the photo credits are:

1, 3, 5, 10:
> Photographer: James (@chongliss@mastodon.ie), Cats: Jiji (1), Luna (3, 5), and Felix (10).

2, 11:
> Photographer: Cassian Lodge (@cassolotl@eldritch.cafe), Cat: Rosa.

4:
> Photographer: Marin Benčević (@marinbenc@sigmoid.social)

6:
> Photographer: Asta Halkjær From (@ahfrom@fedi.ahfrom.synology.me), Cat: Betty Rambo.

7:
> Photographer: Victor Zverovich (@vitaut@mastodon.social), Cat: Luna (no relation).

---

1. https://cheriot.org/book

8:

> Photographer: Michael McWilliams (@MichaelMcWilliams@mas.to), Cat: Scotchy.

9:

> Photographer: jarkman (@jarkman@chaos.social), Cat: Jack.

12:

> Photographer: Isaac Freund (@ifreund@hachyderm.io), Cat: Marzipan.

No generative AI was used in the creation of this image. No artist's work was appropriated without their consent.

2. Reading and using examples

Code listings in this book specify the file that they come from in the book's examples. You can find the examples in a stand-alone examples git repository on GitHub[2].

You can clone this repository with the following command:

```
$ git clone --branch first-edition
  --recursive
  https://github.com/CHERIoT-Platform/book-examples
Cloning into 'book-examples'...
```

This will clone exactly the version used in the first edition. If you check out the first-edition-update branch, then you will have a version that may not exactly match the listings in the book, but which has been updated to work with a newer version of the RTOS. Any differences in this branch will be listed in the errata section of the online edition of the book.

The examples are provided as a stand-alone repository containing a snapshot of the RTOS and network stack each as a *git submodule*. It provides a *development container* configuration (discussed in more detail in Section 3.2) that provides all of the tools required to build the examples. This is discussed in more detail in Chapter 3.

Example code in the book is pulled in from complete source files to ensure that everything that you see as a listing is valid code that will, at the very least, compile (and hopefully work). You should be able to build and run all of the example code yourself.

Listings have line numbers on the left. These are the line numbers in the file, so you can read the extracted listings in context.

2.   https://github.com/CHERIoT-Platform/book-examples

When you read the files that contain these listings, you will see comments like `// something#begin` and `// something#end`. These are the markers for regions extracted and used in the book.

Syntax highlighting for this book is done by libclang (for C/C++) or TreeSitter (for Lua and Rego).

Chapter 1.
CHERIoT Concepts

The CHERIoT platform is an embedded environment that provides a number of low-level features via a mixture of hardware and software features.

1.1. Introducing memory safety

Memory in a modern computer is usually arranged as a flat set of storage locations. At the lowest level, you may do a load or store operation on addresses in this space. Every location in memory is identified by a number and locations are treated as adjacent if their addresses are one apart. When you start a process or a virtual machine, this abstraction is preserved and *virtual memory* lets you pretend that you have a (very large) flat address space.

When you use a programming language that's higher-level than assembly, memory looks a little bit different. Rather than being a flat set of one-byte storage locations, the language exposes memory as *objects*. An object may be something simple, such as an integer, or something large, such as an array of complex structures. On most hardware, this is purely a software abstraction. You may specify that you have an on-stack array of twelve integers, or a heap allocation containing a buffer for a network packet, but the compiled program will use numbers referring to locations in a flat memory space to represent these locations.

The term *memory safety* applies to a variety of properties. It is somewhat difficult to define because the problems arise when you *don't* have memory safety. When you do have memory safety, things simply work as you expect them to. It's therefore easier to think about *memory unsafety*.

Memory safety is usually split into two subcategories: *temporal memory safety* and *spatial memory safety*. When you don't have spatial memory safety, you can think that you are accessing one object, but you may be accessing an adjacent one. For example, if you allocate a 12-byte on-stack buffer and then try to write 16 bytes into it, a memory-safe system will raise some kind of error. An unsafe system will instead let you write four bytes over some adjacent location, possibly a return address. This is the simplest example of how a *buffer overflow* can lead to arbitrary-code execution. If an attacker can overwrite the return address on the stack then they can cause the function to return somewhere else. They can chain several of these together to build rich exploits.

When you don't have temporal memory safety (sometimes called *lifetime safety*) it is possible to access (read or write) an object after its lifetime ends. In most language implementations, memory is *reused* and so accessing an object after its lifetime really means accessing an unrelated object that happens to be stored at the same place in memory.

Languages such as C and C++ are typically categorised as memory-unsafe but this really means that they *allow unsafe implementations*. In both languages, violations of memory safety are specified as *undefined behavior*. This means that an implementation is allowed to do anything if they happen. The language specifications allow this because, on most conventional hardware, dynamically checking that there are no memory-safety violations is too expensive. It is completely valid for an implementation to decide to provide reliable, deterministic, error reporting when these happen, and that's what CHERI C and C++ do.

Higher-level languages usually impose some constraints that make it easier to efficiently guarantee memory safety. For example, Java references are usually implemented as simple numerical addresses just like C pointers, but the language doesn't allow you to do arithmetic on them. This means that you can't ever do some arithmetic to turn a Java reference into a reference to another object. Similarly, it means that the Java Virtual Machine can accurately locate all references to objects. This makes it possible to implement *automatic garbage collection* in Java, finding all of the objects that are not reachable and deleting them rather than relying on the programmer to explicitly deallocate them.

In most C and C++ implementations there are a lot of ways of violating memory safety. For example, you can manufacture pointers from arbitrary integers that happen to match addresses and access *any* object.

The lack of memory safety is responsible for around 70% of critical security vulnerabilities. Memory-safety errors are usually the worst kinds of bug because it is impossible to reason about their impacts from the program source code. By definition, you are accessing some memory that you don't think that you're accessing. This memory may be an object that's completely unrelated to the running code or even something that's part of the implementation of the language and not normally directly accessible from within the language.

Attackers usually find it easy to use memory-safety vulnerabilities for arbitrary-code execution attacks. At this point, the program that is running is no longer the program that you thought you had started, but something different and under the attacker's control.

1.2. Understanding CHERI capabilities

CHERI (pronounced 'cherry') defines an abstract set of features that can be applied to a base architecture, such as AArch64, x86, or RISC-V, to provide fine-grained memory safety that can be used as a building block for compartmentalisation. CHERIoT is a concrete instantiation of the CHERI ideas that is tailed and extended for use in low-cost embedded devices. It makes sense to understand CHERI before you try to understand CHERIoT.

CHERI stands for *Capability Hardware Enhanced RISC Instructions*. This is a somewhat contrived acronym but it captures a few key ideas in CHERI. It's an extension to existing hardware and it doesn't require any complex microcode or look-aside structures to implement (it can be applied to RISC instruction sets). Most importantly, it's an extension that adds a *capability* model to the base instruction set.

A capability, in the abstract sense, is an unforgeable token of authority that must be presented to perform an operation. Capabilities exist in the physical world in various forms. For example, a key to a padlock is a capability to unlock that padlock. When the key is presented, the padlock can be unlocked. Without the key the padlock cannot be unlocked without exploiting some security vulnerability, such as using lock picks or a bolt cutter. It doesn't matter to the padlock who presents the key, only that the correct key has been presented. Some complex building locks have different keys that authorise unlocking different sets of doors. For example, a team leader may have a key that unlocks the offices of everyone on their team and the building manager may hold a key that unlocks everything.

Capabilities can be delegated. The building manager may loan their key to someone else to unlock a door. The key and the door don't care who is holding them. You can create a copy of a capability that you hold and give it to someone else, just as you could go to a key cutter and have a copy made of a key that you own.

A lot of capability systems (including CHERI) allow you to reduce the rights that a capability grants. This breaks the key metaphor somewhat. If you have a master key for a building, you can't easily use it to create a key that allows just locking but not unlocking doors, or create one that opens all of the doors on the ground floor but no others, but capability systems usually do permit this kind of operation.

Some kinds of capabilities can also be *revoked*. This is traditionally the hardest operation to perform on capabilities. In our key analogy, this is equivalent to someone performing an audit of all of the keys and removing some of them from people that shouldn't have them anymore. This is often solved in capability systems by adding a layer of indirection. Rather than allowing capabilities to be stored anywhere, the system places them in one or more centralised tables. When you use a capability, you do so by referring to a location in a table. This makes it easy to revoke capabilities by removing them from the tables. UNIX file descriptors work like this: you refer to them by number and the kernel can invalidate them by simply removing the entry at that location in your process's file-descriptor table.

Some hardware capability systems have used a similar approach to capability storage and revocation but it has a significant disadvantage: every time that you use a capability, the hardware must find it in the relevant table. This can turn a single memory access into several. Implementations can mitigate this somewhat by caching, but these caches quickly introduce significant power overheads. CHERI avoids this entirely, which makes the common operations easier, but makes revocation somewhat more challenging. CHERIoT includes some additional hardware extensions for revocation, which we'll discuss in Chapter 7.

On a CHERI system, capabilities are used to authorise access to memory. Any instruction that takes an address in a conventional architecture takes a *CHERI capability* as the operand instead. The CHERI capability both describes a location in memory and grants access to it. For example, the following RISC-V snippet loads four bytes from offset eight relative to the address in register a1 and places the result in s0.

```
lw s0, 8(a1)
```

On a CHERIoT system, which is a CHERI RISC-V variant, this instruction looks slightly different:

```
clw s0, 8(ca1)
```

Now, it is loading a word into s0 from offset eight relative to the *capability* (not address) in register ca1 (a1 extended to hold a capability.) This instruction will check that the capability in ca1 is a valid capability, check that it has load permission, and check that the range covered by the four-byte load starting at offset eight from the current address is all in bounds. If, and only if, all of these checks pass, will it do the same load as the original version. If any of these fail, the instruction will trap. The next section explains what it means for a capability to be valid and what permissions a capability can hold.

Most of the time, hopefully, you will not be writing assembly and so this is simply a detail for the compiler to worry about. You can think of a CHERI memory capability as a pointer that the hardware understands. In C, if you hold a pointer to an object then you are allowed to access the object that it points to. If you do some pointer arithmetic that goes out of bounds of the object, C says that this is undefined behaviour. CHERI says more concretely that it will trap: you are not authorised to access that memory *with this capability*. If you hold two pointers to objects that are adjacent in memory, then you may be authorised to access the memory, but not with the pointer that you are using.

This highlights the two key security principles that capability systems are able to enforce:

- *The principle of least privilege*, which states that a piece of running code should have the rights to do what it needs to do and no more.
- *The principle of intentional use*, which states that any privileged operation must be performed by intentionally exercising the specific right that is needed.

Capability systems make it easy to implement least privilege by providing running code only with the minimal set of capabilities (with the limited set of rights) that they need. They make it easy to implement intentionality by requiring the specific capability to be presented along with each operation. The latter avoids a large category of confused deputy attacks, where a component holding one privilege is tricked into exercising it on behalf of a differently trusted component.

> In a CHERIoT system, *every* pointer in a higher-level language such as C, and every implicit pointer (such as the stack pointer, global pointer, and so on) used to build the language's abstractions, is a CHERI capability. If you have used other CHERI systems then you may have seen a hybrid mode, where only some pointers are capabilities and others are integers relative to an implicit capability. CHERIoT does not have this hybrid mode. The hybrid mode is intended for running legacy binaries but makes it harder to provide fine-grained sandboxing. CHERIoT assumes all code will be recompiled for the new target.

The phrase 'differently trusted' in the previous paragraph is not an attempt to extend political correctness to software components. Capability systems do not imply hierarchical trust models. Two components may hold disjoint or overlapping sets of capabilities that allow each to perform some set of actions that the other cannot. In a CHERI system, this can include one component having read access to an object and another write access, or two components having access to different fields of the same structure.

1.3. Restricting memory access with compressed bounds

The original CHERI prototypes used a 256-bit capability that stored a full 64-bit base and length. This was useful for research and prototyping but replacing 64-bit pointers with 256-bit ones was an unacceptable overhead when CHERI started to move from research to production. Newer CHERI implementations reduce this overhead by taking advantage of redundancy. The base, top, and address of a capability all have some common bits in the top of their address.

Consider a pointer to memory location 0x08000234, in an allocation that starts at 0x08000230 and is 64 bytes long. The base, top, and address all start 0x080002, so you can store that part separately and then you just need to store the low bits for each of the three values. Modern CHERI encodings work somewhat like this. They store the address of the pointer as a full 32- or 64-bit value and then use a *floating-point bounds encoding* to store the distance from that value to the top and the bottom.

The floating-point representations use a shared exponent but different mantissas for the top and bottom. In the previous example, this means that you'd store the address as the full 32-bit value: 0x08000234. The top is 0x3c bytes above and the base 0x4 bytes below this address. Even on the most space-constrained CHERI encodings, these will fit entirely in the mantissa and so the exponent will be zero.

CHERIoT uses a nine-bit mantissa. If the distance to the top and base can't be expressed in nine bits then you may not be able to store a precise value. For example, imagine that you want a 1024-byte allocation. You can express this, but only if the base and top are at least four-byte aligned.

The larger a memory region you want to represent, the more strongly aligned the base and top must be. The compiler or memory allocator will handle this for you if capabilities correspond to complete allocations but this can be a problem when you are creating *sub-object capabilities*. For example, if you want to pass a capability to a region within a reusable buffer as a function argument, you may not be able to express the bounds precisely. When this happens, you must choose between splitting the operation into two calls that each use part of the buffer, or trusting the callee with slightly larger bounds.

1.4. Decomposing permissions in CHERIoT

Any CHERI system provides a set of permissions on capabilities. Permissions, along with bounds, are *capability metadata*, as shown in Figure 1. CHERI systems typically use double the size of the platform's native address for capabilities, so all of the metadata needs to fit in the size of one address. As well as this metadata, there is a non-addressable *tag bit*, sometimes called a *valid bit* that differentiates between capabilities and other data. If a memory location or a register has its valid bit set, then it holds a capability and the hardware promises that this was derived from a valid sequence of operations from some more powerful capability.

A lot of capability systems, particularly software capability systems, store capabilities in tables or special memory locations. CHERI could not take this approach because it was designed to allow C implementations to use capabilities to represent pointers and C allows interleaving pointers and data. Any memory location in a C program that is large enough and sufficiently aligned to hold a pointer may hold a pointer or some other data. CHERI systems support this arbitrary interleaving with a tag bit. On a CHERIoT system, addresses are 32 bits but capabilities are 65 bits. Normal data operations see only 64 of these bits but capability operations see all 65. If you store data (for example, a 32-bit word or an 8-bit byte) somewhere in a 65-bit chunk, the data will be stored and the tag bit will be cleared. If you load a capability-sized chunk of memory into a capability register, the tag bit will be loaded along with the other 64 bits and will determine whether you've loaded a capability or just 64 bits of data. When you store this back to memory, the tag bit is propagated out again.

Tag bits and their accompanying data are moved between registers and memory *atomically*. This guarantees that you can't write part of a capability and some data to the same location and end up with a valid capability.

 The very earliest CHERI research prototypes used a 256-bit capability on a 64-bit architecture. The versions aimed at production have all used no more than double the address size to store a capability.

Most prior CHERI systems have 64-bit addresses (and therefore 128-bit capabilities) and so have a lot of space for permissions as an orthogonal bitfield. The CHERIoT platform has 32-bit addresses (and therefore 64-bit capabilities) and so has to compress the permissions. This is done, in part, by separat-

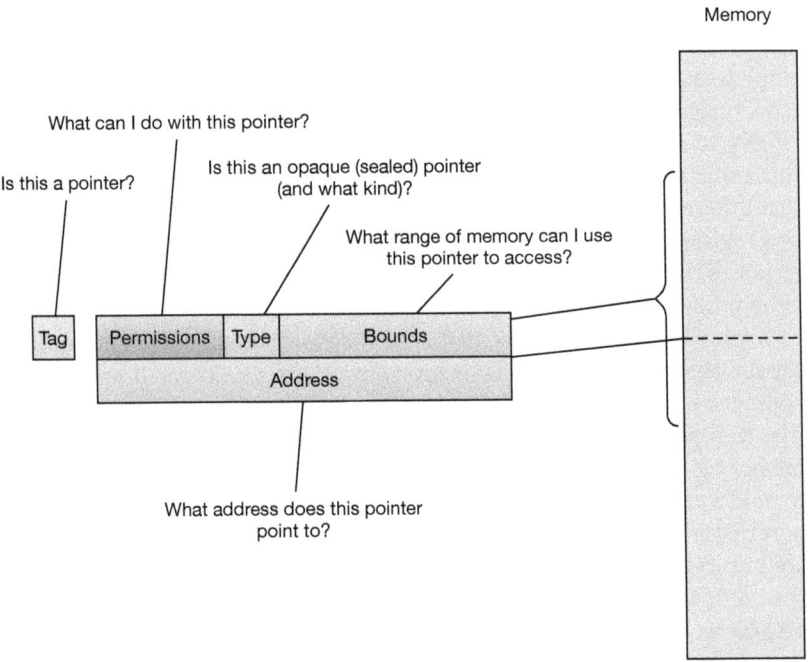

FIGURE 1. A CHERIoT capability grants access to a range of memory.

ing the permissions into primary and dependent permissions. The primary permissions (listed in Table 1) have meaning by themselves. If you use the CHERIoT RTOS logging support (described in Chapter 8) to print capabilities, the permissions will be listed using the letters in the first column.

Read and write permission allow the capability to be used as an operand to load and store instructions, respectively. Execute allows the capability to be used as a jump target, where it will end up installed as the *program counter capability* and used for instruction fetch. We'll cover the sealing and unsealing permissions later.

Global is a bit unusual. The other permissions affect what you can do with the memory that the capability refers to, whereas global affects what you can do with this capability. This should make more sense when we look at the permissions that interact with the global permission.

Debug output letter	Permission name	Meaning
G	Global	May be stored anywhere in memory.
R	Load (Read)	May be used to read.
W	Store (Write)	May be used to write.
X	Execute	May be used to as a jump target (executed).
S	Seal	May be used to seal other capabilities (see Section 1.6).
U	Unseal	May be used to unseal sealed capabilities.
0	User 0	Reserved for software use.

TABLE 1. CHERIoT primary permissions

The dependent permissions (listed in Table 2) provide more fine-grained control. Dependent permissions are ones that depend on the existence of some other permission. Without that permission (or, in the case of load / store capability, at least one of the possible primary permissions), they would be meaningless.

For many of these, it's more useful to think about what can't be done if you lack the permission than to think about what can be done if you have it. By default, the load and store permissions authorise instructions to load and store non-capability data. With the load / store capability permission, they also allow loading and / or storing capabilities. Removing this permission is useful for pure-data buffers. You can't accidentally store a valid pointer into them, and if they already contain a valid pointer then no one can load it via this capability.

You can use a capability that has the load-global permission to load capabilities that have the global permission. Any capability loaded via a capability without this permission will have its global (and load-global) permission

Debug output letter	Permission name	Depends on	Meaning
c	Load / Store Capability	R / W	May be used to load or store capabilities as well as non-capability data.
g	Load Global	R	May be used to load capabilities with the global permission.
m	Load Mutable	R	May be used to load capabilities with write permission.
l	Store Local	W	May be used to store capabilities that do *not* have global permission.
a	Access System Registers	X	Code run via this capability may access reserved special registers.

TABLE 2. CHERIoT dependent permissions

stripped. It can then be stored only via a capability that has the store-local permission.

These permissions are complex but they exist to support language-level features that are much simpler. These language-level properties work because CHERIoT RTOS provides the store-local permission exclusively to stacks and stack capabilities are not global. This combination initially guarantees *thread isolation* in CHERIoT. Pointers to stack allocations are derived from the stack capability, and so lack global, and can therefore be stored only on the stack (the only thing with store-local permission).

Removing the global permission from any other capability gives it the same property: you can store it only on the stack. If you pass it to another function then that function cannot store it in a global or on the heap, which gives you a *shallow no-capture* guarantee: The callee cannot hold onto a copy of the pointer after the end of the call. This is shallow because the callee can capture pointers to objects that are reachable via pointers stored in the original object. Removing the load-global permission makes this a *deep no-capture* guarantee. Any pointer loaded, at any level of indirection, from the original pointer will have the property that it can be stored only on the stack.

Similarly, store and load-mutable permissions are intended to give similar language-level guarantees for mutability. If you have a capability without store permission then you cannot use it to modify the object that the capability points to. If that object contains pointers then you may be able to load one of those and modify an object reachable from the original capability. This gives a *shallow immutability*. Removing the load-mutable permission turns this into a *deep immutability* guarantee, stripping both store and load-mutable permissions from any capability that you load. This lets you share a read-only view of a complex data structure.

The access-system-registers permission controls access to a small number of privileged registers and is never handed out to code other than a tiny trusted component in the core of the RTOS.

The CHERIoT encoding stores 12 permissions in five bits by excluding meaningless combinations and some that are not normally useful. This comes with a few limitations, most notably that execute permission implies load. It is not possible to remove load permission from an executable capability. Some modern platforms support *execute-only memory* as a security feature. CHERIoT cannot express this but this does not cause practical problems for security. The sentry mechanism (described in Section 1.6) lets you have memory that is readable *only* while executing from it, which is a more useful security property. Execute-only memory normally aims to prevent information leaks that lead to code-reuse attacks. These attacks, in turn, are triggered via pointer injection or other memory-safety violations, which CHERIoT deterministically mitigates.

1.5. Building memory safety

Memory safety is a property of a source-level abstract machine. Memory safety for C, Java, or Rust mean different things. At the hardware level, CHERIoT is designed to enable implementations of languages to enforce memory safety, in the presence of untrusted code such as inline assembly or code written in a different language. Most importantly, it provides the tools that allow code in a compartment (see Section 1.8) to protect itself from arbitrary code in a different compartment. This means protecting objects such that code from a different security context cannot:

- Access objects unless passed pointers to them.
- Access outside the bounds of an object given a valid pointer to that object.
- Access an object (or the memory that was formerly used for the object) after the object has been freed.
- Hold a pointer to an object with automatic storage duration (an 'on-stack' object) after the end of the call in which it was created.
- Hold a temporarily delegated pointer beyond a single call.
- Modify an object passed via immutable reference.
- Modify any object reachable from an object that is passed as a deeply immutable reference.
- Tamper with an object passed via opaque reference.

The hardware provides tools for enforcing all of these properties but it's up to the compiler and the RTOS to cooperate to use them correctly. For example, in the CHERIoT ABI, each compartment has a single capability in a register that spans all of its globals and a single capability that grants access to its entire stack. The compiler will derive capabilities from these that are bounded to individual globals or on-stack objects. Inline assembly that references the global-pointer or stack-pointer registers directly can bypass spatial memory safety for these objects, but only from within the same compartment. None of the properties relating to heap objects make sense in the absence of a heap. CHERIoT RTOS provides a shared heap (see Chapter 7) which enforces spatial and temporal safety for heap objects.

1.6. Sealing pointers for tamper proofing

We have discussed all of the primary permissions from Table 1 with the exception of those related to *sealing*. Sealing a capability transforms it from something that conveys rights and can be used to exercise those rights into an opaque token. It can be transformed back with the converse unseal operation.

Capabilities have one field that we have not yet discussed: an *object type*. This is normally zero, representing an unsealed capability. Any non-zero value indicates a sealed capability.

When you seal a capability, you use a capability with permit-seal permission. The sealing operation sets the object type of the newly sealed capability to the address of the capability that authorised the seal operation. With a non-zero object type, the sealed capability cannot be modified. Any attempt to change the address, bounds, or permission will clear the tag and give an invalid capability. It can be copied but is always treated as an opaque value. Unsealing is the only operation that can modify a sealed capability. This requires a valid capability with permit-unseal permission and the same address as the capability that was used in the original seal operation. The unseal operation results in a capability that is identical to the one that was sealed.

If you attempt to unseal a capability that is not sealed with the value of the permit-unseal capability then you will get back an untagged value. Sealed capabilities can therefore be used as trusted handles that can be shared with untrusted code. If the untrusted code tries to modify the value in any way, you can detect the tampering, either by inspecting the tag bit after unsealing or by trying to use it and getting a trap.

Sealing is the building block for a lot of the higher-level security properties in the CHERIoT system. Being able to hand out opaque tokens that can be validated when handed back is a very powerful primitive. Sealed capabilities are a core part of the cross-compartment call mechanism as well as the building block for software-defined capabilities throughout the RTOS.

The CHERIoT encoding has space for only three bits of object type (in contrast with 'big CHERI' systems such as Morello that typically have 18 bits). This is sufficient for a small number of core parts of the ABI but not enough for general-purpose use. To mitigate this limitation, the CHERIoT memory allocator provides a set of APIs (see Section 7.7) that virtualise the sealing mechanism. The same mechanism is also used to build software-defined capabilities.

The object type in a CHERIoT capability is interpreted differently depending on whether the sealed capability is executable or not. For executable capabilities, most of the object types are reserved for sealed entry (*sentry*) capabilities. A sentry capability can be unsealed automatically by jumping to it. Return addresses are automatically sealed by the jump-and-link instructions, so you cannot modify a return address, you can only jump to it.

Beyond that, return addresses are sealed as a different kind of sentry. If you substitute a return address on the stack with a function pointer (or vice versa) you will get a trap in the jump. This makes control-flow hijacking attacks very hard to mount on a CHERIoT system.

Sentries are also used as a building block for cross-compartment calls. A sentry can point to a region of memory that contains both code and data. The data is accessible via PC-relative addressing only after jumping into the code.

1.7. Controlling interrupt status with sentries

In conventional RISC-V (and most other architectures) the interrupt status is controlled via a special register. This register can be modified only in a privileged mode. The CHERIoT ISA allows this register to be modified only by code running with the Access System Registers permission in the program counter capability.

Embedded software often wants to disable interrupts for short periods but granting the permission to toggle interrupts makes auditing availability guarantees between mutually distrusting components almost impossible. Instead, CHERIoT provides three kinds of sentries that control the interrupt status. These either enable or disable interrupts, or leave the interrupt enabled state untouched. The branch-and-link instruction captures the current exception state in the return sentry.

This allows you to provide function pointers to functions that will run with interrupts disabled and guarantee that, on return, the interrupt status is reset as it should be. In effect, this brings structured programming to interrupt status.

In the RTOS, for example, the atomics library provides a set of functions that (on single-core systems without hardware atomics) perform simple read-modify-write operations with interrupts disabled. A compartment can use these without having the ability to arbitrarily toggle interrupts, giving a limit on the amount of time that it can run with interrupts disabled.

1.8. Isolating components with threads and compartments

Most mainstream operating systems have a process model that evolved from mainframe systems. This is built around isolation, with sharing as an afterthought. The primary goal for process isolation was to allow consolidation, replacing multiple minicomputers with a single mainframe. These abstractions were designed with the assumption that they ran independent workloads that wanted to share computational resources. Gradually, communication mechanisms have been added on top.

CHERIoT starts from a fundamental assumption that *isolation is easy, (safe) sharing is hard*. Particularly in the embedded space, it's easy to provide a separate core and SRAM if you want strong isolation without sharing. Most useful workloads involve communication between distrusting entities. For example, if you want to connect an IoT device to a back-end service, your ethernet driver needs to communicate with the TCP/IP stack, which needs to communicate with the TLS stack, which needs to communicate with a higher-level protocol stack such as MQTT, which needs to communicate with your device-specific logic.

CHERIoT provides two composable abstractions for isolation:
- Compartments are units of spatial isolation
- Threads are units of temporal isolation

A compartment owns some code and some globals. It exports a set of functions as entry points and may import some entry points from other compartments. A thread owns a register state and a stack and is a schedulable entity.

At any given point, the core is executing one thread in one compartment. Threads move between compartments via function call and return. When code in one compartment calls another, it loses access to everything that was not explicitly shared. Specifically:
- All registers except argument registers are zeroed.
- The stack capability is truncated to exclude the portion used by the caller.
- The portion of the stack that is delegated from the caller to the callee is zeroed.

On return, the stack becomes accessible again but a similar set of state clearing guarantees confidentiality from the callee to the caller.

Arguments that are passed from one compartment to another may include capabilities. At the start of execution, each compartment has a guarantee that nothing else can see or modify its globals. If one compartment passes a pointer to one of its globals to another, you now have shared memory. This can be useful with restricted permissions for sharing read-only epoch counters and similar.

1.9. Sharing code with libraries

Invoking reusable components does not always involve a change of security context. The CHERIoT software model provides *shared libraries* for sharing code without a security boundary.

Unlike compartments, shared libraries do not have mutable globals. They are reusable code and read-only data, nothing else. Because of this they are invoked via a much lighter-weight mechanism than a full cross-compartment call. This mechanism doesn't clear the stack or registers.

Using a CHERIoT shared library is conceptually equivalent to copying the code that implements it into every compartment that uses it. Unlike simple copying, shared libraries are independently auditable (see Chapter 10) and require only a single copy of the code in memory. All entry points exported from a shared library are invoked via sentries. This means that they can enable or disable interrupts for the duration of the call.

Some shared libraries expose very simple functions, others are a lot more complex. For example, the atomics library provides some functions that are only a handful of instructions long. In contrast, the shared library that packages Microvium[1] provides a complete JavaScript interpreter.

1.10. Auditing firmware images

When a CHERIoT firmware image starts, the loader initialises all of the capabilities that each compartment holds at boot. It does this using metadata provided by the linker. This means that everything that leads to capabilities being provided is visible to the linker. The CHERIoT linker, in addition to providing the firmware image, provides a report about this structure. The report includes:

- The hashes of the sections that form each compartment.
- The list of exports from each compartment and each library.
- The list of functions imported for each compartment and each library.
- Whether each entry point runs with interrupts enabled, disabled, or inherited.
- The list of memory-mapped I/O (MMIO) regions accessible by any compartment.
- How much memory each compartment is permitted to allocate.
- The initial entry point, stack size, and priority for each thread.

This allows automated build time auditing of various high-level security policies. For example, you can check that a single compartment, containing a known binary (for example, one that has been approved by regulators), is the only thing that is able to access a specified device. You can require that nothing runs with interrupts disabled except a specific set of permitted library functions. Or you can say that users can provide their own logic for controlling their IoT device, but require that only compartments that you trust can have the permission to connect to your cloud servers.

---

1. https://microvium.com

Chapter 2.
The RTOS Core

The core of the RTOS is a set of privilege-separated components. Each core component runs with some privileges that mean that it is (at least partially) in the trusted computing base (TCB) for other things.

2.1. Starting the system with the loader

The *loader* runs on system startup. A firmware image contains everything that needs to end up in memory when the system starts, as well as an image header that contains metadata describing its layout. The loader reads the header and populates each compartment with the set of capabilities that it needs. The loader exists so that the system can be started from a firmware image that does not embed capabilities. This is a useful property even if a particular target has persistent storage (non-volatile RAM) that *can* hold capabilities because it ensures that there is an on-device *pointer provenance* flow for the firmware.

Pointer provenance ensures that pointers in the system were derived from other pointers via a chain that makes sense. Pointers cannot be made up from thin air. When a CHERI system boots, it starts with one or more capabilities in registers that convey the full set of permissions. If you call a function like malloc there is a chain of derivations that leads back to these initial capabilities. For example, the loader will create a capability to the heap region that has a subset of permissions (for example, not execute permission) that covers the region that will be used for the heap, and then the memory allocator will reduce the bounds to hand out a capability for a single object. CHERI doesn't let you reconstruct that chain but it does guarantee that it, or some equivalent chain, must have existed.

If a device has non-volatile storage that holds tags, you will typically run the loader once at install time or on first boot of a new firmware image. This ensures that the initial state for each component's memory contains only capabilities that the loader explicitly grants to it. This, in turn, enables multi-stage boot where some functionality, such as attestation, secure key storage, and so on, are provided by a bootloader. These abstractions can all be built from capabilities and so, unlike systems based on protection rings such as TrustZone, an arbitrary number can be nested.

If a compartment contains a global that is a pointer, initialised to point to another global, the loader will initialise the pointer by deriving a capability from one out of either the compartment's code or data capabilities. Again, this enforces provenance properties, this time within a firmware image. A malicious compartment may provide a relocation that points to a global outside its own memory, but the loader will attempt to derive the capability only from the compartment's initial pcc (code) and cgp (globals) regions and so will fail. Globals may point to other globals owned by the compartment; the loader will fail to derive a valid capability if they point elsewhere.

The loader must also provide all capabilities to compartments that allow them to communicate outside of their own private space. This includes access to *memory-mapped I/O* (MMIO) regions, capabilities for pre-shared objects, for software-defined capabilities, and any capabilities for calling entry points exposed by other compartments or libraries. The loader also creates the stacks and trusted stacks for each thread and creates their initial entry points.

The loader is the most privileged component in the system. When a CHERIoT CPU boots, it will have a small set of *root capabilities* in registers. These, between them, convey the full set of rights that can be granted by a capability. Every capability in the running system is derived (often via many steps) from one of these. As such, the loader is able to do anything.

 In a system with a multi-stage boot, the initial capabilities provided to the loader may be restricted, rather than the omnipotent set from CPU boot. For example, an early loader may implement A/B booting by providing the RTOS loader with capabilities to only half of persistent memory.

The risk from the loader is mitigated by the fact that it does not run on untrusted data. The loader operates only on the instructions generated by the linker and so it is possible to audit precisely what it will do (see Chapter 10). It is also possible to validate this by running the loader in a simulator and capturing the precise memory state after it has run.

The loader enforces some of the guarantees in the initial state. It is structured to be able to enforce some of these by construction. For example, only stacks and trusted stacks (accessible only by the switcher, see Section 2.2) have store-local permission and these do not have global permission. The scheduler derives these from a capability that has store-local but not global permissions and derives all other capabilities from one that has the store-local permission removed.

Before starting the system, the loader erases almost all of its code (leaving the stub that handles this erasure), its stack, and clears its registers. The last bit of the loader's code becomes the idle thread (a wait-for-interrupt loop). The loader's stack is used for the scheduler stack. The memory that held the loader's code is used for heap memory.

2.2. Changing trust domain with the switcher

The *switcher* is the most privileged component that runs after the system finishes booting. It is responsible for transitions between threads (context switches) and between compartments (cross-compartment calls and returns). The switcher is a very small amount of code—under 500 instructions —that is expected to be amenable to formal verification.

 Work is underway to formally verify the security properties of the switcher, but is still in early stages at the time of writing.

The switcher is the only component in a running CHERIoT system that has access-system-registers permission. It uses this primarily to access a single reserved register that holds the capability that defines the *trusted stack* for the current thread. A trusted stack is a region of memory containing the register save area for context switches and a small frame for every cross-compartment call that allows a safe return even if the callee has corrupted all state that it has access to.

Trusted stacks are set up by the loader. The loader passes the scheduler (see Section 2.3) a sealed capability to each of these on initialisation. The switcher holds the only permit-unseal capability for the type used to seal trusted stacks.

The context switch path in the switcher spills all registers to the current trusted stack's save area and then invokes the scheduler, which returns a sealed capability to the next thread to run. It then restores the register file from this thread and resumes. If the scheduler returns an invalid capability (one not sealed with the correct type) then the switcher will raise a fault. When an interrupt is delivered, a copy of the program counter capability for the interrupted state is saved in the *exception program counter capability* register. If the exception program counter capability on exception entry is within the switcher's capability, the switcher will terminate. The switcher is written to avoid trapping and so any trap is assumed to be an active attack trying to exploit a bug in the switcher.

On the cross-compartment call path, the switcher is responsible for un-sealing the capability that refers to the export table of the callee, clearing unused argument registers, pushing the information about the return to the trusted stack, subsetting the bounds of the stack, and zeroing the part of the stack passed to the callee. On return, it zeroes the stack again, zeroes unused return registers, and restores the callee's state.

This means that the switcher is the only component that has access to either two threads', or two compartments', state at the same time. As such, it is in the TCB for both compartment and thread isolation. This risk is mitigated in several ways:

- The switcher is small. It contains a similar number of instructions compared to the amount of unverified code in seL4.
- The switcher is defensive. Most errors simply forcibly unwind to the previous trusted stack frame, so a compartment that attempts to attack the switcher exits to its caller.
- Like everything else in the system, it must follow the capability rules. Unlike an operating system running in a privileged mode on mainstream hardware, it does not get to opt out of memory protection, it is not able to access beyond the bounds of capabilities passed to it or access any memory to which it does not have an explicit capability.
- It is largely stateless. All state that it modifies is held in the trusted stack for the current thread.

The switcher appears to the rest of the system as a library. It can expose functions for inspecting or, in a small number of cases, modifying state. These are defined in switcher.h. For example, prior to performing a cross-compartment call, you may want to check that there is sufficient space on the trusted stack for the number of calls that it will need to make. The trusted_stack-_has_space function exposed by the switcher lets you query if the trusted stack has enough space for a specified number of cross-compartment calls. The amount of (normal) stack space is directly visible in a compartment and so normal stack checks do not require the switcher to be involved.

The switcher also implements the thread_id_get function, which provides a fast way for compartments to determine which thread they are currently running on. This function is used in the implementation of priority-inheriting locks (see Section 6.7). Implementing efficient priority-inheriting locks requires a fast mechanism for getting the current thread ID so that it can be stored in the lock.

Documentation for the `trusted_stack_has_space` function

`_Bool trusted_stack_has_space(int requiredFrames)`

Returns true if the trusted stack contains at least `requiredFrames` frames past the current one, false otherwise.

Note: This is faster than calling either `trusted_stack_index` or `trusted_stack_size` and so should be preferred in guards.

Documentation for the `thread_id_get` function

`uint16_t thread_id_get()`

Return the thread ID of the current running thread. This is mostly useful where one compartment can run under different threads and it matters which thread entered this compartment.

User threads (that is, those defined in the xmake firmware configuration) are 1-indexed, with 0 indicating primordial idle and scheduling contexts. User code never runs in these contexts and so anything using this result to index into a per-thread array may wish to subtract one and avoid allocating an array element for the idle thread.

This is implemented in the switcher.

2.3. Time slicing with the scheduler

When the switcher receives an interrupt (including an explicit yield), it delegates the decision about what to run next to the *scheduler*. The scheduler has direct access to the interrupt controller but, in most respects, is just another compartment.

The switcher also holds a capability to a small stack for use by the scheduler. This is not quite a full thread. It cannot make cross-compartment calls and is not independently schedulable. When the switcher handles an interrupt, it invokes the scheduler's entry point on this stack.

The scheduler also exposes other entry points that can be invoked by cross-compartment calls. These fulfil a role similar to system calls on other operating systems, for example waiting for external events or performing inter-thread communication. The scheduler implements blocking operations by moving the current thread from a run queue to a sleep queue and then issuing a software interrupt instruction to branch to the switcher. When the switcher then invokes the scheduler to make a scheduling decision, the scheduler will discover that the current thread is no longer runnable and pick another. Once the thread becomes runnable again, the switcher resumes the thread from the point where it yielded, at which point it can return from the scheduler.

The scheduler is, by definition, in the TCB for availability. It is the component that decides which threads run and which do not. A bug in the scheduler (with or without an active attacker) can result in a thread failing to run.

It is not, however, in the TCB for confidentiality or integrity. The scheduler has no mechanism to inspect the state of an interrupted thread. When invoked explicitly, it is called with a normal cross-compartment call and so has no access to anything other than the arguments.

As with the switcher, the scheduler mitigates these risks by being small (though larger than the switcher). It currently compiles to under 4 KiB of object code. This small size is accomplished by providing only a small set of features that can be used as building blocks for other tasks.

For example, some embedded operating systems provide features such as message queues in their kernel. In CHERIoT RTOS, these are provided by a separate library, which relies on the *futex* (see Section 6.5) facility exposed by the scheduler to allow a producer to block when the queue is full and allow consumers to block when the queue is empty.

Futexes are the *only* mechanism that the scheduler provides for blocking. Interrupts are mapped to futexes and so threads wait for hardware or software events in exactly the same way. This narrow interface and clear separation of concerns helps improve overall system security.

2.4. Sharing memory from the allocator

The final core component is the memory allocator, which provides the heap used for all dynamic memory allocations. This is discussed in detail in Chapter 7. Sharing memory between compartments in CHERIoT requires nothing more than passing pointers (until you start to add availability requirements in the presence of mutual distrust). This means that you can allocate objects (or complex object graphs) from a few bytes up to the entire memory of the system and share them with other compartments.

The allocator has access to the shadow bitmap and hardware revocation engine that enforce temporal safety for the heap, and is responsible for setting bounds on allocated memory. It is therefore trusted for confidentiality and integrity of memory allocated from the heap. If it incorrectly sets bounds, a compartment may gain access to memory belonging to another allocation. If it incorrectly configures revocation state or reuses memory too early then a use-after-free bug may become exploitable.

The allocator is not able to bypass capability permissions, it simply holds a capability that spans the whole of heap memory. As such, it is in the TCB only with respect to heap allocations. It cannot access globals (or code) held in other compartments so a compartment that does not use the heap does not need to trust the allocator.

The allocator also provides a rich set of mechanisms (described in Chapter 7) for two mutually distrusting compartments to ensure that memory is not deallocated at inconvenient times.

2.5. Building a C/C++ environment

So far, this chapter has discussed the components of the system that provide distinct trust domains. CHERIoT RTOS also provides several *shared libraries*. As discussed in Section 1.9, CHERIoT shared libraries do not have private globals, they provide functions that can be invoked from multiple compartments but which has no mutable state of its own.

A C freestanding environment needs a small set of standard-library functions to exist. These are memcpy, memset, and so on. The compiler may insert different calls to these for things like struct assignment or initialisation, and any C code may assume that they exist.

These functions are fairly small (less than 0.5 KiB), but we do not want every compartment that contains them to have to include a copy of them because that small size can add up quickly when you have very large numbers of compartments. Instead, the RTOS includes a freestanding library that includes these functions.

C++ expects slightly more from a freestanding environment. CHERIoT RTOS does not provide support for exceptions, but does support thread-safe initialisation of statics. In C++, function-local static variables that have non-trivial constructors are initialised lazily the first time that they are invoked. The compiler emits a guard word that is used to mark whether the object is initialised and to act as a lock to protect initialisation. The compiler also emits a branch on the initialised bit at the point where the variable comes into scope. In the uninitialised case, this inserts a call to __cxa_guard_acquire to acquire the lock and then a call to __cxa_guard_release to release the lock. The acquire function also checks whether another thread has initialised the variable between the initial check and the call, preventing double initialisation. These are provided by the cxxrt library.

 In environments that support exceptions, there is a third function for static initialisation. The __cxa_guard_abort function is called when a constructor throws an exception. This is not supported on CHERIoT.

For both C and C++ (and other languages that use the same compiler back end), there are some sequences that compilers prefer to generate as calls to helper functions. For example, if you divide one 64-bit number by another, this is a single operator in C. On most 64-bit processors, it's a single divide instruction but on 32-bit processors it requires a much longer sequence. Similarly, GCC and Clang provide a *population count* built-in function that examines an integer and counts the number of bits that are set to one. This is a single instruction on most modern application processors, but requires some shifting and masking on microcontrollers.

CHERIoT RTOS provides the crt library to implement these functions. Not every compartment will need all of them, but the library is around 1.5 KiB of code and so duplicating it across every compartment that does need them would be likely to increase code size significantly.

Although the code sizes in this section may look small, moving a function to a separate compartment typically adds only a handful of bytes to the final binary size. It's quite feasible to have a compartment that is of the order of a hundred bytes in total size. Adding another copy of a function such as memcpy into such a small compartment, rather than simply calling the shared-library version, could more than double the overhead of extracting a function into a library.

2.6. Supporting atomic operations

C11 and C++11 introduced atomic operations. In C, these use the _Atomic qualifier, in C++ they use the std::atomic<> template. Recently, these were somewhat unified so that _Atomic(T) can be a macro that expands to std::atomic<T> when compiling in C++ mode and a built-in type qualifier in C mode. In both languages, these are often referred to as the C++11 model because the C++ version was introduced first and then ported to C.

Compilers implement these with a set of built-in functions that, on most application cores, are lowered in the back end to atomic instructions. Most microcontrollers are single core and so may lack atomic instructions. The CHERIoT Ibex, for example, does not implement any atomic instructions. This does not matter because atomic instructions need to be atomic only with respect to the CPU core itself.

On single-core systems, atomic operations can be implemented by simply disabling interrupts, performing the read-modify-write sequence, and then enabling interrupts. As we saw in Section 1.7, CHERIoT has a simple mechanism for allowing a single function to run with interrupts disabled, without granting it the power to arbitrarily disable interrupts. This mechanism makes it possible to implement the atomic helpers as trivial C functions that just do the non-atomic operations but run with interrupts disabled. Each atomic operation on 1, 2, 4, and 8-byte values is defined as a separate function.

On larger cores, these simple helpers are unnecessary, but C and C++ specified that *any* type could be atomic. Operations such as load, store, exchange and compare-and-exchange are expected to work even if the object is enormous. The compiler expects functions that implement these operations on arbitrary-sized data.

> For types larger than a capability, CHERIoT's representations of _Atomic(T) and std::atomic<T> differ. The C version will use the variable-sized atomic helpers that run with interrupts disabled. The C++ version uses an inline lock in the object and performs atomic operations by acquiring and releasing the lock as needed. This prevents the C++ version from monopolising the CPU and breaking realtime guarantees but breaks interoperability between the two languages.
>
> In general, it is a good idea to avoid _Atomic(T) for any type that is larger than a pointer in C.

Many firmware images use only a small subset of these sizes. 32-bit atomic values are common, and are the size supported for the futex operations (see Section 6.5). The RTOS provides a family of libraries for implementing atomics. The atomic1, atomic2, atomic4 and atomic8 libraries each provide atomic operations for one fixed-size type. As a convenience, there is also an atomic_fixed pretend library that simply acts as if you'd depended on all of the fixed-sized versions. Finally, there is a general atomic library, which also introduces the variable-sized types. The last of these is very rarely used.

2.7. Adding more standard-library functions

A freestanding C is the minimum for an embedded system but it's far from a pleasant development environment. The C strings.h header contains functions such as strlen and strcpy, which do not depend on any operating-system functionality but are also not required by a freestanding environment. On CHERIoT RTOS, these are provided by the strings library.

Similarly, we provide a minimal implementation of a subset of stdio.h that is useful for debugging via the stdio library. In most C implementations there is a single libc or similar that provides all of the standard library. CHERIoT prefers to decompose this so that firmware images can adopt useful subsets.

Most of the C++ standard library that we provide is header-only, but where shared implementations are useful these will be similarly decomposed.

2.8. Exploring other RTOS features

The lib directory in the RTOS SDK contains all of the libraries. Some of these have been discussed already because they are part of a core environment that you might expect to be available for any compartment to use.

Others correspond more to operating system features and will be discussed in later chapters. For example, those related to locking, message queues, and so on will be discussed in Chapter 6. The features for debugging are discussed in Chapter 8.

Others, such as the port of the Microvium JavaScript interpreter, are not discussed in the book at all. This book does not aim to provide an exhaustive list of everything that the RTOS provides as libraries, and more will be added after the book is published. Please look in the RTOS repository to see what has been added.

Chapter 3.
Getting started writing CHERIoT software

Now that you understand the abstract ideas in CHERIoT, you almost certainly want to start writing some real code. CHERIoT is a complete hardware-software platform, which means that you will need at least the following:

- A device or simulator that implements the ISA.
- A copy of the CHERIoT RTOS software to run on the device.
- A CHERIoT toolchain to compile and link the software.

The whole software stack, the ISA specification, and a reference implementation of a CHERIoT core are all open source and so these should be easy to acquire.

This is not the complete list of software in the CHERIoT ecosystem. For example, the auditing tool (see Chapter 10) is separate and there are other open-source components maintained as part of the project.

3.1. Getting the RTOS source code

CHERIoT RTOS is developed on GitHub[1]. This is also the home for the project's issue tracker, please report any bugs that you find there! You will need to clone this repository to get the latest version.

 The RTOS has not quite reached 1.0 at the time of writing. After the 1.0 release, you should also be able to download the RTOS source as a release. Please see the README.md file in the repository for the latest instructions.

The RTOS repository uses *git submodules* for some third-party components. This means that you must do a *recursive* clone:

```
$ git clone --recursive https://github.com/CHERIoT-Platform/
cheriot-rtos
Cloning into 'cheriot-rtos'...
```

This will create a directory called cheriot-rtos. Inside this you will find a directory called sdk, which contains the SDK. There are also some examples and exercises to help you get started.

If you forgot to do a recursive clone, you can run the following command from the cheriot-rtos directory to initialise the submodules:

```
$ git submodule update --init --recursive
```

1.   https://github.com/CHERIoT-Platform/cheriot-rtos

3.2. Using the CHERIoT development container

The CHERIoT project provides a *development container*, usually referred to as a *dev container*. This is an Open Container Initiative (OCI) container image that has all of the tools required for building CHERIoT software preinstalled. This includes the toolchain, auditing tools (see Chapter 10) and some simulators (see Section 3.4).

OCI containers are sometimes referred to as Docker Containers, because the standards evolved from the model supported by the Docker tools, but they are now supported by a range of software including containerd, podman, and so on. A *container instance* (often referred to simply as a container) is an isolated environment that is instantiated from a *container image*. The image is a filesystem built from a set of layers, which allows different containers to share on-disk (and in-cache) space for different images that share a common base.

Dev containers are intended to be used with an editor that supports them but can also be used directly as if they were any other kind of container. Most of what makes a container image a dev container is not part of the container image. The RTOS repository contains a .devcontainer/devcontainer.json file that describes how to find and use the image. This includes scripts to run when the container is created, editor plugins to install, and so on.

This means that, if you use an editor that supports dev containers directly, the experience is largely seamless. If you open the RTOS repository in Visual Studio Code and have the Dev Containers plugin installed, it will prompt you to reopen the repository in a container. This will then fetch the container for you, configure plugins for syntax highlighting, autocomplete, and so on.

 If you're using Windows, you may find that git has mangled line endings or failed to create symbolic links (which require Developer Mode to be enabled). Visual Studio Code will offer an option to clone the repository in a new volume. Docker and Podman on Windows run containers in a Linux virtual machine and volumes are implemented as folders in the VM's filesystem, rather than as Windows folders mounted into the VM. You will probably find that this works better.

If, like me, your preferred development environment is a lightly modernised version of a 1970s minicomputer, you can still use the dev container. The container image is ghcr.io/cheriot-platform/devcontainer:latest.

You can run this directly from the directory where you checked out the RTOS repository:

```
$ docker run --rm -it \
  --mount \
  source=$(pwd),target=/home/cheriot/cheriot-rtos,type=bind \
  ghcr.io/cheriot-platform/devcontainer:latest
```

This command will create a single instance of the container with the current directory mounted as /home/cheriot/cheriot-rtos. This creates an ephemeral instance. You can create persistent instances with docker create.

In the dev container, all of the CHERIoT tools are installed in /cheriot-tools/bin/.

> The dev container also exists to support *GitHub Code Spaces*. These run a Visual Studio Code instance in a browser, attached to a dev container deployed in an Azure VM. If you create a Code Space from the CHERIoT RTOS repository, it will be set up with everything that you need to develop for CHERIoT in the browser. GitHub Code Spaces are a good way to start playing with CHERIoT, but the free tier is limited to 120 CPU hours (60 hours on the smallest VM tier) so you will probably want to install the toolchain locally for serious development.

3.3. Setting up a development environment

Having a copy of the RTOS software does not enable you to build it. You will also need a *toolchain*: a compiler, linker, and other associated tools that can take source code and turn it into a firmware image that can run on a device. If are using the dev container, these tools are all installed for you.

The CHERIoT toolchain is based on LLVM, which used to stand for 'Low Level Virtual Machine' until it became clear that none of those words actually applied to the project and it is now just a name. LLVM is a generic set of building blocks for writing compilers, structured around the *LLVM Intermediate Representation* (LLVM IR). It includes a mature C/C++ front end, a component that transforms C and C++ (and Objective-C) into LLVM IR. This front end, clang, is the default compiler on Apple platforms, Android, and FreeBSD. LLVM also includes a linker, lld. These two are sufficient to turn source code into something that can run on a system. LLVM also provides some other components that are useful for development. For example, llvm-objdump is used to disassemble a binary, which is useful when you have some telemetry that tells you that you've taken a CHERI bounds exception at address 0xbaadc0de but you would quite like to know what that corresponds to in the source code where you might be able to fix the issue. It also includes llvm-objcopy, which is used on some targets to turn an *Executable and Linkable Format* (ELF) file into a raw stream of bytes to be loaded into memory.

 The CHERIoT LLVM toolchain aims to upstream all of the CHERIoT support in mainline LLVM. We hope to have the majority of this work done in 2025, so by the time that you read this it's possible that a generic LLVM install will be sufficient. We expect to do new-feature development in the CHERIoT LLVM repository so you may prefer to use it even if upstream works.

You can build LLVM yourself, though it takes quite a lot of CPU time and memory. Make sure you have at least 10-20 GiB of disk space available if you want to do this. You will find instructions in the CHERIoT RTOS Getting Started guide[2]. Generally, building the toolchain yourself is recommended only if you have software supply-chain concerns or if you are working on the toolchain. For everyone else, it's better to use a pre-built version from the dev container.

These days, a compiler is expected to do more than simply compile code. It is also expected to talk the *language server protocol* (LSP) and provide syntax highlighting, autocompletion, cross-referencing, and so on.

The build system used by CHERIoT RTOS is intended to make this easy to support. Figure 2 shows the result in Visual Studio Code. All of the CHERIoT-specific extensions (see Chapter 4) are correctly highlighted.

This support is not limited to Visual Studio Code. It can work with any editor that supports the language-server protocol. The parsing code from the clang front end is also part of the clangd dæmon, which implements the server part of this protocol.

The dev container includes a .vimrc that (if you install Vim) uses the Asynchronous Lint Engine[3] plugin to connect to our clangd build. Simply run

2. https://github.com/CHERIoT-Platform/cheriot-rtos/blob/main/docs/GettingStarted.md#build-ing-cheriot-llvm
3. https://github.com/dense-analysis/ale

The CHERIoT Ibex is, at the time of writing, the only available core that supports the CHERIoT ISA, though we expect more to appear in the next few years. The Ibex is a three-stage in-order core, which is optimised for area, rather than performance. As part of the original CHERIoT research project, we also added the CHERIoT extensions for Flute, a RISC-V core implemented in BlueSpec. Flute was not production quality, but did demonstrate that a five-stage core that was (slightly) more optimised for performance could eliminate most of the CHERIoT-specific overhead. Ibex is expected to be slower than a similar-complexity non-CHERI microcontroller, but is only very slightly larger.

Google has also contributed an emulator based on their MPACT simulation environment. MPACT is intended for integration with Renode for simulating complex SoCs. Google has created a clean-slate implementation of the CHERIoT ISA in this. This is currently, by quite a large margin, the fastest of the available simulators or emulators. The Sail model is directly translated from the formal model and typically manages 200–400 KIPS (thousand instructions per second) on a fast machine. The SAFE simulator is a cycle-accurate simulation of a chip and is typically a bit over 50% of the performance of Sail. The MPACT simulator can usually manage over 5 MIPS, at least an order of magnitude faster than Sail.

Beyond software simulators there are currently two mature options for FPGA simulation. The SAFE project, as previously mentioned, can be run on the Arty A7. Unfortunately, Microsoft does not provide FPGA bitfiles so you must build this yourself.

lowRISC has produced an FPGA development board designed specifically for CHERIoT, using a slightly smaller version of the same FPGA as the Arty A7. This has a rich set of peripherals, including an LCD display. It also has set of LEDs that can display CHERI exceptions directly for the CHERIoT Ibex core, as shown in Figure 3. These will glow red and gradually fade when a CHERIoT-specific exception is triggered in software.

At the time of writing, there are not yet any CHERIoT chips commercially available. SCI Semiconductor has announced their ICENI line of CHERIoT microcontrollers, the first of which should be available in 2025.

3.5. Building firmware images

CHERIoT RTOS uses the xmake[5] build system. Xmake is a build system im-

5.   https://xmake.io/#/

FIGURE 3. CHERIoT exception LEDs on the Sonata FPGA development board.

plemented in Lua. It was chosen because it is easy to add new kinds of build targets.

In a typical system that uses the compile-link process invented by Mary Allen Wilkes in the 1960s, you compile source files to object code and then link object code to produce executables. You may have an intermediate step that produces libraries.

The CHERIoT build process was designed to enable separate compilation and binary distribution of components. Each source file is compiled either for use in a shared library or for use in a specific compartment. This means that, when building compartments, the compiler invocation must know the compartment in which the object file will be used.

Next, compartments and libraries are linked. This requires a special invocation of the linker that produces a relocatable object file with the correct structure. At this point, the only exported symbols are those for exported functions and the only undefined symbols should be those for MMIO regions or exports from other compartments (see Chapter 5 for more information).

 The build system produces a .library or .compartment file for each shared library and each compartment.

In theory, these can be distributed as binaries and linked into a firmware image but this is not yet handled automatically by the build system.

The final link step produces a firmware image. It also produces the JSON report that describes all cross-compartment interactions and is used for auditing.

Using the RTOS build system involves writing an xmake.lua file that describes the build. This starts with some boilerplate:

```
4 set_project("CHERIoT example")
5
6 sdkdir = os.getenv("CHERIOT_SDK") or
7  "../../cheriot-rtos/sdk/"
8 includes(sdkdir)
9
10 set_toolchains("cheriot-clang")
```

LISTING 1. Build system code for importing the CHERIoT RTOS SDK
[from: examples/hello_world/xmake.lua]

The set_project call gives a name to the project.

Lines 6–8 import the RTOS SDK. This first tries to use the CHERIOT_SDK environment variable and, if not, tries a relative file. The sdkdir variable should point to the location of the sdk directory from the RTOS repository. Finally, line 10 selects the CHERIoT toolchain. Ideally this line would not be needed, but xmake's scoping rules require it to be provided here.

This boilerplate snippet will exist at the top of most xmake.lua files for CHERIoT. Only the name of the project (and possibly the path to the SDK) will be different.

The SDK file provides rules for building the various kinds of CHERIoT components (compartments, libraries, and firmware) and also includes all of the libraries that are part of the RTOS. These libraries include the core definitions for a freestanding C implementation (memcpy and friends), the atomic helpers for cores without atomic instructions, and the C runtime things that are called from compiler builtins. See the lib directory in the SDK for a full list.

If you want your firmware built to support running on more than one CHERIoT implementation then you will typically want to expose a build-configuration option that selects the target board, as shown in Listing 2. This exposes a --board option at the configure stage.

```
14 option("board")
15 set_default("sail")
```

LISTING 2. Build system code for allowing the board to be selected at configure time [from: examples/hello_world/xmake.lua]

You can set a default and we use "sail" here for the simulator build from our Sail formal model of the ISA. This refers to a board description file (see Chapter 12). If you're usually targeting a particular hardware platform, setting the default here allows users to avoid specifying it manually on every build. If you're *always* targeting a particular hardware platform then you can avoid this entirely.

Next, you need to add any compartments and libraries that are specific to this firmware image. In most cases, you can do this in just two lines, the first providing the name of the compartment and the second providing the list of files, as shown in Listing 3. For this example, we'll have two compartments. One is our entry point, the other is a function that we'll use as a simple example of a cross-compartment call.

```
19 -- An example compartment that we can call
20 compartment("example_compartment")
21  add_files("compartment.cc")
22
23 -- Our entry-point compartment
24 compartment("hello")
25  add_files("hello.cc")
```

LISTING 3. Build system code for building compartments
[from: examples/hello_world/xmake.lua]

This example is going to make a cross-compartment call from the "hello" compartment to the "example_compartment" compartment and then print the result using printf, which is provided by the stdio library from the RTOS. The cross-compartment call is exposed from compartment.hh as shown in Listing 4. The only difference between this and a normal C/C++ function pro-

The name of the compartment in the xmake.lua must match the name used for the exported function as described in Section 4.1. If they do not match, the compiler will raise an error that a function is defined in the wrong compartment.

totype is the __cheriot_compartment macro. This is explained in detail in Section 4.1.

```
 7 /**
 8  * Example of a function in a compartment.
 9  */
10 __cheriot_compartment(
11   "example_compartment") int exported_function(void);
```

LISTING 4. Exporting a function for use by other compartments
[from: examples/hello_world/compartment.hh]

The implementation of this function is trivial (see Listing 5), it just returns 42. Note that, aside from the annotation from the function prototype, we don't need any changes to expose this for use from other compartments. The same is true on the caller's side, as shown in Listing 6. Functions exported from a compartment are called just like any other C function.

```
 5 #include "compartment.hh"
 6
 7 int exported_function()
 8 {
 9   return 42;
10 }
```

LISTING 5. A trivial implementation of an exported function
[from: examples/hello_world/compartment.cc]

```
 8 /// Thread entry point.
 9 void __cheriot_compartment("hello") entry()
10 {
11   printf("compartment returned %d\n", exported_function());
12 }
```

LISTING 6. A simple compartment entry point that does a cross-compartment call [from: examples/hello_world/hello.cc]

The entry function is also annotated as a function exported from a compartment. This is because it's a *thread entry point*, a function that is called at the start of a thread. In CHERIoT RTOS, threads are statically defined. This is described in more detail in Chapter 6.

Returning to the build system, Listing 7 shows how the firmware block defines everything that's combined together to create a firmware image. First, the add_deps lines are defining the compartments and libraries that are linked. The first add_deps adds two libraries provided by the RTOS, implementing the core functions for a freestanding C environment and a minimal subset of stdio.h functions, respectively. The next add_deps adds the two compartments that we defined earlier.

Not all of the metadata that we set can be defined in the declarative syntax of xmake, and so we have to implement a function using the on_load hook to set the remaining properties. The "board" property is set from the option that we declared. This is where, if you don't need to support multiple targets, you could directly specify the board that you wish to target.

```
29  -- Firmware image for the example.
30  firmware("hello_world")
31    -- RTOS-provided libraries
32    add_deps("freestanding", "stdio")
33    -- Our compartments
34    add_deps("hello", "example_compartment")
35    on_load(function(target)
36      -- The board to target
37      target:values_set("board", "$(board)")
38      -- Threads to select
39      target:values_set("threads", {
40        {
41          compartment = "hello",
42          priority = 1,
43          entry_point = "entry",
44          stack_size = 0x400,
45          trusted_stack_frames = 2
46        }
47      }, {expand = false})
48    end)
```

LISTING 7. Build system code for linking the final firmware image
[from: examples/hello_world/xmake.lua]

The "threads" property is set to an array (as a Lua array literal) of thread descriptions. Each thread must set five properties:

compartment
The compartment in which this thread starts.

priority
The priority of this thread. Higher numbers indicate higher priorities.

entry_point

> The name of the function for this thread's entry point. This must be a function that takes and returns void, exported from the compartment specified by the compartment key.

stack_size

> The number of bytes of stack space that this thread has allocated.

trusted_stack_frames

> The number of trusted stack frames. Each cross-compartment call pushes a new frame onto this stack and so this defines the maximum cross-compartment call depth (including the entry point) for this thread.

3.6. Running firmware images

Many of the board targets provide a run command. This is simple for simulators: it runs the simulator.

If you have built the example from the last section then you can run it simply with xmake run, like this:

```
$ xmake run
Running file hello_world.
ELF Entry @ 0x80000000
tohost located at 0x800061e0
compartment returned 42
SUCCESS
```

> The current version of xmake does not automatically build the target so it's good to get into the habit of using xmake && xmake run, which will build (if necessary) before running. This is expected to be changed in a future version of xmake.

In some cases, these commands may depend on external configuration. For example, Sonata has a nice mBed-inspired loader that runs on a Raspberry Pi 2040, which configures the FPGA and loads firmware images. This exposes the flash filesystem so that you can just copy a firmware file into the SONATA device and the 2040 will reboot the FPGA and load the firmware. The run script provided for Sonata looks for the SONATA device in some common mount locations and, if that fails, simply prints the location of the file and tells you to copy it yourself.

If you are working in the dev container, the host filesystems are not automatically available and must be explicitly added. You can add extra mount locations to the .devcontainer/devcontainer.json file. If you're on macOS, the SONATA filesystem will be mounted in /Volumes, so you can add the following snippet (in the top-level object in the JSON file) to expose it to the container:

```
"mounts": [
  "source=/Volumes/SONATA,target=/mnt/SONATA,type=bind"
]
```

On other operating systems, modify the source part to the correct location. This should prompt for the dev container to be restarted, which is required for new mount points to take effect.

If you are running the dev container directly, you will need to add this instruction directly to the invocation of docker or podman. For example, from the cheriot-rtos directory:

```
$ docker run -it --rm \
--mount source=$(pwd),target=/cheriot-rtos,type=bind \
--mount source=/Volumes/SONATA/,target=/mnt/SONATA,type=bind \
ghcr.io/cheriot-platform/devcontainer:latest
/bin/bash
```

Either of these approaches will mount the SONATA filesystem as /mnt/SONATA, where the run script for Sonata can find it.

 On Windows, Docker containers run in WSL2, which is a specialised Hyper-V virtual machine. Host folders are exposed via 9p over VirtFS. It appears that this is either too slow, or lacks the correct sync commands, for writes to the Sonata flash storage to be reliable from Docker on Windows. Docker and Podman both work reliably for Sonata on Linux and macOS.

The run command typically provides a convenient default. Some simulators provide various options if you invoke them directly. For example, both the Sail and SAFE simulators provide instruction-level tracing.

The Sail simulator is installed in the dev container as /cheriot-tools/bin/cheriot_sim. This will directly run an ELF binary, so you can recreate the behaviour of the xmake run command like this:

```
$ cheriot-tools/bin/cheriot_sim  build/cheriot/cheriot/release/
hello_world
Running file hello_world.
ELF Entry @ 0x80000000
tohost located at 0x800061e0
compartment returned 42
SUCCESS
```

If you add the --trace flag, you will get a *lot* more output. This enables all possible tracing. Every memory access, every register update, and every executed instruction will be traced. You can select a subset of this by providing an argument to --trace=. For example, passing --trace=instr will trace only instructions. The most useful option here is --trace=exception. This will provide a line of output for exceptions, which includes the address of the faulting instruction. This is very useful for finding out where CHERI exceptions have happened.

 If you use xmake run to run a simulator then it will run only the simulator that the firmware image was built for. If you invoke a simulator directly, you will not get this check. Most targets have sufficiently different memory layouts that you cannot use the same firmware image between them.

The SAFE simulator is built with Verilator, which requires tracing to be enabled or disabled as a compile-time option. The dev container therefore installs two versions cheriot_ibex_safe_sim and cheriot_ibex_safe_sim_- trace. Unlike the Sail simulator, this cannot simply run an ELF file, it needs a VHX file for each memory containing a hex dump of the initial contents of that memory. The run script for SAFE first creates this and then invokes the simulator. The scripts/ibex-build-firmware.sh script takes the ELF file as an argument and then creates the firmware directory containing the two required VHX files. The simulator expects a firmware directory to exist in the current directory and does not take any arguments.

For both simulators, tracing provides a lot of output and redirecting this to a file may be useful.

The MPACT simulator also provides an interactive mode, enabled with -i. This provides a debugging environment. You can use help inside the interactive mode to see the commands, which include breakpoints, watchpoints, and so on.

Chapter 4.
C/C++ extensions for CHERIoT

The CHERIoT platform adds a small number of C/C++ annotations to support the compartment model.

4.1. Exposing compartment entry points

Compartments are discussed in detail in Chapter 5. A compartment can expose functions as entry points via a simple attribute.

The cheri_compartment({name}) attribute specifies the name of the compartment that defines a function. This is used in concert with the -cheri-compartment= compiler flag. This allows the compiler to know whether a particular function (which may be in another compilation unit) is defined in the same compartment as the current compilation unit, allowing direct calls for functions in the same compilation unit and cross-compartment calls for other cases.

This can be used on either definitions or declarations but is most commonly used on declarations.

If a function is defined while compiling a compilation unit belonging to a different compartment, the compiler will raise an error. In CHERIoT RTOS, this attribute is always used via the __cheriot_compartment({name}) macro. This makes it possible to simply use #define __cheriot_compartment(x) when compiling for other platforms.

Most of the time, you will not need to worry about the compiler flags directly. The xmake provided by CHERIoT RTOS will set the compiler flags for you automatically. Listing 8 shows the prototype of a trivial function that increments an integer that is private to a compartment.

```
 7  /**
 8   * A function to increment a private variable inside a
 9   * compartment.
10   */
11  __cheriot_compartment(
12    "example_compartment") int increment();
```

LISTING 8. Exporting a function for use by other compartments from a header.
[from: examples/compartment_annotation/interface.h]

The body of this function is then shown in Listing 9. Note that this does not require the attribute, it is inherited from the prototype. If you forget to include the header, you will see a linker error about a missing symbol.

```
13  int increment( )
14  {
15    counter++;
16    return 0;
17  }
```

LISTING 9. The body of a function that is exposed for cross-compartment calls.
[from: examples/compartment_annotation/compartment.cc]

The build system specifies the -cheri-compartment= flag based on the compartment target definition in the xmake.lua. Listing 10 shows this for the simple example compartment.

```
15  -- An example compartment that we can call
16  compartment("example_compartment")
17    add_files("compartment.cc")
```

LISTING 10. Build system code for defining a compartment.
[from: examples/compartment_annotation/xmake.lua]

If you get the compartment name wrong, the compiler will generate an error. For example, if you change the compartment name in Listing 8 to "wrong_compartment", you will see the following error when compiling compartment.cc, which contains the definition of this function:

```
error: compartment.cc:21:5: error: CHERI compartment entry declared
for compartment 'wrong_compartment' but implemented in
'example_compartment' (provided with -cheri-compartment=)
   21 | int monotonic(Callback callback)
      |     ^
```

4.2. Passing callbacks to other compartments.

The cheri_callback attribute specifies a function that can be used as an entry point by compartments that are passed a function pointer to it. This attribute must also be used on the type of function pointers that hold cross-compartment invocations. Any time the address of such a function is taken, the result will be a sealed capability that can be used to invoke the compartment and call this function.

The compiler does not know, when calling a callback, whether it points to the current compartment. As such, calling a CHERI callback function will *always* be a cross-compartment call, even if the target is in the current compartment.

This attribute can also be used via the __cheriot_callback macro, which allows it to be defined away when targeting other platforms.

Listing 11 shows both how to declare a typedef for a function pointer type that can be used for cross-compartment callbacks and how to expose a function that takes one. This is a simple function that will increment a private counter and invoke the callback.

```
16  /**
17   * A cross-compartment callback that takes an integer and
18   * returns an integer.
19   */
20  typedef __cheriot_callback int (*Callback)(int);
21
22  /**
23   * Example of a function that takes a cross-compartment
24   * callback as an argument.
25   */
26  __cheriot_compartment("example_compartment") int monotonic(
27     Callback);
```

LISTING 11. Exposing a function that takes a cross-compartment callback for use by other compartments. [from: examples/compartment_annotation/interface.h]

The implementation of this function (Listing 12) calls it just as it would call any other function pointer. The difference is dealt with entirely by the compiler. For a normal call, the compiler will emit a simple jump-and-link to the address, whereas in this case it will invoke the switcher (see Section 2.2) with the callback as an extra argument.

Every function that's exposed for cross-compartment invocation has an entry in the compartment's *export table*, containing the metadata that the switcher will use. Every function that is directly called by another compartment will then have an entry in the calling compartment's *import table* that the loader will initialise with a sealed capability to the export table entry. Callback functions work in a similar way, except that the import table entry is for the compartment that exposes the callback.

When you take the address of a callback function, the compiler simply inserts a load of the import table entry, giving exactly the same kind of sealed capability that you would use for direct cross-compartment calls. At the call site, the only difference between a direct cross-compartment call and a call-back is that the former will contain the load from the import table, whereas the latter will simply move the callback into the register that is used to pass the callee to the switcher.

```
21 int monotonic(Callback callback)
22 {
23   return callback(++counter);
24 }
```

LISTING 12. The body of a function that invokes a cross-compartment callback.
[from: examples/compartment_annotation/compartment.cc]

The callback is then declared just like any other function, but with the correct attribute, as shown in Listing 13.

 The function attributes can be provided either before the start of the function or before the function name (after the return type). In some cases, the latter can avoid ambiguity (the attribute definitely applies to the function, not to the return type), but both are equivalent the rest of the time.

```
8 int __cheriot_callback callback(int counter)
9 {
10   printf("Counter value: %d\n", counter);
11   return 0;
12 }
```

LISTING 13. A function that can be invoked as a cross-compartment callback.
[from: examples/compartment_annotation/entry.cc]

The callback function is passed just like any other function pointer, as shown in Listing 14. Note that the two ways of taking the address of a function in C/C++ (callback and &callback) are equivalent. Both work; some people prefer the former because it is more concise, others prefer the latter because it is a visual marker that a pointer is being constructed.

When you run this example, you should see:

```
Counter value: 2
Counter value: 3
```

The callback is invoked in the compartment that implements it and has access to the copy of the counter (passed by value) that the caller provides, but it cannot modify the counter.

```
19  increment();
20  monotonic(callback);
21  monotonic(&callback);
```

LISTING 14. A function that can be invoked as a cross-compartment callback.
[from: examples/compartment_annotation/entry.cc]

4.3. Exposing library entry points

Libraries are discussed in detail in Chapter 5. Like compartments, they can export functions via a simple annotation. Unlike compartments, they are simply a mechanism for code sharing, not a security boundary. Libraries do not have mutable globals and each call to a library is assumed to have access to everything in the caller. Libraries are intended to provide almost the same abstraction as if you'd copied and pasted code into each compartment that calls them, though without the accompanying code duplication.

The cheri_libcall attribute specifies that this function is provided by a library (shared between compartments). This attribute is implicit for all compiler built-in functions, including memcpy and similar freestanding C environment functions. As with cheri_compartment( ), this may be used on both definitions and declarations.

Unlike the compartment annotation, the library annotation does not specify the library that provides the function (though you can validate this later with the auditing tools, as described in Chapter 10). This allows library functions to be moved between libraries easily, a refactoring that does not affect most of the security model. For example, the RTOS used to provide a library that implemented all of the helpers for atomic operations. This was later split into separate libraries for different sized objects, allowing code to link only the atomic operations for types that it uses.

This attribute can also be used via the __cheriot_libcall macro, which allows it to be defined away when targeting other platforms. This is how it is used in Listing 15, which declares a simple library function.

```
7  /**
8   * A simple example library function.
9   */
10 __cheriot_libcall void library_function();
```

LISTING 15. A declaration of a library function
[from: examples/library_annotation/interface.h]

As with the compartment annotations, these don't need to be placed on both the prototype and the declaration. Listing 16 shows the definition, which omits the attribute.

```
10 void library_function()
11 {
12   // Print the stack capability from within the library.
13   Debug::log("Stack pointer: {}",
14             __builtin_cheri_stack_get());
15 }
```

LISTING 16. A definition of a library function
[from: examples/library_annotation/library.cc]

Both the library function and the call site, shown in Listing 17, use the CHERIoT RTOS debugging APIs that are described in detail in Chapter 8. Among other things, these allow you to pretty-print capabilities. These use a compiler builtin to get the capability to the stack and print it.

```
11 /// Thread entry point.
12 void __cheriot_compartment("entry") entry()
13 {
14   // Print the current stack capability.
15   Debug::log("Stack pointer: {}",
16             __builtin_cheri_stack_get());
17   // Call the function exported from the library.
18   library_function();
19 }
```

LISTING 17. Calling a simple library function.
[from: examples/library_annotation/entry.cc]

When you run this example, you should see the stack capability printed twice, once by the entry compartment and once by the library. The library is called from the compartment so you should see the stack pointer move, but the bounds will remain the same. When you run it, you should see something like this:

```
Entry compartment: Stack pointer: 0x80000af0 (v:1
0x80000720-0x80000b20 l:0x400 o:0x0 p: - RWcgml -- ---)
Library: Stack pointer: 0x80000ad0 (v:1 0x80000720-0x80000b20
l:0x400 o:0x0 p: - RWcgml -- ---)
```

The bounds (0x80000720-0x80000b20) remain constant across the call. This means that malicious code in the library could inspect or modify everything on the caller's stack. In contrast, if you try the same thing in a compartment, you will see this stack truncated.

Try modifying this example to place the function in a compartment instead of a library. Don't forget to modify the xmake.lua file to change the library target to compartment.

4.4. Interrupt state control

The cheriot_interrupt_state attribute (commonly used as the C++11 / C23 attribute cheriot::interrupt_state) is applied to functions and takes an argument that is one of the following:

enabled
> Interrupts are enabled when calling this function.

disabled
> Interrupts are disabled when calling this function.

inherit
> The interrupt state is unchanged (inherited from the caller) when invoking this function.

For most functions, inherit is the default. For cross-compartment calls, enabled is the default and inherit is not permitted.

The compiler may not inline functions at call sites that would change the interrupt state and will always call them via a sentry capability set up by the loader. This makes it possible to statically reason about interrupt state in lexical scopes.

 If a compartment is able to provide arbitrary interrupt-disabled functions, that compartment is in the TCB for availability. It is a good idea to move interrupt-disabled code into library functions where the contents of the library can be audited and the exact binary for the interrupt-disabled function can be part of a *software bill of materials* (SBOM), which can then allow you to reason about the whole system's availability guarantees.

If you need to wrap a few statements to run with interrupts disabled, you can use the convenience helper CHERI::with_interrupts_disabled. This is annotated with the attribute that disables interrupts and invokes the passed lambda. This maintains the structured-programming discipline for code running with interrupts disabled: it is coupled to a lexical scope.

Documentation for the `with_interrupts_disabled` function

```
template<typename T>
  [[cheriot::interrupt_state(disabled)]] auto
with_interrupts_disabled(T &&fn)
```

Invokes the passed callable object with interrupts disabled.

You need to be very careful using this attribute. Listing 18 shows a very simple example of how disabling interrupts can have adverse effects. The `spin_for_ticks` function in this example will simply spin for the requested number of ticks, reading the cycle counter until enough time has elapsed. This is called by a thread entry-point function that runs with low priority, with increasing tick counts.

The `rdcycle64` function reads the cycle timer. The `thread_sleep` call is sleeping for a single scheduler tick. This function and the meaning of a scheduler tick are explained in more detail in Chapter 6. For now, assume that the thread is attempting to sleep for the number of cycles shown by the `printf` call at the start, outside of the loop.

The other thread in this program is shown in Listing 19. This runs with high priority and so will always preempt the low-priority thread when it is able to, but disabling interrupts means that preemption is impossible. Timer interrupts do not fire and so the scheduler cannot interrupt the function.

When you run this, you will see that the actual time spent sleeping increases each iteration:

```
One tick is 10000 cycles
low-priority thread running
Cycles elapsed with high-priority thread yielding: 23461
low-priority thread running
Cycles elapsed with high-priority thread yielding: 33450
low-priority thread running
Cycles elapsed with high-priority thread yielding: 43449
low-priority thread running
Cycles elapsed with high-priority thread yielding: 53448
```

The low-priority thread is allowed to start running when the high-priority thread yields but then prevents any other thread in the system from running. If you did anything like this in a realtime system, this would guarantee that you would would miss your realtime deadlines.

```
30
31  /**
32   * A function that runs with interrupts disabled and
33   * consumes CPU for the requested number of ticks.
34   */
35  [[cheriot::interrupt_state(disabled)]] void
36  spin_for_ticks(uint32_t ticks)
37  {
38    uint64_t end =
39      rdcycle64() + (uint64_t(ticks) * TIMERCYCLES_PER_TICK);
40    while (rdcycle64() < end) {}
41  }
42
43  /// Low-priority thread entry point.
44  void __cheriot_compartment("interrupts") low()
45  {
46    int sleeps = 2;
47    while (true)
48    {
49      printf("low-priority thread running\n");
50      spin_for_ticks(sleeps++);
51    }
52  }
```

LISTING 18. A low-priority thread that uses an interrupts-disabled function to consume CPU. [from: examples/interrupts_disabled/interrupts.cc]

```
10  /// High-priority thread entry point.
11  void __cheriot_compartment("interrupts") high()
12  {
13    printf("One tick is %d cycles\n", TIMERCYCLES_PER_TICK);
14    while (true)
15    {
16      // Get the current cycle time
17      uint64_t start = rdcycle64();
18      // Sleep for one scheduler tick
19      Timeout t{1};
20      thread_sleep(&t);
21      // Report how long the sleep was
22      printf("Cycles elapsed with high-priority thread "
23             "yielding: %lld\n",
24             rdcycle64() - start);
25    }
26  }
```

LISTING 19. A high-priority thread that is starved by an interrupts-disabled function called from a low-priority thread.
[from: examples/interrupts_disabled/interrupts.cc]

The key problem here is that the interrupts-disabled function has an unbounded run time. It will consume the CPU for a data-dependent amount of time with no practical upper bound. When you are building realtime systems, even very soft realtime systems, you must ensure that the worst-case execution time for responding to events is bounded.

4.5. Importing MMIO access

The MMIO_CAPABILITY({type}, {name}) macro is used to access memory-mapped I/O devices. These are specified in the board definition file by the build system. The DEVICE_EXISTS({name}) macro can be used to detect whether the current target provides a device with the specified name.

The type parameter is the type used to represent the MMIO region. The macro evaluates to a volatile {type} *, so MMIO_CAPABILITY(struct UART, uart) will provide a volatile struct UART * pointing (and bounded) to the device that the board definition exposes as uart. This is precisely what happens in Listing 20, which prints 'Hello world!' to the UART directly.

```
10  static const char hello[] = "Hello world!\n";
11  for (char c : hello)
12  {
13    MMIO_CAPABILITY(Uart, uart)->blocking_write(c);
14  }
```

LISTING 20. Retrieving a pointer to a UART's MMIO space and using it.
[from: examples/raw_uart/raw_uart.cc]

4.6. Sealing opaque types

Sealed capabilities were introduced in Section 1.6. They provide a simple hardware-enforced mechanism for providing type-safe *opaque types*.

You normally implement opaque types in C/C++ by forward-declaring a struct type and then handing out pointers to that type. For example, you might write something like this:

```
struct MyType;
MyType *create_my_type();
```

This function will return a new instance of some type, but the caller can't see the implementation details. They can, of course, cast it to a char* or similar and read and write the underlying data. The opaque type is a software-engineering boundary telling the caller that they should not depend on the representation of this type.

Sealing on CHERIoT makes it easy to turn that software-engineering boundary into a security boundary. The same interface can be written for CHERIoT as:

```
struct MyType;
MyType *__sealed_capability create_my_type();
```

The returned value is marked as being tamper proof. The hardware ensures that the caller cannot modify the underlying object. If the caller casts this to a char* and tries to modify it then they will get a run-time trap. The __sealed_capability qualifier ensures that callers don't do this accidentally. The compiler will error if you try to dereference a sealed capability.

You can implicitly cast the MyType *__sealed_capability to void* but not to a MyType *. You can explicitly cast away the __sealed_capability qualifier but that just lets you compile things that will trap at run time.

The builtins for sealing and unsealing respect these types, as do the RTOS APIs (Section 7.7) that use them. This means that you can write a function that expects a MyType *__sealed_capability and preserve type safety throughout your code and untrusted code. When a caller gives you back this kind of pointer and you unseal it, you will get a MyType * that is either a valid value or untagged.

4.7. Manipulating capabilities with C builtins

The compiler provides a set of built-in functions for manipulating capabilities. These are typically of the form __builtin_cheri_{noun}_{verb}. You can read all of the fields of a CHERI capability with get as the verb and the following nouns:

address
> The current address that's used when the capability is used as a pointer.

base
> The lowest address that this authorises access to.

top
> The address immediately after the end of the range that this authorises access to.

length
> The distance between the base and the top.

perms
> The architectural permissions that this capability holds.

sealed
> Is this a sealed capability?

tag
    Is this a valid capability?

type
    The type of this capability (zero means unsealed).

The verbs vary because they express the *guarded manipulation* guarantees for CHERI capabilities. You can't, for example, arbitrarily set the permissions on a capability, you can only remove permissions. Capabilities can be modified with the nouns and verbs listed in Table 3.

Noun	Modification verb	Operation
address	set	Set the address for the capability.
bounds	set	Sets the base at or below the current address and the length at or above the requested length, as closely as possible to give a valid capability
bounds	set_exact	Sets the base to the current address and the length to the requested length or returns an untagged capability (one that will trap if used) if the result is not representable.
perms	and	Clears all permissions except those provided as the argument.
tag	clear	Invalidates the capability but preserves all other fields.

TABLE 3. CHERI capability manipulation builtin functions

Setting the object type for sealed capabilities is more complex and requires a second capability that authorises sealing. The address field for capabilities with permit-seal or permit-unseal permissions refers to the object-type space, rather than the memory address space. The __builtin_cheri_seal function takes an authorising capability (something with the permit-seal permission) as the second argument and sets the object type of the result to the address of the sealing capability. Conversely, __builtin_cheri_unseal uses a capability with the permit-unseal permission and an address matching the object type to restore the original unsealed value.

Most of the time, C code will avoid using the builtins directly and instead use the wrappers defined in cheri-builtins.h. This file contains a set of macros that wrap the builtins to remove the __builtin_ prefix.

 Although most of the macros in cheri-builtins.h match the names of the underlying builtins, the permissions macros follow the CHERIoT RTOS coding convention of avoiding abbreviations and so use permissions instead of perms. The predicates prefix the operation with _is so __builtin_cheri_equal_exact becomes cheri_is_equal_exact.

You can see how to use most of the introspection builtins via their macro wrappers in Listing 21. This prints a capability, showing its address, tag (valid) bit, length, bounds, and permissions. The permissions are expanded as the letters from the tables in Section 1.4. The builtins are thing wrappers around the instructions, which represent the permissions as a bitmask. Individual bits must be extracted by a bitwise AND operation.

Listing 22 uses this function to print some initial capabilities from both heap and stack memory and then manipulates them. First, it explicitly sets the bounds of the heap capability to 23 bytes, then removes all permissions except load.

```
35  // A stack allocation
36  char stackBuffer[23];
37  print_capability(stackBuffer);
38  // A heap allocation
39  char *heapBuffer = malloc(23);
40  print_capability(heapBuffer);
41  // Setting the bounds of a heap capability
42  char *bounded = cheri_bounds_set(heapBuffer, 23);
43  print_capability(bounded);
44  // Removing permissions from a heap capability
45  bounded = cheri_permissions_and(bounded, CHERI_PERM_LOAD);
46  print_capability(bounded);
47  print_capability(heapBuffer);
```

LISTING 22. Manipulating capabilities using the C builtin wrappers.
[from: examples/manipulate_capabilities_c/example.c]

When you run this example, you should see something like this (the exact addresses may vary):

```
 6 void print_capability(void *ptr)
 7 {
 8   unsigned permissions = cheri_permissions_get(ptr);
 9   printf(
10     "0x%x (valid:%d length: 0x%x 0x%x-0x%x otype:%d "
11     "permissions: %c "
12     "%c%c%c%c%c%c %c%c %c%c%c)\n",
13     cheri_address_get(ptr),
14     cheri_tag_get(ptr),
15     cheri_length_get(ptr),
16     cheri_base_get(ptr),
17     cheri_top_get(ptr),
18     cheri_type_get(ptr),
19     (permissions & CHERI_PERM_GLOBAL) ? 'G' : '-',
20     (permissions & CHERI_PERM_LOAD) ? 'R' : '-',
21     (permissions & CHERI_PERM_STORE) ? 'W' : '-',
22     (permissions & CHERI_PERM_LOAD_STORE_CAP) ? 'c' : '-',
23     (permissions & CHERI_PERM_LOAD_GLOBAL) ? 'g' : '-',
24     (permissions & CHERI_PERM_LOAD_MUTABLE) ? 'm' : '-',
25     (permissions & CHERI_PERM_STORE_LOCAL) ? 'l' : '-',
26     (permissions & CHERI_PERM_SEAL) ? 'S' : '-',
27     (permissions & CHERI_PERM_UNSEAL) ? 'U' : '-',
28     (permissions & CHERI_PERM_USER0) ? '0' : '-');
29 }
```

LISTING 21. Pretty-printing a capability using the C builtin wrappers.
[from: examples/manipulate_capabilities_c/example.c]

```
0x80000ae1 (valid:1 length: 0x17 0x80000ae1-0x80000af8 otype:0
permissions: - RWcgml -- -)
0x80006710 (valid:1 length: 0x18 0x80006710-0x80006728 otype:0
permissions: G RWcgm- -- -)
0x80006710 (valid:1 length: 0x17 0x80006710-0x80006727 otype:0
permissions: G RWcgm- -- -)
0x80006710 (valid:1 length: 0x17 0x80006710-0x80006727 otype:0
permissions: - R----- -- -)
0x80006710 (valid:1 length: 0x18 0x80006710-0x80006728 otype:0
permissions: G RWcgm- -- -)
```

First, note the difference between the permissions on the stack and heap allocation. The heap allocation has global permission: it may be stored anywhere. The stack allocation lacks global, but has store-local permission, which allows it to be used to store other capabilities providing they don't have the global permission. These two conditions ensure that stack pointers (which lack global) can be stored only on the stack (the only memory that has store-local permission).

The bounds on the original heap allocation are rounded up to a multiple of the heap's allocation granule size. The CHERIoT allocator allocates 8-byte chunks, so this is rounded up to 24 (0x18) bytes. For a capability this small, CHERIoT can precisely represent the desired size and so the bounds-setting operation succeeds and you can derive a capability with the precise bounds that we requested.

Next, this removes all permissions except load. This pointer now provides a read-only view of the data, which cannot be stored anywhere except on the stack and which cannot be used to load capabilities.

Finally, this example prints the heap allocation again to remind you that these permissions and bounds apply to the *pointer* and not to the *object*. We have not removed permissions from an object, we have created a pointer that has fewer permissions to that object. There is no limit to the number of pointers that can exist to a single object.

4.8. Comparing capabilities with C builtins

By default, the C/C++ == operator on capabilities compares only the address.

This is subject to change in a future revision of CHERI C. It makes porting some existing code easier, but breaks the substitution principle (if a == b, you would expect to be able to use b or a interchangeably).

You can compare capabilities for exact equality with the `__builtin_cheri_equal_exact`, or the `cheri_is_equal_exact` macro that wraps the builtin. This returns true if the two capabilities that are passed to it are identical, false otherwise. Exact equality means that the address, bounds, permissions, object type, and tag are all identical. It is, effectively, a bitwise comparison of all of the bits in the two capabilities, including the tag bits.

You can see the difference between the two in Listing 23. This creates a capability with a small offset into an on-stack buffer and then restricts the bounds and removes permissions from it, then compares them for equality using both the == operator and the `cheri_is_equal_exact` macro.

When you run this example, you should see output that looks something like this:

```
33   // A stack allocation
34   char   stackBuffer[23];
35   char *offset = stackBuffer + 4;
36   print_capability(offset);
37   // Reduce the bounds
38   char *bounded = cheri_bounds_set(offset, 4);
39   print_capability(bounded);
40   printf("Equal? %d\n", bounded == offset);
41   printf("Exactly equal? %d\n",
42           cheri_is_equal_exact(bounded, offset));
43   // Remove permissions
44   char *restricted =
45     cheri_permissions_and(bounded, CHERI_PERM_LOAD);
46   print_capability(restricted);
47   printf("Equal? %d\n", bounded == restricted);
48   printf("Exactly equal? %d\n",
49           cheri_is_equal_exact(bounded, restricted));
50   char *untagged = cheri_tag_clear(restricted);
51   print_capability(untagged);
52   printf("Equal? %d\n", untagged == restricted);
53   printf("Exactly equal? %d\n",
54           cheri_is_equal_exact(untagged, restricted));
```

LISTING 23. Comparing two capabilities for equality.

[from: examples/compare_capabilities/example.c]

```
0x80000ae5 (valid:1 length: 0x17 0x80000ae1-0x80000af8 otype:0
permissions: - RWcgml -- -)
0x80000ae5 (valid:1 length: 0x4 0x80000ae5-0x80000ae9 otype:0
permissions: - RWcgml -- -)
Equal? 1
Exactly equal? 0
0x80000ae5 (valid:1 length: 0x4 0x80000ae5-0x80000ae9 otype:0
permissions: - R----- -- -)
Equal? 1
Exactly equal? 0
0x80000ae5 (valid:0 length: 0x4 0x80000ae5-0x80000ae9 otype:0
permissions: - R----- -- -)
Equal? 1
Exactly equal? 0
```

First it shows the original capability, which grants complete access to a stack allocation and has its address four bytes offset into the object. Then the bounded capability, which has the same address and permissions, but different bounds. These compare equal with address-based comparison but not exactly equal.

Next it removes permissions from the derived capability and compares these. Again, the difference in permissions is not reflected in the address-based equality but is in the exact equality.

The final case is the most interesting and the one where this can be the most confusing. The last pointer constructed in this example is not a capability. This is constructed by clearing the tag, which is the bit that indicates that the capability-sized word is, in fact, a capability. Losing the tag bit means that this is not a capability at all, merely 64 bits of data that happen to be loaded into a capability register. With the C equality operator, this *still* compares equal to any of the other capabilities, but the exact-equality comparison fails.

Ordered comparison, using operators such as less-than or greater-than, always operate with the address. There is no total ordering over capabilities. Two capabilities with different bounds or different permissions but the same address will return false when compared with either < or >.

This is fine according to a strict representation of the C abstract machine because comparing two pointers to different objects is undefined behaviour. It can be confusing but, unfortunately, there is no good alternative. Comparison of pointers is commonly used for keying in collections. For example, the C++ std::map class uses the ordered comparison operators for building a tree and relies on it working correctly for keys that are pointers. Ideally, these would explicitly operate over the address, but that would require invasive modifications when porting to CHERI platforms.

You can see the case that can make this confusing in Listing 24. This compares two capabilities using the ordered operators and then exact equality.

```
58  if (bounded > offset)
59  {
60    printf("bounded > offset\n");
61  }
62  else if (bounded < offset)
63  {
64    printf("bounded < offset\n");
65  }
66  else if (cheri_is_equal_exact(bounded, offset))
67  {
68    printf("bounded exactly equals offset\n");
69  }
70  else
71  {
72    printf("bounded is not greater than, less than, nor "
73           "equal to, offset\n");
74  }
```

LISTING 24. Trying to construct an ordering over two capabilities.
[from: examples/compare_capabilities/example.c]

When you run this example, it will print:

```
bounded is not greater than, less than, nor equal to, offset
```

This highlights that, within the C abstract machine, there is no good choice for what == should do on capabilities. In the current version, it breaks the substitution principle: you cannot use a and b interchangeably if a == b. In the alternative version, existing code that does a < b and a > b and assumes that a == b holds if both ordered comparisons fail would now be incorrect.

In general, in new code, you should avoid comparing pointers for anything other than exact equality, unless you are certain that they have the same base and bounds. Instead, be explicit about exactly what you are testing. Do you care if the permissions are different? Do you care about the bounds? Do you care if the value is tagged? Or do you just want to care about the address? In each case, you should explicitly compare the components of the capability that you care about.

You can also compare capabilities for subset relationships with __built-in_cheri_subset_test. This returns true if the second argument is a subset of the first. A capability is a subset of another if every right that it conveys is held by the other. This means the bounds of the subset capability must be smaller than or equal to the superset and all permissions held by the subset must be held by the superset.

You can see this for the capabilities that we've been looking at in Listing 25.

```
78   printf("bounded ⊂ offset? %d\n",
79         cheri_subset_test(offset, bounded));
80   printf("restricted ⊂ bounded? %d\n",
81         cheri_subset_test(bounded, restricted));
82   printf("untagged ⊂ restricted? %d\n",
83         cheri_subset_test(restricted, untagged));
84   printf("offset ⊂ bounded? %d\n",
85         cheri_subset_test(bounded, offset));
```

LISTING 25. Subset relationships over two capabilities.
[from: examples/compare_capabilities/example.c]

When you run this, the output is:

```
bounded ⊂ offset? 1
restricted ⊂ bounded? 1
untagged ⊂ restricted? 0
offset ⊂ bounded? 0
```

Most of these lines should not be a surprise. The bounded capability is a subset of the original, it was created by subsetting the bounds. The capability that was created by subsetting the rights on the bounded version is, in turn, a subset of the bounded version. Finally, the original is not a subset of the bounded version.

The surprising entry might be that the untagged capability is not a subset of the original. In a set-theoretic sense, this would be incorrect: The empty set is a subset of any other set. In practice, this degenerate case is not useful.

The test-subset operation gives a unidirectional substitution property (i.e. any operation that is safe to do with the subset is safe to do with the superset) but this is not usually something that you care about. The test is most useful for telling if one capability is *derived from* another (or, at least, could have a derivation path from a specific common root). For example, we can tell that (ignoring stack lifetime errors) bounded and restricted are both derived from the original stack allocation. It happens that, in this specific case, unbounded was derived from the same stack allocation but the lack of a tag bit means that there are no *provenance* guarantees. For untagged values, we can make no claims about whether they were derived from any other capabilities.

This is useful to check if a particular pointer that you've been given is derived from something that you already own. The claims mechanisms (described in Section 7.8) uses this, for example, to allow threads to keep an object alive if you hold a pointer derived from the original object pointer. The temporal-safety properties of CHERIoT ensure that any dangling pointer to a heap object will be untagged and so any valid (tagged) pointer that is a subset of a heap allocation must be derived from the return from the original call to malloc or some similar function.

4.9. Sizing allocations

CHERI capabilities cannot represent arbitrary bases and bounds. The original CHERI prototypes, with a 64-bit address, encoded a 64-bit top address and a 64-bit base. This made capabilities 256 bits in total (four times the address size), which was not feasible for production implementations (though having lots of space was very useful for prototyping). Fortunately, there is a lot of redundancy between these three values. Generally, for any allocation, the high bits of the base, top, and some in-bounds address will all be the same.

CHERI systems since around 2016 have used compressed bounds encodings that take advantage of this redundancy. Rather than storing a complete address for the top and bottom, they store a floating-point value that is the distance from the address to the top and from the address to the base. The exponent bits are shared between the two. This means that, the larger the bounds, the more strongly aligned the base and bounds must be.

The current CHERIoT encoding gives byte-granularity bounds for objects up to 511 bytes, then requires one more bit of alignment for each bit needed to represent the size, up to 8 MiB. Capabilities larger than 8 MiB must be aligned on an 8 MiB boundary for their base and top. This is ample for small embedded systems where most compartments or heap objects are expected to be under tens of KiBs.

This is a slightly simplified version of the original CHERI scheme, which simplifies critical-path lengths on short pipelines. A microcontroller may have a simple pipeline with only the traditional fetch, decode, and execute phases (or even less). The critical path is the path with the most logic chained together in a single stage. This limits the maximum clock speed for the device because a signal must be able to propagate through all of this logic in a single cycle.

Future versions of CHERIoT are likely to support slightly more expressive formats on longer pipelines, where the decoding can be split between two or more stages. Other CHERI systems make different trade-offs.

Calculating the length can be non-trivial and can vary across CHERI systems. The compiler provides two builtins that help.

The first, `__builtin_cheri_round_representable_length`, returns the smallest length that is larger than (or equal to) the requested length and can be accurately represented. The compressed bounds encoding requires both the top and base to be aligned on the same amount and so there's a corresponding mask that needs to be used for alignment. The `__builtin_cheri_representable_alignment_mask` builtin returns the mask that can be applied to the base and top addresses to align them.

Listing 26 shows how to use these builtins via their wrappers to find the smallest representable size for a requested size.

The allocator is using these internally when it determines the size to provide for a request and the alignment that it needs to find. When you run it, you may see something like this.

```
34  const size_t Size = 160000;
35  printf("Smallest representable size of %d-byte "
36         "allocation: %d (0x%x). Alignment mask: 0x%x\n",
37         Size,
38         cheri_round_representable_length(Size),
39         cheri_round_representable_length(Size),
40         cheri_representable_alignment_mask(Size));
41  void *allocation = malloc(Size);
42  print_capability(allocation);
```

LISTING 26. Rounding up sizes for representable allocations.
[from: examples/bounds_lengths/example.c]

```
Smallest representable size of 160000-byte allocation: 160256
(0x27200). Alignment mask: 0xfffffe00
0x80006800 (valid:1 length: 0x27200 0x80006800-0x8002da00 otype:0
permissions: G RWcgm- -- -)
```

The requested size needs to be rounded up to 160,256 bytes. The hex representation makes it easier to see the alignment is 0x200, or 512 in decimal. The top and bottom of an allocation that can accurately represent the requested size must be 512-byte aligned. The alignment mask is simply another way of representing this, it is nine zeroes in the low bits and ones in all of the high bits.

When the allocator returns a value for this requested size, the length is rounded up as you'd expect. If you bitwise AND the base and top with the alignment mask, you will see no change. Both are, in this specific case, slightly more strongly aligned than required, most likely because this is the first malloc call in the program and so these are as strongly aligned as the heap base. You can test that the alignment is adequate by doing a bitwise AND (C operator: &) of the base or top with the alignment mask. This should leave the value unmodified.

4.10. Manipulating capabilities with CHERI::Capability

The raw C builtins can be somewhat verbose. CHERIoT RTOS provides a CHERI::Capability class in cheri.hh to simplify inspecting and manipulating CHERI capabilities.

These provide methods that are modelled to allow you to pretend that they give direct access to the fields of the capability. The manipulate_capabilities_cxx example shows how to do the same things as the manipulate_capabilities_c example, this time with the C++ APIs. First, Listing 27 reimplements the print_capability function using CHERI::Capability. This is slightly more verbose because it's printing with the printf function, which is a C variadic and so cannot take the result of ptr.address(), which is a proxy that allows you to manipulate the address.

```
6  void print_capability(CHERI::Capability<void> ptr)
7  {
8    using P                      = CHERI::Permission;
9    ptraddr_t        address     = ptr.address();
10   CHERI::PermissionSet permissions = ptr.permissions();
11   printf("0x%x (valid:%d length: 0x%x 0x%x-0x%x otype:%d "
12          "permissions: %c "
13          "%c%c%c%c%c%c %c%c %c%c%c)\n",
14          address,
15          ptr.is_valid(),
16          ptr.length(),
17          ptr.base(),
18          ptr.top(),
19          ptr.type(),
20          (permissions.contains(P::Global)) ? 'G' : '-',
21          (permissions.contains(P::Load)) ? 'R' : '-',
22          (permissions.contains(P::Store)) ? 'W' : '-',
23          (permissions.contains(P::LoadStoreCapability))
24             ? 'c'
25             : '-',
26          (permissions.contains(P::LoadGlobal)) ? 'g' : '-',
27          (permissions.contains(P::LoadMutable)) ? 'm' : '-',
28          (permissions.contains(P::StoreLocal)) ? 'l' : '-',
29          (permissions.contains(P::Seal)) ? 'S' : '-',
30          (permissions.contains(P::Unseal)) ? 'U' : '-',
31          (permissions.contains(P::Global)) ? '0' : '-');
32 }
```

LISTING 27. Pretty-printing a capability using the C++ APIs.
[from: examples/manipulate_capabilities_cxx/example.cc]

 The using P = CHERI::Permission is not good style. It is done here so that the example code fits in a narrow page. In normal code, a mode descriptive name would be better.

Note the CHERI::PermissionSet class here. This is a (constexpr) class that encapsulates a CHERI permission set. The C version of this exposed the permissions in their raw form as a word where each bit represented a permission. The C++ version uses a rich type, with methods for subsetting. This can be used as a template parameter and can be used in static assertions for compile-time validation of derivation chains. The loader makes extensive use of this class to ensure correctness, with compile-time checks that operations on permission-set objects are valid.

This part of the example uses the `contains()` method to query whether a specific permission is present. This is strongly typed; it takes a `CHERI::Permission`, not an arbitrary integer. It is also a variadic template function: you can pass it multiple permissions and it will return true if and only if the permission set has all of them.

Next, Listing 28 does the same set of manipulations as Listing 22. This uses a `CHERI::Capability<void>` rather than a `void*` to hold the pointers.

```
38  // A stack allocation
39  char stackBuffer[23];
40  print_capability(stackBuffer);
41  // A heap allocation
42  CHERI::Capability<void> heapBuffer = new char[23];
43  print_capability(heapBuffer);
44  // Setting the bounds of a heap capability
45  auto bounded     = heapBuffer;
46  bounded.bounds() = 23;
47  print_capability(bounded);
48  // Removing permissions from a heap capability
49  bounded.permissions() &= CHERI::Permission::Load;
50  print_capability(bounded);
51  print_capability(heapBuffer);
```

LISTING 28. Manipulating capabilities using the C++ APIs.
[from: examples/manipulate_capabilities_cxx/example.cc]

The `bounded.bounds() = 23` expression shows how the methods act like fields. This is doing a set-bounds operation on the capability. Similarly, the `&=` operation on the result of calling `permissions()` is an and-permissions operation. This lets you operate on the permissions as a `CHERI::PermissionSet` directly.

The equality comparison for `CHERI::Capability` uses exact comparison, unlike raw C/C++ pointer comparison. This is less confusing for new code (it respects the substitution principle) but users may be confused that a `==` b is true but `Capability{a} == Capability{b}` is false. Listing 29 shows the various forms of comparison.

When you run this, you will see:
```
heapBuffer == bounded? 0
heapBuffer == bounded (as raw pointers)? 1
heapBuffer == bounded (as address comparison)? 1
```

```
55  printf("heapBuffer == bounded? %d\n",
56         heapBuffer == bounded);
57  printf("heapBuffer == bounded (as raw pointers)? %d\n",
58         heapBuffer.get() == bounded.get());
59  printf(
60    "heapBuffer == bounded (as address comparison)? %d\n",
61    heapBuffer.address() == bounded.address());
```

LISTING 29. Comparting capabilities using the C++ APIs.
[from: examples/manipulate_capabilities_cxx/example.cc]

The last two comparisons are equivalent, but the third is more explicit. If you want to compare two pointers for equality as address comparison, comparing their addresses makes the intent clear.

See cheri.hh for more details and for other convenience wrappers around the compiler builtins.

Chapter 5.
Compartments and libraries

In most conventional operating systems, you share code with shared libraries and you isolate running code with processes. Compartments in CHERIoT are somewhere between these two abstractions. Unlike a process, they do not own threads, which are an independent concept in CHERIoT, described more in Chapter 6.

Communication between compartments looks a lot more like communication between shared libraries than like inter-process communication (IPC). They can export functions to be called from other compartments and can call functions exported from other compartments. Like a shared library, they have code and globals associated with them, but a *cross-compartment call* crosses a security boundary, in the same way that an IPC message would.

CHERIoT shared libraries are a lightweight way of reusing code without duplicating it into different compartments. They provide a very similar programmer model to simply copying and pasting a function into every compartment that uses it, without the space overhead. Calling a library function does not involve crossing a security boundary. Libraries contain code and read-only data but do not have mutable globals. It is possible for libraries to hold secrets but, unless library functions are written in very careful assembly, they should assume that any (immutable) globals in the library can leak to callers. Each library entry point is exposed as a sentry capability (see Section 1.6) to the callers, which means that the caller cannot directly read its code or (immutable) data.

5.1. Compartments and libraries export functions

In a UNIX-like system, a shared library can export any kind of symbol. This includes functions and global variables. In CHERIoT, compartments and libraries can export only functions as entry points. Global variables are always private to a compartment or library, unless a pointer is explicitly passed out as a function argument or return in a cross-compartment call. This design is intended to make it easier to reason about sharing between compartments.

If you declare a global in a header and define it in a library or a compartment, you may see linker errors if you try to use it in other compartments or libraries. This holds even for const globals exported from libraries. You can place a static const global in a header for a library, but that will introduce

If a library traps, the error handler for the caller compartment may see the register file for the middle of the library. Similarly, the compiler may spill arbitrary values onto the stack or leave them in registers at the end of a library function. As such, you should assume that anything processed in a library written in a compiled language will leak to the caller and anything written in assembly must be *very* careful to avoid leaking secrets. This is not normally a problem because most libraries just exist as an alternative to compiling the same functions into multiple compartments. For example, the functions that implement locks on top of futexes (see Section 6.5) are in a library to reduce overall code size, but simply copying the implementations of these functions into each caller would have no security implications.

tight coupling: the value in the header may be inlined at any use site. For very large globals, this may also increase code size significantly.

As mentioned previously, (read-only) globals in a library are hidden in a software-engineering sense, but may be leaked to callers and should not be considered private in a security sense.

You can still use a compartment's globals to share data but you must explicitly expose them via an accessor function. This makes CHERIoT compartments and libraries similar to Smalltalk-style objects, with public methods and private instance variables. You can also create globals that are shared between compartments (see Section 5.7) but that are not part of any compartment.

If you expose an interface that returns a pointer to a global, you can use CHERI permissions to restrict access. Returning a read-only pointer to a global is a common idiom for building a lightweight broadcast communication channel. The owning compartment can write to the global and other compartments can read from their copy of the pointer, with guarantees that only the owning compartment is making changes.

To see the differences, Listing 30 shows a header that exports two functions, one from a compartment and one from a library.

The exported functions both contain the implementation shown in Listing 31, which uses the debug APIs (see Chapter 8) to print the capabilities in three registers. This listing shows the version in the library but the code in

```
 7  /**
 8   * A simple example library function.
 9   */
10  __cheriot_libcall void library_function();
11
12  /**
13   * A simple example compartment function.
14   */
15  __cheriot_compartment(
16    "compartment") int compartment_function();
```

LISTING 30. A header defining library and compartment exports.
[from: examples/library_or_compartment/interface.h]

the compartment is identical. There are two compartments in this example, the entry compartment and the compartment that it calls.

The exported (library and compartment) functions will print the stack, code, and globals regions, respectively. The compiler provides builtin functions to copy two of these (the program counter and stack capabilities) but the third, the globals pointer, requires some inline assembly. The inline assembly needs to run at the start of the function because this function does not reference any globals, so the compiler will otherwise spill this register to use it as a temporary.

When you run this code, you should see output something like this:

```
Entry: Stack pointer: 0x80000d30 (v:1 0x80000750-0x80000d50 l:0x600
o:0x0 p: - RWcgml -- ---)
Entry: Program counter: 0x80005f18 (v:1 0x80005ee0-0x80005fe8
l:0x108 o:0x0 p: G R-cgm- X- ---)
Entry: Globals pointer: 0x80006202 (v:1 0x80006200-0x80006204 l:0x4
o:0x0 p: G RWcgm- -- ---)
Library: Stack pointer: 0x80000d20 (v:1 0x80000750-0x80000d50
l:0x600 o:0x0 p: - RWcgml -- ---)
Library: Program counter: 0x80005d48 (v:1 0x80005d20-0x80005df8
l:0xd8 o:0x0 p: G R-cgm- X- ---)
Library: Globals pointer: 0x80006202 (v:1 0x80006200-0x80006204
l:0x4 o:0x0 p: G RWcgm- -- ---)
Compartment: Stack pointer: 0x80000cf0 (v:1 0x80000750-0x80000d10
l:0x5c0 o:0x0 p: - RWcgml -- ---)
Compartment: Program counter: 0x80005e20 (v:1 0x80005df8-0x80005ee0
l:0xe8 o:0x0 p: G R-cgm- X- ---)
Compartment: Globals pointer: 0x800061fe (v:1 0x800061fc-0x80006200
l:0x4 o:0x0 p: G RWcgm- -- ---)
```

Ignore the exact memory addresses, these may change depending on where you run the example. First, note that the program counter capability (the capability used for instruction fetch) is different in all three cases and

```
12  register void *cgp asm("cgp");
13  asm("" : "=C"(cgp));
14  // Print the stack capability from within the library.
15  Debug::log("Stack pointer: {}",
16              __builtin_cheri_stack_get());
17  Debug::log("Program counter: {}",
18              __builtin_cheri_program_counter_get());
19  Debug::log("Globals pointer: {}", cgp);
```

LISTING 31. A simple print function to introspect compartment state.
[from: examples/library_or_compartment/library.cc]

the bounds do not overlap. In this particular build, the called compartment is placed in code memory immediately after the entry compartment, so the address 0x80005df8 is the boundary between the two.

Next, observe that the globals pointer is different between the entry compartment and the one that is called in the last three lines of the output. This example includes a single int global, to make sure that these are non-zero (two compartments may have the same zero-length capabilities for globals if they have no globals). In contrast, the library prints the same globals pointer as the caller. As previously mentioned, a malicious library can access any globals in the caller.

Finally, look at the stack pointers. The first thing to note is that the *start* address is 0x80000750 in all cases. This is because the stack belongs to the thread and not the compartment. Stacks grow downwards and the *end* of the stack is the same for each. The *address* of the stack pointer is different in each because they run at different depths on the stack. The initial value is very close to the top of the stack, then the library and compartment calls are deeper. A compartment call needs to save more state (two callee-save registers and the old global pointer, which are preserved across normal calls) and so entry to the compartment call is slightly (48 bytes) lower. The top of the stack is the most interesting place. In the compartment call, the top of the stack is at address 0x80000d10, 64 bytes below its location in the entry compartment and the library. Anything above that point is unreachable in the compartment before then. The length shows this truncation another way. The original had 0x600 bytes of stack but this is reduced to 0x5c0 after the cross-compartment call.

This may all be easier to understand visually. Figure 4 shows the memory ranges that each compartment points to, in each of the three places. The lines marked with a 1 indicate the initial values on entry, those marked 2 indicate the values in the library call and those marked 3 show the values in the cross-compartment call.

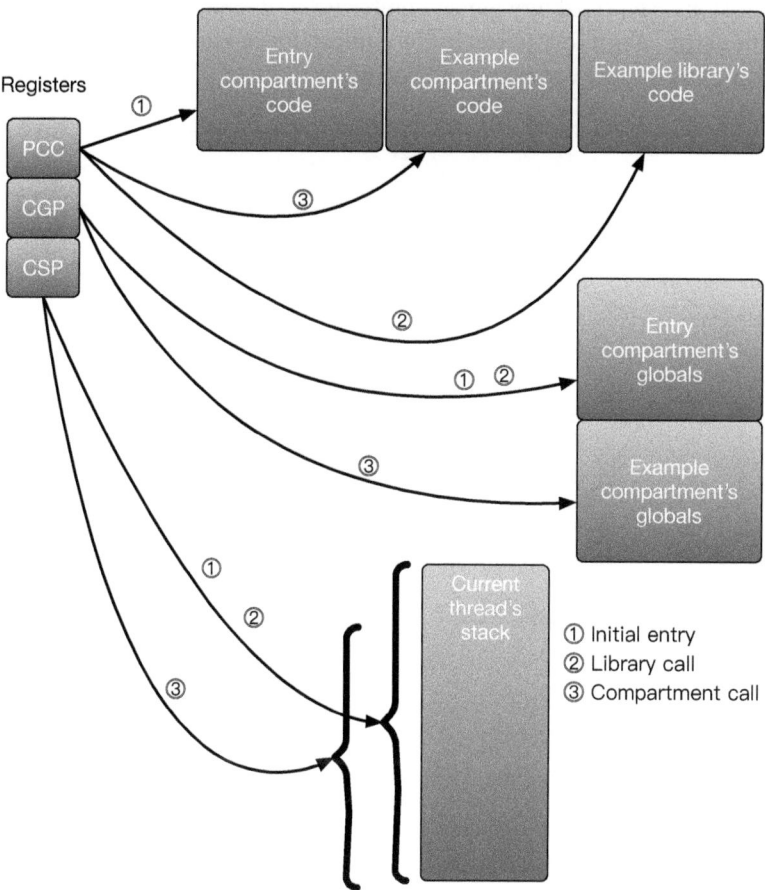

FIGURE 4. An illustration of memory pointed to by each register in the compartment-call example.

5.2. Understanding the structure of a compartment

From a distance, a compartment is a very simple construct. The core of a compartment is made of just two capabilities. The program counter capability (PCC) defines (and grants access to) the range of memory covering the compartment's code and read-only globals. This has read and execute permissions. The capability global pointer (CGP) defines (and grants access to) the range of memory covering the compartment's mutable globals. The full structure is more complex and is shown in Figure 5.

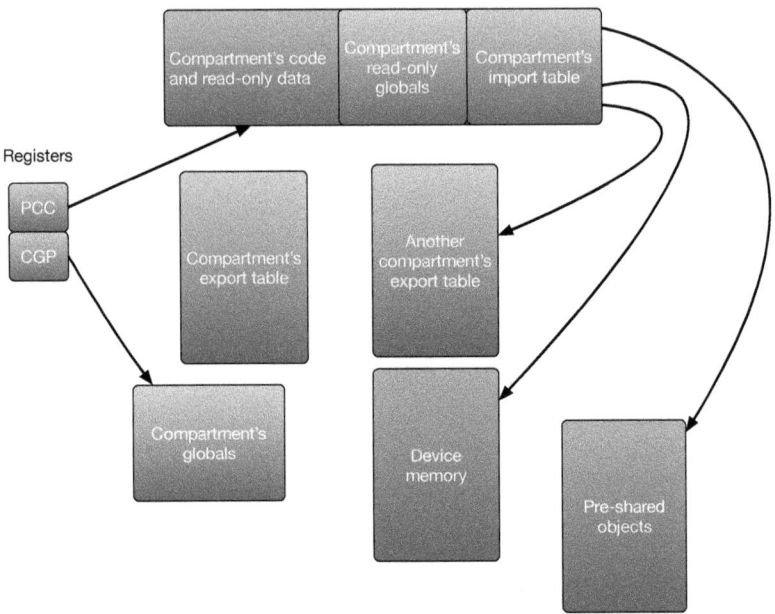

FIGURE 5. The structure of a compartment.

 A future version of the ABI may move read-only globals out of the program counter capability region but this requires some ISA changes to be efficient and so will likely not happen before CHERIoT 2.0.

If a compartment didn't need to interact with anything else, these two regions would be sufficient. In practice, compartments are useful only because they interact with other compartments or the outside world. The read-only data region contains an *import table*. This is the only region of memory that, at system start, is allowed to contain capabilities that grant access outside of the PCC and CGP region for the compartment. The instructions for the loader to populate these are in the firmware image and are amenable to auditing.

The import table contains three kinds of capabilities. MMIO capabilities are conceptually simple: they are just pointers that grant access to specific devices. This mechanism allows byte-granularity access to device registers and so it's possible to provide a compartment with access to a single device register from a large device.

Import tables also contain sentry capabilities for library functions. A shared library has its own PCC region (like a compartment) but does not have a CGP region. Library routines are invoked by loading the sentry from the import table and jumping to it.

Finally, import tables contain sealed capabilities referring to other compartments' *export tables*. If a compartment exports any entry points for other compartments to call, it has an export table. This contains the PCC and CGP for the compartment and a small amount of metadata for each exported function describing:

- The location of the entry point.
- Whether interrupts are enabled or disabled when invoking this function.
- How many argument registers are used (conversely, how many are unused and should be zeroed).

This is all of the information that the switcher needs to transition from one compartment to another. Libraries have similar export-table entries, though they are used by the loader rather than the switcher. The final element, the number of registers to use, is not used for libraries because library calls are not a transition between security domains.

Extracting code and moving it to a new compartment adds a very small amount of memory overhead, on the order of a dozen words for a typical compartment.

5.3. Adding compartments to the build system

The build system makes adding compartments trivial. An xmake build file (xmake.lua) uses a declarative Lua-like syntax at the top level. This defines targets as sections. Listing 32 shows the build system logic for the example compartments and libraries from earlier. Defining a new target implicitly ends the definition of the previous one. This example implicitly ends the library and entry targets, but uses target_end() to explicitly end the compartment target.

```
15  -- An example compartment that we can call
16  compartment("compartment")
17    add_files("compartment.cc")
18  target_end()
19
20  -- An example compartment that we can call
21  library("library")
22    set_default(false)
23    add_files("library.cc")
24
25  -- Our entry-point compartment
26  compartment("entry")
27    add_files("entry.cc")
28    add_deps("compartment", "library")
```

LISTING 32. Build system code for defining compartment and library targets
[from: examples/library_or_compartment/xmake.lua]

Inside each target definition, you can add files, dependencies on other targets, and so on. The "library" target, for example, sets itself as a non-default target. xmake will build every default target, whether it is used or not. Marking a target as non-default allows it to be defined, but built only if it is used. This is useful for reusable components. The RTOS provides build-system logic for a set of libraries, but each is built only if it is added as a dependency of something that is built.

 The compartment, library, and firmware target markers are syntactic sugar over the xmake target command. The first two simply set the default rules to build as the correct kind of target. The firmware target definition is more complex because it also implicitly instantiates core parts of the RTOS, constructs the linker script, and so on. If you are reading the xmake documentation[1], simply treat these as if they were target definitions.

 If your xmake.lua file contains compartment or library definitions but no firmware, then it can be reused. Each of the optional libraries and compartments shipped with the RTOS is defined like this, in a separate xmake.lua that is then included. As long as the components are set as non-default, they will simply be available for firmware to add as dependencies.

---

1. https://xmake.io

Once you have defined the rules to build each compartment and library, they need to be combined into a firmware image. Any library or compartment that is a direct or indirect dependency of a firmware image will be built and linked into the final image. For this example, we show both forms. The entry compartment lists both the library and the example compartment as explicit dependencies because it calls both of them. The firmware definition (Listing 33) adds the entry compartment as an explicit dependency, which then pulls in the other two. This firmware also depends on two libraries from the core RTOS, the freestanding library, which provides the core of the C run-time environment, and the debug library which pretty-prints the debug messages.

```
32  -- Firmware image for the example.
33  firmware("library_or_compartment")
34    -- RTOS-provided libraries
35    add_deps("freestanding", "debug")
36    -- Our compartments
37    add_deps("entry")
```

LISTING 33. Build system code for adding dependencies on compartment and library targets [from: examples/library_or_compartment/xmake.lua]

5.4. Choosing a trust model

There are three trust models that are commonly applied to compartments:

Sandbox

A sandbox is a compartment that is used to isolate untrusted code. This model is used to protect the rest of the system. Typically, a sandbox will trust values passed to it as arguments to exported functions or return values from functions that it calls in other compartments.

Safebox

A safebox is a compartment that holds some secret or sensitive data that must be protected from the outside. For example, a safebox may be used to protect a key and expose functions that use it to encrypt or sign data on behalf of callers. A safebox does not trust any data provided from outside of the compartment, but callers may trust it to behave correctly.

Mutual distrust

Mutual distrust is the strongest model. A compartment in a mutual-distrust relationship protects itself from attacks from the outside by careful handling of inputs and expects other compartments to protect themselves from it in the same way.

This is the start of defining a threat model for your code. A compartment may simply be used for fault isolation, to limit the damage that a bug can do. You may assume that an attacker will be able to compromise some compartments (for example, those directly processing network packets) and defend yourself accordingly.

In the core of the RTOS, the scheduler is written as a safebox. It does not trust anything on the outside and assumes that everything else is trying to make it crash. The memory allocator is also written as a safebox, assuming that everything else is trying to either make it crash or leak powerful capabilities. For some operations, the scheduler invokes the allocator. The scheduler trusts the allocator to enforce heap memory safety. It does not, for example, try to check that the memory allocator is returning disjoint capabilities (it can't see every other caller of heap_allocate, so it couldn't validate this). It is, however, written to assume that other compartments may try to maliciously call allocator APIs to cause it to crash, for example by freeing memory that the scheduler is using. When thinking about trust, it's worth trying to articulate the properties that other code is trusted to enforce or preserve. For example, everything in the CHERIoT system trusts the scheduler for availability. Most things trust the allocator to enforce spatial and temporal memory safety for the heap.

5.5. Implementing a safebox

The safebox abstraction is trivial to implement in CHERIoT. Listing 34 shows the build system for a safebox. Note that there's nothing in this that indicates the trust model. From the perspective of the build, all compartments are just compartments. Trust relationships between them are a property of how you write the code in the compartments.

Listing 35 shows a complete implementation of a simple safebox for a guess-the-number game. This generates a (very weak!) pseudorandom number using the cycle counter and allows callers to guess it.

This is called from the runner compartment, shown in Listing 36. This compartment talks directly to the outside world and so is part of the attack surface. It's quite unlikely that a compartment that simply reads individual bytes and ignores anything not in the ASCII digit range could be vulnerable, but the same techniques can protect much more realistic examples.

When you run this, you will see output something like the following:

```
Runner: Guess a number between 0 and 9 (inclusive)
Safebox: Guess was 3, secret was 4
Safebox: Guess was 1, secret was 8
Safebox: Guess was 9, secret was 4
Safebox: Guess was 4, secret was 3
Safebox: Guess was 8, secret was 6
Safebox: Guess was 1, secret was 0
Safebox: Guess was 2, secret was 8
Safebox: Guess was 3, secret was 5
Safebox: Guess was 5, secret was 2
Safebox: Guess was 2, secret was 3
Safebox: Guess was 1, secret was 6
Runner: Correct!  You guessed the secret was 3
```

```
16  -- The safebox compartment
17  compartment("safebox")
18   add_files("safebox.cc")
19
20  compartment("runner")
21   add_files("runner.cc")
22
23  -- Firmware image for the example.
24  firmware("safebox_example")
25   -- RTOS-provided libraries
26   add_deps("freestanding", "cxxrt", "debug")
27   -- Our compartments
28   add_deps("runner", "safebox")
29   on_load(function(target)
30     -- The board to target
31     target:values_set("board", "$(board)")
32     target:values_set("threads", {
33       {
34         compartment = "runner",
35         priority = 1,
36         entry_point = "entry",
37         stack_size = 0x400,
38         trusted_stack_frames = 2
39       },
40     }, {expand = false})
41   end)
```

LISTING 34. Build system code for the safebox example.
[from: examples/safebox/xmake.lua]

In this example, the extra compartmentalisation doesn't really buy us anything. You could combine these two compartments and have similar functionality. Perhaps more importantly, separating them adds little additional complexity to the code, yet respects the *principle of least privilege*. The code

```
 6 using Debug = ConditionalDebug<true, "Safebox">;
 7
 8 bool check_guess(int guess)
 9 {
10   static int secret = rdcycle64() % 10;
11   if (guess != secret)
12   {
13     Debug::log(
14       "Guess was {}, secret was {}", guess, secret);
15     secret = rdcycle64() % 10;
16     return false;
17   }
18   return true;
19 }
```

LISTING 35. A safebox for a guess-the-numbers game
[from: examples/safebox/safebox.cc]

```
 6 using Debug = ConditionalDebug<true, "Runner">;
 7
 8 __cheriot_compartment("runner") void entry()
 9 {
10   Debug::log("Guess a number between 0 and 9 (inclusive)");
11   while (int c =
12            MMIO_CAPABILITY(Uart, uart)->blocking_read())
13   {
14     if ((c < '0') || (c > '9'))
15     {
16       Debug::log("Invalid guess: {}", c);
17       continue;
18     }
19     c -= '0';
20     if (check_guess(c))
21     {
22       Debug::log("Correct!  You guessed the secret was {}",
23                  c);
24     }
25   }
26 }
```

LISTING 36. The runner compartment for the guess-the-numbers game
[from: examples/safebox/runner.cc]

that handles I/O does not need to know the secret and the code that knows
the secret does not need to be able to read via the UART.

A safebox assumes that its caller is malicious. A compartment may start
malicious or become malicious as the result of a compromise. Try modifying only runner.cc in this example to leak the secret without any incorrect

guesses. Hopefully, you will find it impossible.

5.6. Building software capabilities with sealing

The CHERI capability mechanism can be used to express arbitrary software-defined capabilities. Recall that a capability, in the abstract, is an unforgeable token of authority that can be presented to allow some action. In UNIX systems, for example, file descriptors are capabilities. A userspace process cannot directly talk to the disk or the network, but if it presents a valid file descriptor to system calls such as read and write then the kernel will perform those operations on its behalf.

CHERIoT provides a mechanism to create arbitrary software-defined capabilities using the *sealing* mechanism (see Section 1.6). CHERIoT provides almost a few billion sealing types for use with software-defined capabilities. You can allocate one of these dynamically by calling token_key_new.

> There is no mechanism to reuse sealing capabilities. As such, once you have allocated 4,278,190,079, you will be unable to create new ones. A 20 MHz core doing nothing other than allocating new sealing capabilities could exhaust this space in around a day. If untrusted code is allowed to allocate dynamic sealing capabilities then you may wish to restrict its access to this API and instead give it access to a wrapper that limits the number that it may allocate.

You can also statically register a sealing type with the STATIC_SEALING_-TYPE( ) macro. This takes a single argument, the name that you wish to give the type. This name is used to refer to the static sealing capability and is the name that will show up in auditing reports.

Documentation for the STATIC_SEALING_TYPE macro

STATIC_SEALING_TYPE(name)

Macro that evaluates to a static sealing type that is local to this compartment.

Documentation for the `token_key_new` function

`SKey token_key_new( )`

Create a new sealing key.

This function is guaranteed to complete unless the allocator has exhausted the total number of sealing keys possible (2^32 - 2^24). After this point, it will never succeed. A compartment that is granted access to this entry point is trusted not to exhaust this resource. If you wish to allow a compartment to seal objects, but do not wish to allow it to allocate new sealing keys, then you should insert a proxy compartment that guarantees that it will call this API once and return a single key to the caller.

The return value from this is a capability with the permit-seal and permit-unseal permissions. Callers may remove one or both of these permissions and delegate the resulting capability to allow other compartments to either seal or unseal the capabilities with this key.

If the sealing keys have been exhausted then this will return null. This API is guaranteed never to block.

You can access the sealing capability within the compartment that exported it using the STATIC_SEALING_VALUE( ) macro. You can also refer to it in other compartments, but *only* when constructing *static sealed objects*. A static sealed object is like a global defined in a compartment, but that compartment can access it only via a sealed capability.

Static sealed objects are declared with DECLARE_STATIC_SEALED_VALUE and defined with DEFINE_STATIC_SEALED_VALUE. These macros take as arguments both the name of the sealing type and the compartment that exposes it. This ensures that there is no ambiguity and that accidental name collisions don't lead to security vulnerabilities.

This gives a building block that can be used to define arbitrary software-defined capabilities at system start. A compartment that performs some action exposes a sealing type and a structure layout that it expects. Static instances of this structure can be baked into the firmware image and then passed as sealed capabilities into the compartment that wishes to use them

---

Documentation for the DECLARE_STATIC_SEALED_VALUE macro

`DECLARE_STATIC_SEALED_VALUE(type, compartment, keyName, name)`

Forward-declare a static sealed object. This declares an object of type type that can be referenced with the STATIC_SEALED_VALUE macro using name. The pointer returned by the latter macro will be sealed with the sealing key exported from compartment as keyName with the STATIC_SEALING_TYPE macro.

The object created with this macro can be accessed only by code that has access to the sealing key.

Documentation for the DEFINE_STATIC_SEALED_VALUE macro

`DEFINE_STATIC_SEALED_VALUE(type, compartment, keyName, name, initialiser, ...)`

Define a static sealed object. This creates an object of type type, initialised with initialiser, that can be referenced with the STATIC_SEALED_VALUE macro using name. The pointer returned by the latter macro will be sealed with the sealing key exported from compartment as keyName with the STATIC_SEALING_TYPE macro.

The object created with this macro can be accessed only by code that has access to the sealing key.

---

as capabilities. They can be unsealed using the token APIs described in Section 7.7. Often, you'll use this via a type-specific wrapper, as in Listing 37. The macro (DECLARE_AND_DEFINE_COUNTER) lets users of this API define a new counter with the sealing type that the compartment exposes.

The increment function from this header is defined in Listing 38. This uses token_unseal to unseal the sealed argument. This will return a valid unsealed object, or null if the unseal fails. Note that this uses the static sealed value via the STATIC_SEALING_TYPE macro. The sealing type doesn't need to be declared, simply using it here ensures that it is exported from the compartment.

```
 8 using MonotonicCounterState = std::atomic<int64_t>;
 9
10 #define DECLARE_AND_DEFINE_COUNTER(name)                         \
11   DECLARE_AND_DEFINE_STATIC_SEALED_VALUE(                        \
12     MonotonicCounterState, monotonic, CounterKey, name, 0)
13
14 typedef MonotonicCounterState
15   *__sealed_capability MonotonicCounter;
16
17 /**
18  * Increments a monotonic counter and returns the new value.
19  *
20  * Returns a negative value for errors.
21  */
22 int64_t __cheriot_compartment("monotonic")
23   monotonic_counter_increment(
24     MonotonicCounter allocatorCapability);
```

LISTING 37. A header defining an interface using sealed objects.

[from: examples/software_capability/monotonic_counter.hh]

Trying to use a sealing type that isn't exported from a function will result in a linker error.

```
 9 int64_t
10 monotonic_counter_increment(MonotonicCounter sealedCounter)
11 {
12   if (auto *counter = token_unseal(
13           STATIC_SEALING_TYPE(CounterKey), sealedCounter))
14   {
15     return ++(*counter);
16   }
17   return -EINVAL;
18 }
```

LISTING 38. The increment function for a monotonic counter.

[from: examples/software_capability/monotonic.cc]

This function follows the convention of returning -EINVAL if passed an invalid value. If the unseal succeeds, this function knows that it can trust the contents of the object. You can see this being called in Listing 39.

The caller starts by declaring a monotonic counter and then tries calling the increment function twice with a valid (sealed) value. It then tries again with two kinds of invalid values. The first is a value of the correct underlying type, but which is not sealed. The lack of sealing means that the callee can't trust that the rules for this type are followed. In this example, the type of a

```
 9  // Declare and define a counter for this to use.
10  DECLARE_AND_DEFINE_COUNTER(aCounter)
11
12  void __cheriot_compartment("caller") entry()
13  {
14    // Get a pointer to the valid counter.
15    auto validCounter = STATIC_SEALED_VALUE(aCounter);
16    // Create an unsealed value of the correct type
17    MonotonicCounterState invalidCounterState;
18    auto invalidCounter = reinterpret_cast<MonotonicCounter>(
19        &invalidCounterState);
20    auto invalidSealedCounter =
21        reinterpret_cast<MonotonicCounter>(MALLOC_CAPABILITY);
22
23    // Try the valid capability
24    printf("Valid counter increment returned %lld\n",
25          monotonic_counter_increment(validCounter));
26    printf("Valid counter increment returned %lld\n",
27          monotonic_counter_increment(validCounter));
28    // Try the invalid ones
29    printf("Invalid counter increment returned %lld\n",
30          monotonic_counter_increment(invalidCounter));
31    printf("Invalid counter increment returned %lld\n",
32          monotonic_counter_increment(invalidSealedCounter));
33    // Try manipulating the counter directly
34    auto underlyingCounter =
35        reinterpret_cast<MonotonicCounterState *>(validCounter);
36    (*underlyingCounter)++;
37  }
```

LISTING 39. Calling the atomic increment function for a monotonic counter.
[from: examples/software_capability/caller.cc]

monotonic counter guarantees that the counter increments monotonically but an unsealed value would allow the caller to set it to arbitrary values. This should fail to unseal because it is not a sealed value.

The second invalid value *is* a sealed value, but it is not sealed with the correct type. This is the default capability used for memory allocations in this compartment. In this case, sealing should fail because the type is incorrect. This shows how sealing enforces *type safety* even in the presence of untrusted code.

Finally, this casts away the sealed type qualifier and tries to access the underlying type directly. The compiler will permit this (it's a reinterpret_-cast, which tells the compiler that you're doing something that might be unsafe but that it should trust you) but then the hardware will prevent you from using the result.

When you run this, you should see the following output:

```
Valid counter increment returned 1
Valid counter increment returned 2
Invalid counter increment returned -22
Invalid counter increment returned -22
Error handler: SealViolation(0x3) error at 0x80003dd8 (v:0
0x80003d88-0x80003e48 l:0xc0 o:0x0 p: G R-cgm- X- ---) (return
address: 0x80006358 (v:1 0x80006110-0x80006da0 l:0xc90 o:0x5 p: G
R-cgm- X- ---)), with capability register CA0(0xa): 0x800079f0 (v:1
0x800079f0-0x80007a00 l:0x10 o:0xc p: G RWcgm- -- ---)
```

The first two calls worked and incremented the monotonic counter. The last two calls, with invalid objects, were detected in the caller and the errors were handled gracefully. Finally, the attempt to directly access the sealed object trapped and invoked the compartment's error handler (see Section 5.11), which printed a helpful message for debugging the failure.

The monotonic counter is valid as long as the counter starts at zero (overflowing a 64-bit signed counter will take an infeasible amount of time). What would happen if a malicious caller initialised a counter with a non-zero value? The full contents of any object created in this way shows up in the audit log. You can audit these in a firmware image to ensure that they are valid (see Chapter 10). Once you've read Chapter 10, try writing a policy for this example that ensures that all counters start at zero.

Most of the token APIs are implemented as cross-compartment calls into the allocator, but token_obj_unseal (called here via the token_unseal wrapper) is a fast path implemented as a library. This makes it fast to unseal objects (no cross-compartment call). It also removes any dependency on the allocator from things that rely on static sealing.

The RTOS' allocator provides a more detailed example of a real-world use for this feature. When you allocate memory, you pass the allocator a static sealed object that represents your allocation capability, which authorises allocating memory up to a quota. These contain a quota that is decreased on allocation and increased on deallocation. A compartment can allocate memory only if it has an allocation capability and any allocation capability that it holds shows up in the audit report when linking a firmware image.

5.7. Sharing globals between compartments

CHERIoT supports a notion of pre-shared objects. Each pre-shared object is allocated in a dedicated region of memory and can be imported into one or more compartments. Each import can have a different set of permissions.

This model lets you define a global that is, for example, writeable by one compartment but readable from many, with no control flow between the communicating compartments.

Currently, the syntax for importing a pre-shared object is more verbose. A future version of the CHERIoT compiler will incorporate this into the type system and control imports via attributes on extern declarations.

You can import a pre-shared object with the SHARED_OBJECT(type, name) macro. This takes the type of the object and its name (which must be globally unique across the firmware image) as arguments. This evaluates to a pointer to the object. Objects imported with this macro have the full set of permissions for imported objects.

You can also disable individual permissions using the SHARED_OBJEC-T_WITH_PERMISSIONS macros. This takes an additional four boolean arguments that define the following set of permissions:

- Load
- Store
- Load or store capabilities
- Load mutable

Note that load-mutable depends on both load and load/store capability permissions. You cannot load a capability that has store permission if you cannot load a capability.

Shared objects are defined in the build system, by setting the shared_objects value on a target (typically a compartment). For example:

```
on_load(function(target)
    target:values_set("shared_objects", { exampleK = 1024,
test_word = 4 }, {expand = false})
end)
```

You don't need to define this on every compartment that imports the object, a single definition is all that is necessary. This example is from the test suite and defines a test_word object that is a single 32-bit value and an exampleK object that is 1024 bytes. Note that the objects are defined as sizes, not as types. The type cannot be enforced by CHERI and depends on the compartment that imports the object. If a single compartment has write access to an object then that compartment forms the TCB for type safety of that object.

5.8. Refining trust

It seems conceptually easy to say 'this code is trusted' and 'this code is untrusted', but that rarely tells the whole story. At a high level, components are typically trusted (or not) with respect to three properties:

Confidentiality
How does information flow out of this component?
Integrity
How can information be modified by this component?
Availability
What can this component prevent from working?

 Compartments and threads are both units of isolation in a CHERIoT system. Threads are scheduled independently and provide a building block for availability guarantees. Only a higher-priority thread or code running with interrupts disabled can prevent an unrelated thread from making progress.

The relative importance of each of these varies a lot depending on context. For example, you often don't care at all about confidentiality for encrypted data, but you would not want the plain text form to leak and you definitely wouldn't want the encryption key to leak. If you're building a safety-critical system, availability is often key. Dumping twenty tonnes of molten aluminium onto the factory floor will probably kill people and cost millions of dollars, so preventing that is far more important than ensuring that no one unauthorised can inspect the state of your control network.

This kind of model helps understand where you should put compartment boundaries. If an attacker can compromise one component, what damage can they do to these properties in other compartments and in the system as a whole?

For example, consider the simplest embedded application, which just flashes an LED in a pattern. Where should you put compartment boundaries here? You might put the piece that prepares the pattern in one compartment and the part that interacts directly with the LED in another. Doing this does not add security value. Neither compartment is exposed to an attacker and so you're just protecting against bugs. The compartment with direct access to the device is just passing a value from a function argument to the device. It is unlikely that there will be a bug in this code that can affect the rest of the system. Conversely, the code that can call this can do everything that this compartment can do, so you haven't reduced the damage that a bug can cause.

Now imagine a slightly more complex device where, rather than lighting a single LED, you are driving an LED strip that takes a 24-bit colour value for each LED in the strip, encoded as a waveform down a two-wire serial line.

If you generate the wrong waveform, you'll get the wrong pattern and so there is an availability property that you can protect by moving the code that pauses and toggles a GPIO pin into a separate driver compartment. This driver routine needs to run with interrupts disabled (context switching in the middle of programming the strip would cause it to reprogram the first part twice). Running with interrupts disabled has availability implications on the rest of the system because nothing else can run while this is happening. If you put the driver in a separate compartment then you are protected in both directions:

- The driver is the only thing that can touch the relevant GPIO pin, so if the code in that driver is correct, nothing can cause the strip to be incorrectly programmed.
- The driver runs with interrupts disabled but the rest of the application runs with interrupts enabled, so you can audit the driver code to ensure that it doesn't cause problems for anything else that the microcontroller is doing.

This then gives you something to build on if you decide, for example, that you want to be able to update the lighting patterns from the Internet. Now you want to add a network stack to be able to fetch the new patterns and an interpreter to run them. What does the threat model look like?

The network stack is exposed to the Internet and so is the most likely place for an attack to start. If this needs to interact with the network hardware with interrupts disabled then you probably want to put that part in a separate network driver compartment so that an attacker can't cause the network stack to sit with interrupts disabled forever. A lot of common attacks on network stacks will simply fail on a CHERIoT system because they depend on violating memory safety, but it's possible that an attacker will find novel techniques and compromise the network stack.

You will want narrow interfaces between the network stack and the TLS stack, so that the worst that an attacker with full control over the network stack compartment can do is provide invalid packets (and an attacker can do that from the Internet anyway). The TLS stack will decode complete messages and forward them to the interpreter compartment. TLS packets have cryptographic integrity protection so anything that comes through this path is probably safe (unless the TLS compartment is compromised) but putting the interpreter in a separate compartment ensures that invalid interpreter code can provide different colours to the LEDs but can't damage the LEDs and can't launch attacks over the network.

5.9. Validating arguments

If a function that is exported from a compartment takes primitive values as arguments, there's little that an attacker can do other than provide invalid values. For things like integers, this doesn't matter; for enumerations it's important to ensure that they are valid values.

Pointers are more complicated. There are a few things that an attacker can do with pointer arguments to invoke a crash:

- Provide a pointer without write permission for an output operand.
- Provide a pointer without read permission for an input operand.
- Provide a pointer without global permission that must be captured and held across calls.
- Provide a pointer with a length that is too small.
- Provide something that isn't a valid pointer at all.
- Provide a pointer that overlaps your stack as an output argument.

Any of these (or similar attacks) will allow an attacker to cause your compartment to encounter a fault when it tries to use the pointer.

In general, you will want to check permissions and bounds on any pointer argument that you're passed. The CHERI::check_pointer function helps here. It checks that a pointer has (at least) the bounds and permissions that you expect and that it isn't in your current stack region. If you don't specify a size, the default is the size of the argument type. You can use this to quickly check any pointer that's passed to you.

 Checking the pointer is not the only option. A CHERI fault will invoke the compartment's error handler (see Section 5.11) and so it may be possible to recover. Some compartments choose to assume that their arguments are valid and just gracefully clean up if they aren't.

If a pointer refers to a heap location, there is one additional attack possible. In general, a pointer cannot be modified after it's been checked, but the memory that a pointer refers to may be freed. When this happens, the pointer is implicitly invalidated. In some cases, you may simply wish to disallow pointers that point to the heap.

You can check whether a pointer refers to heap memory by calling heap_address_is_valid. If this returns true, you can prevent deallocation by using the *claim* mechanism, described in Section 7.8.

Documentation for the `check_pointer` function

```
template<PermissionSet Permissions =
PermissionSet{Permission::Load},
         bool           CheckStack  = true,
         bool           EnforceStrictPermissions = false>
  __always_inline inline bool
  check_pointer(auto  &ptr,
                size_t space =
sizeof(std::remove_pointer<decltype(ptr)>))
```

requires(std::is_pointer_v<std::remove_cvref_t<decltype(ptr)>>
||

IsSmartPointerLike<std::remove_cvref_t<*decltype*(ptr)>>)

Checks that ptr is valid, unsealed, has at least Permissions, and has at least space bytes after the current offset.

ptr can be a pointer, or a smart pointer, i.e., any class that supports a get method returning a pointer, and operator=. This includes Capability and standard library smart pointers.

If the permissions do not include Global, then this will also check that the capability does not point to the current thread's stack. This behaviour can be disabled (for example, for use in a shared library) by passing false for CheckStack.

If EnforceStrictPermissions is set to true, this will also set the permissions of the passed capability reference to Permissions, and its bounds to space. This is useful for detecting cases where compartments ask for fewer permissions than they actually require and callers happen to provide the required permissions. Similarly, if you are calling check_pointer in a function that wraps untrusted code such as a third-party library, this lets you detect cases where your callers are failing to remove permissions that the untrusted code should not have.

This function is provided as a wrapper for the ::check_pointer C API. It is always inlined. For each call site, it materialises the constants needed before performing an indirect call to ::check_pointer.

Alternatively, you can use the ephemeral claim mechanism (also docu-

---

Documentation for the `heap_address_is_valid` function

```
_Bool heap_address_is_valid(const void * object)
```

Returns true if object points to a valid heap address, false otherwise. Note that this does *not* check that this is a valid pointer. This should be used in conjunction with check_pointer to check validity. The principle use of this function is checking whether an object needs to be claimed. If this returns false but the pointer has global permission, it must be a global and so does not need to be claimed. If the pointer lacks global permission then it cannot be claimed, but if this function returns false then it is guaranteed not to go away for the duration of the call.

---

mented in Section 7.8) to ensure that a pointer is either a pointer that cannot be freed, or to ensure that it remains live until the next cross-compartment call. These techniques are all combined in Listing 40, which is a simple function that prints a string to the UART, defensively.

This first uses a lock (see Chapter 6) to ensure that only one thread will access this function at a time. If this compartment exposed more than one function that used the UART then the lock would need to be shared between all of them. Next, it uses heap_claim_ephemeral to prevent concurrent deallocation. After this, it is safe to use check_pointer to ensure that the permissions are correct and that this pointer does not overlap the current compartment's stack (because of the default value of CheckStack). For a C string, this checks only that a single byte is readable. The function then gets the length explicitly and prints either the full length of the buffer, or the buffer up to a null terminator, whichever is shorter.

You can see how well this works with the attacks shown in Listing 41. This tries passing a string that is not null-terminated, a string without load permission, an untagged capability, and finally a valid capability.

When you run this example, you should see output like this:

```
No null
Non-malicious string
```

The string that misses the null terminator is written, but then there's no overflow. The string that has the wrong permissions and the string that is not a valid capability at all are simply not printed. Finally, the non-malicious

```
14  /// Write a message to the UART.
15  int uart_puts(const char *msg)
16  {
17    static FlagLockPriorityInherited lock;
18    // Prevent concurrent invocation
19    LockGuard g(lock);
20    Timeout   t{UnlimitedTimeout};
21    // Make sure that this is not going to be deallocated out
22    // from under us.
23    if (heap_claim_ephemeral(&t, msg) != 0)
24    {
25      return -EINVAL;
26    }
27    // Check that this is a valid pointer with the correct
28    // permissions.
29    if (!check_pointer<PermissionSet{Permission::Load}>(msg))
30    {
31      return -EINVAL;
32    }
33    // Get the bounds (distance from address to top) of the
34    // pointer.
35    Capability buffer{msg};
36    size_t    length = buffer.bounds();
37    // Write the data, one byte at a time.
38    for (size_t i = 0; i < length; i++)
39    {
40      char c = msg[i];
41      if (c == '\0')
42      {
43        break;
44      }
45      MMIO_CAPABILITY(Uart, uart)->blocking_write(c);
46    }
47    MMIO_CAPABILITY(Uart, uart)->blocking_write('\n');
48    return 0;
49  }
```

LISTING 40. Checks to ensure that a function does not crash.
[from: examples/check_arguments/uart.cc]

string is printed correctly, showing that the attacker has not been able to corrupt internal state.

5.10. Ensuring adequate stack space

The stack is shared between compartments invoked on the same thread. The callee has access to the portion of the stack that its callers have not used. This is most important when a compartment is called by an untrusted caller. In

```
13  char unterminatedString[] = {
14    'N', 'o', ' ', 'n', 'u', 'l', 'l'};
15  uart_puts(unterminatedString);
16  Capability invalidPermissions = "Invalid permissions";
17  invalidPermissions.permissions() &= Permission::Store;
18  uart_puts(invalidPermissions);
19  char *invalidPointer = reinterpret_cast<char *>(12345);
20  uart_puts(invalidPointer);
21  uart_puts("Non-malicious string");
```

LISTING 41. Attempting to attack the safe UART.
[from: examples/check_arguments/hello.cc]

this case, a malicious caller may try to consume almost all of the stack before calling a victim compartment. The victim would then trap in a place under the attacker's control.

Before entering a compartment, the switcher will check the amount of stack space against the required amount in the export table. By default, the compiler will fill this value with the amount that is required by the function that serves as an entry point. This is sufficient for leaf functions, but if your function calls others (and they are not inlined) then this will be insufficient.

You can specify the stack space required by an exported function by using the __cheriot_minimum_stack attribute. This is a function attribute that takes a single argument, the number of bytes of stack space that the function requires. Setting this attribute ensures that the switcher will not invoke the exported function unless at least the required amount of stack space is available. The malicious caller from the previous example would see a return value if -ENOTENOUGHSTACK and your code would not be invoked. Using this attribute requires you to know how much stack space the function will use.

CHERIoT CPUs include a feature called a stack high-water mark that tracks the amount of stack that is used so that the switcher can avoid zeroing unused portions of the stack. The switcher provides a function, stack_lowest_used_address, that you can call to find the lowest address. You can then use the difference between the top of the stack capability (accessed via the __builtin_cheri_stack_get built-in function) to determine how much stack space has been used in a particular invocation of a compartment entry point.

The debug.hh header includes a C++ helper class, StackUsageCheck. This takes a template argument allowing it to be disabled, enabled and just log if you use more than the expected amount of stack, or enabled and trap if you

---

Documentation for the `stack_lowest_used_address` function

`ptraddr_t stack_lowest_used_address()`

Returns the lowest address that has been stored to on the stack in this compartment invocation.

 This helper checks the amount of stack usage *of the current compartment.* The switcher check is not intended to ensure that the invocation of the current compartment can succeed, only that failures are detectable and recoverable. If you want to ensure that a called compartment *also* has enough stack then you will need to add its stack requirements to those of your compartment.

use more than the expected amount of stack. This is most commonly used with a macro like this:
```
#define STACK_CHECK(expected)
      StackUsageCheck<StackMode, expected, __PRETTY_FUNCTION__>
stackCheck
```
The StackMode template argument is one of `StackCheckMode::Asserting`, `StackCheckMode::Logging`, or `StackCheckMode::Disabled`. Typically, you will use it in logging mode initially, then disabled mode in production. Use it in asserting mode when running representative tests in CI so that it fails if you have increased your stack requirements and not updated the caller.

It's important that the tests that you run in asserting mode have good coverage. It's typically fine for this to be function-granularity coverage: with the exception of variable-length arrays, functions stack usage does not depend on control flow within the function.

 It's tempting to enable the stack checks in debug builds. This is usually a bad idea because debug builds include extra checks that increase stack usage. Enabling the stack checks in debug builds will cause you to demand more stack space than a release build actually needs, increasing overall memory pressure.

5.11. Handling errors

Asynchronous interrupts are all routed to the scheduler to wake up the relevant threads and schedule the correct thread. Synchronous faults are (optionally) delivered to the compartment that caused them. These include CHERI exceptions, invalid instruction traps, and so on: anything that can be directly attributed to the current instruction.

Compartments have two opportunities to handle these, by implementing at least one of two kinds of error handlers.

Rich

> Rich error handlers that have access to the full state at the point the error occurred. These can be written in C/C++ and can do things like step over faulting instructions and resume, or provide rich diagnostic information about the interrupted context.

Stackless

> Lightweight error handlers that must be written in assembly.

When a hardware exception occurs, the switcher will first look for a *rich error handler* and prepare a call frame for it. If there is not sufficient stack space to invoke a rich error handler, or if one is not provided by the current compartment, the switcher will then look for a *stackless error handler*.

The stackless variant will be passed the stack capability as it was on entry to the compartment and the exception cause, but no other information. Most users will not write these but will instead use one that the platform provides.

5.12. Writing rich error handlers

You can provide a rich error handler by implementing `compartment_error_handler` in your compartment.

Documentation for the `compartment_error_handler` function

```
enum ErrorRecoveryBehaviour compartment_error_handler(struct
ErrorState * frame, size_t mcause, size_t mtval)
```

The error handler for the current compartment. A compartment may choose to implement this. If not implemented then compartment faults will unwind the trusted stack.

This function is passed a copy of the register file and the exception cause registers when a fault occurs. The mcause value will be one of the standard RISC-V exception causes, or 0x1c for CHERI faults. CHERI faults will encode the CHERI-specific fault code and the faulting register in mtval. You can decompose this into its component parts by calling CHERI::extract_cheri_mtval.

Documentation for the `extract_cheri_mtval` function

```
std::pair<CauseCode, RegisterNumber>
extract_cheri_mtval(uint32_t mtval)
```

Decompose the value reported in the mtval CSR on CHERI exception into a pair of CauseCode and RegisterNumber.

Will return CauseCode::Invalid if the code field is not one of the defined causes and RegisterNumber::Invalid if the register number is not a valid register number. Other bits of mtval are ignored.

 The error handler is called with interrupts enabled, even if interrupts were disabled in the faulting code. Latency-critical code should never depend on the error handler for meeting its timing.

The spilled register file does not contain a tagged value for the program counter capability. This is to prevent library functions that run with interrupts disabled or with access to secrets from accidentally leaking on faults. All other registers will be preserved exactly as they are in the register file.

At the end of your error handler, you have two choices. You can either ask the switcher to resume, installing your modified register file (rederiving the PCC from the compartment's code capability), or you can ask it to continue unwinding.

Error handling functions are used for resource cleanup. For example, you may wish to drop locks when an error occurs, or you may wish to reset the compartment entirely. The heap_free_all function, discussed in Chapter 7, helps with the latter.

Error handlers are somewhat similar to UNIX signal handlers, but with some important differences. They are invoked for synchronous faults, not arbitrary event notification. Importantly, they are required only to handle the current compartment's errors. You cannot, for example, call malloc in a signal handler because it would deadlock (or corrupt state) if the signal arrives during a call to malloc or free. In contrast, if a call to heap_allocate fails then that error will be handled in the allocator compartment. Your error handler will never be invoked in the middle of a call to the allocator and so it is fine to use error handlers to release locks and free memory.

5.13. Using scoped error handling

You are unlikely to ever write a stackless error handler. Most of the time, you will want to link the one provided by the unwind_error_handler target. This can be adopted by adding add_deps("unwind_error_handler") to your compartment's target in xmake.lua.

The scoped error handling is built on top of the standard C setjmp and longjmp functions. These are quite unusual because setjmp can return twice. When you call it, it initialises a jmp_buf structure with some state about the current stack frame and returns zero. You can then pass this jmp_buf down the stack to longjmp. This longjmp call will make the original setjmp return a second time (immediately destroying any stack frames between the setjmp and longjmp calls), with the value passed into longjmp as the second argument.

This implementation is intended to be used with a set of macros that provide exception-like error handling. These maintain a stack of jmp_buf structures, as defined by setjmp. The head of the linked list is stored at the top of the region of the stack that is visible to the current compartment invocation, in a gap left by the switcher. Each CHERIOT_DURING macro invocation pushes an entry onto a stack that allows returning and each CHERIOT_END_HANDLER macro pops the top entry.

Between these two, a CHERIOT_HANDLER is the equivalent of the start of a catch block. This defines the start of a region where code will run if an error is triggered. You can see this in action in Listing 42. This uses __builtin_-trap, which the compiler will transform into an invalid instruction, to force a trap. This is a placeholder for anything that might raise an error (including in nested function calls), such as a bounds violation, a use-after-free bug, a null-pointer dereference, and so on.

Documentation for the CHERIOT_DURING macro

CHERIOT_DURING

Simple error handling macros. These are modelled on the OpenStep exception macros and are similarly built on top of setjmp. Code between CHERIOT_DURING and CHERIOT_HANDLER corresponds to a try block. Code between CHERIOT_HANDLER and CHERIOT_END_HANDLER corresponds to a catch block, though no exception value is actually thrown.

Any automatic-storage values accessed in both blocks must be declared volatile.

```
16  Debug::log("About to try something unsafe.");
17  CHERIOT_DURING
18  {
19    Debug::log("In during block");
20    if (shouldTrap)
21    {
22      // This will unconditionally trap.
23      __builtin_trap();
24    }
25  }
26  CHERIOT_HANDLER
27  {
28    Debug::log("Something bad happened!");
29  }
30  CHERIOT_END_HANDLER
31  Debug::log("Finished unsafe block.");
```

LISTING 42. Example of using scoped error handling
[from: examples/error_handling/errors.cc]

If you run this example with shouldTrap set to false then it will generate the following output:

```
Error handling example: About to try something unsafe.
Error handling example: In during block
Error handling example: Finished unsafe block.
```

The code in the CHERIOT_DURING block runs, the code in the CHERIOT_HAN-DLER block is omitted, and control flow resumes after CHERIOT_END_HAN-DLER. In contrast, if shouldTrap is true then the trap will transition into the switcher, which will then invoke the compartment's stackless error handler, which will then transfer control into the CHERIOT_HANDLER block and you'll see output like this:

```
Error handling example: About to try something unsafe.
Error handling example: In during block
Error handling example: Something bad happened!
Error handling example: Finished unsafe block.
```

This lets you do things like release locks or clean up per-call state in case of failure.

5.14. Conventions for cross-compartment calls

If a compartment faults and force unwinds to the caller then the return registers will be set to -1. This makes it easy to use the UNIX convention of returning negative numbers to indicate error codes. The value -1 is -ECOMPARTMENT-FAIL and other numbers from errno.h can be used to indicate other failures.

A CHERIoT capability is effectively a tagged union of a pointer and 64 bits of data. You can take advantage of this in functions that return pointers to return either an integer or, if the result is not tagged, an error code.

To see a slightly less-contrived version of error handling, Listing 43 is a version of Listing 40, rewritten to use error handling instead of checking. The original version checked all of the properties of the string and protected itself against concurrent mutation. This version still uses check_pointer, because this also prevents information disclosure by ensuring that the string does not overlap the current compartment invocation's stack. You could omit this check if you are not worried about information disclosure. For capabilities that you write through, this check is very important because otherwise you may write over parts of your own stack and corrupt internal state by accident.

The example then simply tries to read the bytes, assuming that they are a valid null-terminated C string.

```
15  /// Write a message to the UART.
16  int uart_puts(const char *msg)
17  {
18    // Prevent information disclosure, check that this does
19    // not overlap with our stack region.  Check for obvious
20    // errors at the same time.
21    if (!check_pointer(msg))
22    {
23      return -EINVAL;
24    }
25    static FlagLockPriorityInherited lock;
26    // Prevent concurrent invocation
27    LockGuard g(lock);
28    int       result = 0;
29    // Assume this is a null-terminated string, report an
30    // error on exceptions if not.
31    on_error(
32      [&]() {
33        for (const char *m = msg; *m != '\0'; m++)
34        {
35          MMIO_CAPABILITY(Uart, uart)->blocking_write(*m);
36        }
37      },
38      [&]() { result = -EINVAL; });
39    MMIO_CAPABILITY(Uart, uart)->blocking_write('\n');
40    return result;
41  }
```

LISTING 43. Using structured error handling to ensure that a function does not crash. [from: examples/yolo_arguments/uart.cc]

This version uses the C++ wrappers that take lambdas, rather than the macro versions, but the semantics are the same as described earlier. When you run this, you should see exactly the same output as the original version:

```
No null
Non-malicious string
```

The string that lacks a null terminator will now simply be written looking for one. The attempt to read one byte past the end will trigger a bounds exception. This will then invoke the second lambda passed to on_error, which will set the error code and resume. The other errors are caught by the check_pointer call. If you remove that call, you will instead see the following output:

```
No null

Non-malicious string
```

Now, each call is printing the trailing newline, even if it encountered a fault while reading the message.

Chapter 6.
Communicating between threads

CHERIoT RTOS provides threads as a core abstraction. Threads run until they either yield or are preempted via an interrupt, and then later resume from the same point. There are a small number of scheduler APIs that allow threads to block; higher-level APIs from other compartments may block by indirectly invoking them.

Remember that, in most respects, the scheduler is just another compartment. It doesn't run with elevated privileges. It makes a decision about which thread to run next, but it is not able to see the stacks or register states associated with threads. When another thread calls into the scheduler (for example, to sleep or to wake other threads), the call is just like any other cross-compartment call and uses the same mechanism.

6.1. Defining threads

Threads in CHERIoT RTOS cannot be dynamically created. Creating threads at run time would require allocating stacks at run time. The no-capture guarantees that CHERIoT RTOS enforces are based on the guarantee that no code other than the loader has access to two stacks' memory at a time and so the switcher can zero stacks and avoid leaks. The only store-local capabilities that a thread ever has access to are derived from its current stack. Allowing stack creation would violate that: at least the memory allocator would have access to multiple stacks at once. It would be possible to allocate stacks from a separate pool, but that's not really different from allocating stacks up front and having a small compartment that switches them from one use to another or implements a thread pool. There is an example thread pool in lib/thread_pool in the RTOS SDK, with its interface defined in the thread_pool.h header, that you can either use directly or use as inspiration for your own design, if you want to create new thread-like contexts.

If a thread entry point returns then the thread exits but, importantly, this does *not* free the thread's stack or trusted stack. The memory owned by a thread is assigned to that thread as long as the system runs.

Threads in CHERIoT RTOS are constructed with four properties:
- The size of their stack.
- The size of their *trusted stack*.
- Their priority.
- The entry point where they start executing.

The stack size means the same as on any other platform. Specifically on CHERIoT, the stack-pointer capability will be bounded to this size (rounded up if necessary for alignment) and any overflow of the stack, even by a single byte, will trap. The trusted stack size is the maximum number of cross-compartment calls that this thread can do. Each cross-compartment call invokes the switcher, which pushes a new frame onto the trusted stack describing where to return.

 In the current version, each trusted stack frame is three capabilities (24 bytes). A larger trusted stack does not make much difference to total memory consumption.

The priority of threads matters only in relative terms. Like FreeRTOS (and unlike UNIX), higher numbers mean higher priorities. The scheduler has some data structures whose size depends on the number of priorities, so compiling with fewer priorities can make the scheduler smaller.

The entry point property is a compartment's entry point. It must be exposed as described in Chapter 5. Thread entry points take no arguments and return no arguments.

On most other systems, thread creation functions take a pointer. This does not make sense for threads that are not dynamically created because there is no context for their creation.

6.2. Identifying the current thread

You will sometimes need to know which thread is currently running. This can be for something as simple as debugging but may also be needed for maintaining per-thread data structures. The ID of each thread is stored in the register save area for that thread and the switcher exposes a library call (thread_id_get) to read it.

Thread IDs start at one (not zero!) because zero is used to indicate the idle thread and so is never visible. The thread_count function returns the number of threads that have been created in the system. This is not decremented when threads exit, so it provides the upper bound on the number of threads that may exist. This can be used to size data structures that are indexed by thread ID.

Documentation for the `thread_id_get` function

```
uint16_t thread_id_get()
```

Return the thread ID of the current running thread. This is mostly useful where one compartment can run under different threads and it matters which thread entered this compartment.

User threads (that is, those defined in the xmake firmware configuration) are 1-indexed, with 0 indicating primordial idle and scheduling contexts. User code never runs in these contexts and so anything using this result to index into a per-thread array may wish to subtract one and avoid allocating an array element for the idle thread.

This is implemented in the switcher.

Documentation for the `thread_count` function

```
uint16_t thread_count()
```

Returns the number of user threads (that is, those defined in the xmake firmware configuration), including threads that have exited.

This API never fails, but if the trusted stack is exhausted and it cannot be called then it will return -1. Callers that have not probed the trusted stack should check for this value.

The result of this is safe to cache because it will never change over time.

Somewhat counter intuitively, `thread_id_get` is faster than `thread_count` to call. The former is a libcall that that switcher implements, the latter is a cross-compartment call into the scheduler. This is not normally a problem because the result of `thread_count` does not change and can be cached in a compartment, whereas the result of `thread_id_get` depends on the current thread and cannot be safely cached.

The `current_thread` example shows calling these functions. The entry point function for this is shown in Listing 44 and the thread definitions from the `xmake.lua` file in Listing 45.

```
9  /// Thread entry point.
10 void __cheriot_compartment("current") entry()
11 {
12   for (int i = 0; i < 2; i++)
13   {
14     printf("Current thread: %d of %d (iteration %d)\n",
15             thread_id_get(),
16             thread_count(),
17             i);
18   }
19 }
```

LISTING 44. A simple example that prints the current thread
[from: examples/current_thread/current.cc]

```
30 -- Threads to select
31   target:values_set("threads", {
32     {
33       compartment = "current",
34       priority = 1,
35       entry_point = "entry",
36       stack_size = 0x400,
37       trusted_stack_frames = 2
38     },
39     {
40       compartment = "current",
41       priority = 2,
42       entry_point = "entry",
43       stack_size = 0x400,
44       trusted_stack_frames = 2
45     }
46   }, {expand = false})
```

LISTING 45. The thread definitions for the current-thread example
[from: examples/current_thread/xmake.lua]

Note that the second thread has a higher priority than thread one. When you run this example, you should see output like this:

```
Current thread: 2 of 2 (iteration 0)
Current thread: 2 of 2 (iteration 1)
Current thread: 1 of 2 (iteration 0)
Current thread: 1 of 2 (iteration 1)
```

The higher-priority thread is running until it exits. Normally, a higher-priority thread would *yield* to allow another thread to run, as we'll see later in this chapter.

6.3. Limiting blocking with timeouts

Several RTOS APIs have timeouts. These are expressed as a pointer to a Time-out structure. This design is intended to allow a single timeout to be passed down a chain of operations.

 Timeouts represent time spent blocking (yielding waiting to be runnable), not time spent running (doing useful work).

Timeouts measure time in *scheduler ticks*. A tick is a single scheduling quantum, which depends on the board configuration. This is the minimum amount of time for which it is plausible for a thread to sleep. If a thread sleeps, another thread becomes runnable and is then allowed to run (unless it also yields).

Although ticks exist as a unit of accounting, the CHERIoT RTOS scheduler is a *tickless scheduler*. Traditional schedulers schedule a timer interrupt at a fixed quantum and make a scheduling choice at each call. This can be inefficient because a high-priority thread will be routinely interrupted and then rescheduled (because it remains the highest-priority thread). A tickless scheduler avoids this and instead, before scheduling a thread, sets a timer interrupt to fire at the next point when another thread may be woken.

For example, consider the case where a high-priority thread sleeps for three ticks and a lower-priority thread runs. With a traditional scheduler, a timer interrupt will fire three times. Each time, the scheduler will do some accounting and then reschedule the lower-priority thread. In contrast, a tickless scheduler will configure the timer to fire once, after three ticks have elapsed. At that point, the high-priority thread is runnable and so will be scheduled.

The timeout structure captures the amount of time that is allowed to block and the number of ticks for which it has blocked. Each subsequent call that is passed the same timeout structure may increase the amount of slept time and decrease the remaining time. This means that a timeout is *stateful*. If you pass a pointer to the same timeout to multiple APIs, they will all consume the ticks that were set when the timeout structure was initialised. This is normally useful because it means that a function that calls multiple functions that block can have a timeout parameter and forward it to each of the functions that it calls, but it means that you can't just create one timeout at the start of your thread and keep using it (unless you initialise it to the unlimited timeout value).

A thread may block for more than the permitted limit if it is sleeping while a higher-priority thread runs. Only the highest-priority thread can make strong realtime guarantees in the presence of other runnable threads.

Functions that take a timeout should always expect it as the first argument. This allows it to be forwarded to subsequent calls trivially.

Timeouts may not be stored on the heap. Any function checking timeouts may refuse to accept a heap-allocated timeout. It is difficult to work with heap-allocated timeouts because they may be deallocated while the thread is sleeping, which would then cause it to crash upon updating the timeout structure.

6.4. Sleeping

Sleeping for a bounded number of ticks is the simplest form of blocking available. The thread_sleep call causes the caller to yield until a certain number of ticks have run.

As with other calls that take a Timeout, the number of ticks that have elapsed during the call can be checked by reading the elapsed field of the timeout structure.

Sleeping in a system with an RTOS scheduler conflates two concepts:

- Waiting for some time to elapse.
- Allowing lower-priority threads to run.

The thread_sleep call supports both of these but understanding how they differ requires understanding a little of the scheduler's behaviour. Recall that CHERIoT RTOS has a *tickless scheduler*.

This means that, although it uses ticks as an abstraction for defining scheduling quanta, it does not schedule a regular timer interrupt. When two threads at the same priority level are runnable, the scheduler will request a timer interrupt to preempt the current one and switch to the other. If the running thread has no peers, the scheduler will allow it to run until either it yields or another higher or equal-priority thread's timeout expires. The tick abstraction remains as a convenient way of expressing time to the scheduler, but internally the scheduler tracks only elapsed cycles.

Documentation for the `thread_sleep` function

`int thread_sleep(struct Timeout * timeout, uint32_t flags)`

Sleep for at most the specified timeout (see `timeout.h`).

The thread becomes runnable once the timeout has expired but a higher-priority thread may prevent it from actually being scheduled. The return value is a saturating count of the number of ticks that have elapsed.

A call of `thread_sleep` with a timeout of zero is equivalent to `yield`, but reports the time spent sleeping. This requires a cross-compartment call and return in addition to the overheads of `yield` and so `yield` should be preferred in contexts where the elapsed time is not required.

The `flags` parameter is a bitwise OR of `ThreadSleepFlags`.

A sleeping thread may be woken early if no other threads are runnable or have earlier timeouts. The thread with the earliest timeout will be woken first. This can cause a yielding thread to sleep when no other thread is runnable, but avoids a potential problem where a high-priority thread yields to allow a low-priority thread to make progress, but then the low-priority thread does a short sleep. In this case, the desired behaviour is not to wake the high-priority thread early, but to allow the low-priority thread to run for the full duration of the high-priority thread's yield.

If you are using `thread_sleep` to elapse real time, pass `ThreadSleep-NoEarlyWake` as the flags argument to prevent early wakeups.

By default, if 0 is passed as the `flags` argument to `thread_sleep`, the sleep operation is treated as a *yield*. This is a way for the running thread to communicate to the scheduler that it is happy for other (lower or equal-priority) threads to run for up to the specified number of ticks. The scheduler may wake the yielding thread if no other thread is going to be runnable within that number of ticks. This allows high-priority threads to allow other threads to run, but continue using the CPU if no other thread is runnable.

In some cases, you really want to sleep. For example, if you're updating a clock display, you will want to run once a second or once a minute to update the display. The same applies if you're sending keep-alive packets or periodically monitoring some other component. In these cases you definitely have no useful work to do, irrespective of the state of any other threads that can or cannot run. You can pass ThreadSleepNoEarlyWake as the flags argument to thread_sleep to indicate that you really want to sleep.

You can see the effect of sleeping in the thread_sleep example, as shown in Listing 46. This is a modified version of the current_thread example from earlier, now sleeping in each loop iteration.

```
10 /// Thread entry point.
11 void __cheriot_compartment("current") entry()
12 {
13   for (int i = 0; i < 2; i++)
14   {
15     printf("Current thread: %d of %d\n",
16             thread_id_get(),
17             thread_count());
18     Timeout t{1};
19     thread_sleep(&t);
20   }
21   printf("Cycles elapsed: %lld\n", rdcycle64());
22 }
```

LISTING 46. A simple example of thread sleeping
[from: examples/thread_sleep/current.cc]

If you run this, you should see output that looks somewhat like this:

```
Current thread: 2 of 2
Current thread: 1 of 2
Current thread: 2 of 2
Current thread: 1 of 2
Cycles elapsed: 262193
Cycles elapsed: 265806
```

As before, thread two runs first, but then it yields and allows thread one to run. Thread one then yields and allows thread two to run, and so on. If thread one did *not* yield then it would be preempted after one tick.

Try modifying this example, adding ThreadSleepNoEarlyWake as a second argument to the thread_sleep call. You should now see output that looks very similar, but shows lower cycle counts at the end:

```
Current thread: 2 of 2
Current thread: 1 of 2
Current thread: 2 of 2
Current thread: 1 of 2
Cycles elapsed: 249233
Cycles elapsed: 252273
```

 If you run this with the Sail simulator, do not be surprised if the cycle counts look very small. Sail is not a cycle-accurate model. The cycle count is guaranteed to be monotonic, but not to represent a real system in any way. The snippets in this section are using the Ibex simulator.

Here you see that the total execution time has gone from 265,806 cycles to 252,273. In the original version, when thread one slept (after doing far less than one tick's worth of work), there were no runnable threads so the scheduler does nothing for a while. Eventually, thread two (the high-priority thread) is runnable again and it resumes. In the version with ThreadSleep-NoEarlyWake, thread two can resume as soon as thread one sleeps. Similarly, when thread two yields for the second time, thread one will resume.

6.5. Waiting for events with futexes

The scheduler exposes a set of futex APIs as a building block for various notification and locking mechanisms. Futex is a contraction of 'fast userspace mutex'. This does not quite apply on a CHERIoT system, where there is no userspace, but the core concept of avoiding a privilege transition on fast paths still applies.

A CHERIoT RTOS futex is a 32-bit word where the scheduler provides compare-and-sleep (futex_timed_wait) and notify (futex_wake) operations.

 In C++, std::atomic<uint32_t> provides wait, notify_all, and notify_one methods that expose futex functionality and may be more convenient to call than the raw futex APIs. These include some additional (non-standard) overloads that expose more of the underlying futex functionality.

A futex allows you to use atomic operations on a 32-bit word for fast paths but then sleep and wake threads when they are blocked, rather than spinning.

Documentation for the `futex_timed_wait` function

```
int futex_timed_wait(Timeout * ticks, const uint32_t *
address, uint32_t expected, uint32_t flags)
```

Compare the value at `address` to `expected` and, if they match, sleep the thread until a wake event is sent with `futex_wake` or until the thread has slept for `ticks` ticks.

The value of `ticks` specifies the permitted timeout. See `timeout.h` for details.

The `address` argument must permit loading four bytes of data after the address.

The `flags` argument contains flags that may control the behaviour of the call. This is either `FutexNone` (zero) for the default behaviour or `FutexPriorityInheritance` if the low 16 bits should be treated as a thread ID for priority inheritance.

This returns:
- 0 on success: either `*address` and `expected` differ or a wake is received.
- `-EINVAL` if the arguments are invalid.
- `-ETIMEOUT` if the timeout expires.

Anything that can be implemented with a spin-wait loop can usually be made more efficient with a futex.

For example, consider the simplest possible spinlock, which uses a single word containing a one to indicate locked and a zero to indicate unlocked. When you encounter a one, you sit in a loop doing an atomic compare-and-swap trying to replace a zero with a one. When this succeeds, you've acquired the lock.

On most operating systems running on single-core processors, you will sit in this loop until you exhaust your quantum, then a timer will fire and another thread will run. Your thread may be scheduled before the thread that owns the lock finishes, so you'll then spin for another quantum.

The first simple optimisation on this design is to yield in the spin loop. This will allow other threads to run but the waiting thread remains runnable and so may be rescheduled early. With an RTOS priority scheduler, if the thread

---

Documentation for the `futex_wake` function

`int futex_wake(uint32_t * address, uint32_t count)`

Wakes up to `count` threads that are sleeping with `futex_timed_wait` on `address`.

The `address` argument must be a valid unsealed pointer with a length of at least four after the address but the scheduler does not require any explicit permissions. The scheduler never needs store access to the futex word. Removing store permission means that a compromised scheduler can cause spurious wakes but cannot tamper with the futex word. If, for example, the futex word is a lock then the scheduler can wake threads that are blocked on the lock but cannot release the lock and so cannot make two threads believe that they have simultaneously acquired the same lock.

The return value for a successful call is the number of threads that were woken. `-EINVAL` is returned for invalid arguments.

---

that's waiting is a higher priority than the thread that owns the lock, the thread that owns the lock may never be scheduled.

A futex lets the waiting thread sleep. The `futex_timed_wait` call will compare the value in the futex word to the expected value (one, indicating locked, in this case) and, if they match, will send the thread to sleep and remain asleep until the thread owning the lock does a `futex_wake` call when unlocking.

A more complete futex-based lock uses three values in the lock word to differentiate between locked states with and without waiters. This allows the uncontended case to avoid any cross-compartment calls.

Futexes can be used to build other waiting mechanisms beyond locks. A *barrier* is the simplest primitive that you can build with a futex. This is a very simple primitive that blocks every thread until all threads have reached the same point in the code. Listing 47 shows how a barrier might be implemented, using the `std::atomic` wrapper around futexes.

The counter is set to the number of threads (two in this case). When a thread arrives at the barrier, it decrements the counter. Note that the decrement operator on `std::atomic` is an atomic decrement, so exactly one thread should take the counter to zero. The thread that set the counter to zero then

```
10 /// Thread entry point.
11 __cheriot_compartment("barrier") void entry()
12 {
13   static std::atomic<uint32_t> barrier = 2;
14   printf("Thread: %d arrived at barrier\n",
15          thread_id_get());
16   uint32_t value = --barrier;
17   if (value == 0)
18   {
19     barrier.notify_all();
20   }
21   else
22   {
23     while (value != 0)
24     {
25       barrier.wait(value);
26       value = barrier;
27     }
28   }
29   printf("Thread: %d passed barrier\n", thread_id_get());
30 }
```

LISTING 47. Implementing a barrier with a futex [from: examples/barrier/barrier.cc]

notifies any waiting threads to wake. Other threads, as they arrive, will sit using the wait method, which is a thin wrapper around futex_wait.

The loop on line 23 is important. Imagine that one thread decrements the counter to one and is then preempted. Then another thread decrements it to zero and does the notify_all (futex_wake) call. The first thread, when it resumes will try to wait on the futex, but the value has now changed. Fortunately, futex_wait takes an expected value and so, if the futex word does not have this value then the call will resume immediately.

If this example had three threads, a similar race could occur in the opposite direction. If the first thread decremented from three to two and was then preempted by a second thread, it would call futex_wake with an expected value of two, but the value would now be one. It would then wake, because the value does not match. If this happens, it would reload the value, note that it is not zero, and retry waiting. The futex APIs are designed to allow this combination of wait and atomic operation to work for any interleaving.

Try modifying this example by adding more threads (don't forget to increase the initial value of the counter!).

6.6. Building locks from futexes

The locks library provides a set of futex-based locks. The locks.h header exposes the interface to this library.

Ticket locks

provide guaranteed FIFO semantics for waiters.

Flag locks

are simple locks that wake waiters in the order of their thread priorities. These can optionally provide priority inheritance (see Section 6.7).

Recursive mutexes

wrap a priority-inheriting flag lock and allow the same thread to acquire a lock multiple times.

Semaphores

provide a counting semaphore abstraction.

C++ users may prefer to use the wrappers provided in locks.hh, which implement a uniform interface for different lock types. This header also defines a NoLock class that provides the same interface but does not do any locking so generic data structures can be implemented with and without locking.

You can see the difference between the lock types by running the locking example. This uses a lock declared at the top of the file, as shown in Listing 48. This is using a flag lock in the uncommented version. You can change it to using a ticket lock by commenting out the first declaration and uncommenting the second.

```
10 // Comment out this line and uncomment
11 // the next one to see how ticket locks
12 // behave.
13 FlagLock lock;
14 // TicketLock lock;
```

LISTING 48. Declaring a lock in C++ [from: examples/locking/locking.cc]

The rest of this file contains three versions of the function shown in Listing 49. One of these is defined for each of three threads, which are created with three different priorities. The do_useful_work function in the example just calls thread_sleep with a timeout of one second, but in real code would be doing the work that must be done with the lock held.

```
29 __cheriot_compartment("locking") void low()
30 {
31   while (true)
32   {
33     lock.lock();
34     printf("Low priority thread "
35            "acquired lock\n");
36     do_useful_work();
37     lock.unlock();
38   }
39 }
```

LISTING 49. The low-priority thread entry point for the locking example
[from: examples/locking/locking.cc]

When you run this example, you should see output like this:

```
High priority thread acquired lock
High priority thread acquired lock
High priority thread acquired lock
High priority thread acquired lock
High priority thread acquired lock
```

This is an example of *starvation*. The low- and medium-priority threads are both waiting for the lock, but the high-priority thread is not yielding between releasing and reacquiring the lock and so they are never woken.

If you change this to a ticket lock, the output will change to this:

```
High priority thread acquired lock
Medium priority thread acquired lock
Low priority thread acquired lock
High priority thread acquired lock
Medium priority thread acquired lock
Low priority thread acquired lock
```

Ticket locks are modelled after the ticket dispensers that are used to manage queues of people. When you arrive, you take the ticket with the next number. There is a display showing the current number and you wait until the display matches your number. A ticket lock is implemented with two counters. The first counter is used to assign tickets. When you try to acquire the lock, you atomically fetch-and-increment the counter. The result of the fetch is your ticket number. You then wait until the second counter is equal to your ticket number. When you release the lock, you increment the second counter. This is built from futexes by doing a futex_wait on the counter word to block acquiring the lock and a futex_wake when you release the lock.

In this example, the high-priority thread runs first and acquires the lock. Next, while it's yielding in the middle, the medium-priority thread tries to acquire the lock and blocks. Before blocking, it successfully receives a ticket and so is next in line for the lock. The low-priority thread then does the same. When the high-priority thread resumes, it also acquires a ticket and is now in the queue to run after the other two threads.

Each thread runs in this version, but a high-priority thread is blocked waiting for two lower-priority threads to proceed, which may not be desirable.

6.7. Inheriting priorities

Simple futex-based locks are vulnerable to *priority inversion*, where a high-priority thread is unable to make progress because a lock is held by a lower-priority thread. We saw an example of this with ticket locks but the same is also possible with flag locks, as we'll see in the priority_inheritance example.

This starts with the high-priority thread shown in Listing 50 running. This will sit in a loop, first yielding for up to a second to allow other threads to run, then trying to acquire a lock. This example is using LockGuard, a simple RAII wrapper around the RTOS' locks. The constructor variant here with two arguments takes a timeout in addition to the lock. Lock guards are convertible to bool and convert as true if and only if the lock is acquired. This allows the thread to print whether the lock was acquired, or it timed out waiting for the lock.

While this thread yields, the thread shown in Listing 51 runs. This first yields and then infinite loops. The infinite loop in this example is a placeholder for anything that does long-running work and does not yield.

```
42 __cheriot_compartment("priority_"
43                       "inheritance") void medium()
44 {
45   // Let the low-priority thread run
46   // until it yields
47   Timeout t(MS_TO_TICKS(1000));
48   thread_sleep(&t);
49   printf("Medium priority thread entering infinite loop "
50          "and not yielding\n");
51   while (true)
52   {
53     x++;
54   }
55 }
```

LISTING 51. A medium-priority thread that will starve a high-priority thread
[from: examples/priority_inheritance/priority_inheritance.cc]

```
16 __cheriot_compartment("priority_"
17                       "inheritance") void high()
18 {
19   // Let the low and
20   // medium-priority threads start
21   Timeout t(MS_TO_TICKS(1000));
22   thread_sleep(&t);
23   while (true)
24   {
25     t = Timeout(MS_TO_TICKS(1000));
26     if (LockGuard g{lock, &t})
27     {
28       printf("High-priority thread acquired the lock!\n");
29     }
30     else
31     {
32       printf("High-priority thread failed to acquire the "
33              "lock!\n");
34     }
35   }
36 }
```

LISTING 50. A high-priority thread that will be starved
[from: examples/priority_inheritance/priority_inheritance.cc]

While the medium-priority thread yields, the thread shown in Listing 52 runs. This acquires the lock and also yields. This thread is the lowest priority and so, even without the explicit yield, a similar thread in a more complex program could easily be preempted with the lock held. The yield simply forces it to happen every time, to trigger the problem.

 Prior to C++26, infinite loops are *undefined behaviour* in C++ if they do not have any side effects. The x++ in this loop is simply incrementing an atomic integer to make sure that this loop is not optimised away.

After the low-priority thread yields (or is preempted) the medium-priority thread will resume and infinite loop (or, at least, does something that doesn't yield). The low-priority thread cannot run, because a higher-priority thread is runnable. When the high-priority thread tries to run, it sees that the lock is already acquired and blocks, waiting for it to be finished. Unfortunately, the thread that could release the lock never runs and so you see output like this:

```
59 __cheriot_compartment("priority_"
60                       "inheritance") void low()
61 {
62   while (true)
63   {
64     lock.lock();
65     printf("Low-priority thread acquired the lock\n");
66     Timeout t(MS_TO_TICKS(500));
67     thread_sleep(&t, ThreadSleepNoEarlyWake);
68     printf("Low-priority thread releasing the lock\n");
69     lock.unlock();
70   }
71 }
```

LISTING 52. A low-priority thread that will be preempted with a lock held
[from: examples/priority_inheritance/priority_inheritance.cc]

```
Low-priority thread acquired the lock
Low-priority thread releasing the lock
Low-priority thread acquired the lock
Medium priority thread entering infinite loop and not yielding
High-priority thread failed to acquire the lock!
High-priority thread failed to acquire the lock!
High-priority thread failed to acquire the lock!
```

This example is quite easy to debug, because the starvation is total: the high-priority thread never makes progress. If the medium-priority thread yielded sometimes, this would be much worse because the high-priority thread would make progress but at a far slower rate than its priority would imply.

Priority inheritance is the solution to this kind of problem. With priority inheritance, a thread that blocks on a lock that is held by a lower-priority thread will temporarily loan its priority to the thread the owns the lock. This allows the lower-priority thread run and release the lock. If you change the FlagLock in the example to a FlagLockPriorityInherited, you will see this output:

```
Low-priority thread acquired the lock
Low-priority thread releasing the lock
Low-priority thread acquired the lock
Medium priority thread entering infinite loop and not yielding
Low-priority thread releasing the lock
High-priority thread acquired the lock!
High-priority thread acquired the lock!
High-priority thread acquired the lock!
```

Now, while the medium-priority thread runs, the high-priority thread waits and tries to acquire the lock. The lock is held and so it will try to loan its priority to the thread that owns it. This allows the low-priority thread to run in preference to the medium-priority one. The low-priority thread runs and releases the lock, allowing the high-priority thread to resume and acquire the lock.

The futex APIs implement this by storing the thread ID of the owning thread in the bottom 16 bits of the futex word and passing FutexPriority-Inheritance to the flags argument in the wait call. The specified thread will have its priority set to the highest priority of any of the waiting threads. The priority boost lasts until the waiters time out or the boosted thread releases the lock, whichever happens first. A single thread can hold multiple priority-inheriting locks and receive priority boosts from all of them. Most of the time, you will not use this directly and will instead use the priority-inheriting lock APIs from their C or C++ wrappers.

The priority inheritance mechanism can also be used to build asymmetric locks. These have a fast path that doesn't do any cross-compartment calls and a slow path that does. You can find one example of this in the hazard pointer mechanism for short-lived claims. This must detect when a thread has tried to add a hazard pointer while the allocator is scanning the list, without slowing down the allocator. Before reading the list, the allocator increments the top 16 bits of the futex word and sets the low 16 to the thread ID performing the operation. Threads updating the hazard set check the futex word before and after updating the list. If the top 16 bits have changed, they know that the allocator has scanned the list and they must retry. If the top 16 bits contain an odd value, the allocator is currently scanning the list and they must wait. They can do a priority-inheriting wait with a one-tick timeout *even though the allocator will not ever call futex_wake*. They will yield for one tick, boosting the priority of the thread that's currently in the allocator, but then resume at the end of the tick.

6.8. Securing futexes

Most of the time you will want to use futexes (and the locks that wrap them) to synchronise operations within a single compartment. Futex-based locks rely on the contents of the lock word to be valid. For example, if a flag lock is directly accessible by two mutually distrusting compartments, one can write an invalid value to the word and either prevent the other from waking waiters or cause it to spuriously believe that it has acquired the lock.

This is not normally a limitation because locks typically protect some data structure or other resource that should not be concurrently mutated by multiple threads. Providing mutable views of such a structure to multiple compartments is almost certainly a security vulnerability, even without attacks on the futex.

There is one situation where futexes are safe to share across compartment boundaries. If you have a component that others trust for availability, it can share read-only views of a futex to allow waiting for an out-of-band event. The scheduler does this for interrupts (see Chapter 9), allowing threads to use the futex wait operation to block until an interrupt is ready.

6.9. Using event groups

The event_group library provides an event-group API that is primarily intended for porting code written against FreeRTOS's event-group APIs. The event.h header exposes the interface to this library. These APIs do not have a clear trust model and so should be avoided in new code that is not ported from FreeRTOS. You can build more convenient interfaces atop futexes for most synchronisation operations. You may also simply use multiple futexes and the multiwaiter API (see Section 6.12) to wait for multiple events.

An event group is a set of up to 24 values that can be set or cleared independently. Waiters can wait for any or all of an arbitrary subset of these.

Event groups are created with the eventgroup_create function. This returns an opaque handle to the event group, which can be used for setting, clearing, or waiting on events.

Documentation for the eventgroup_create function

```
int eventgroup_create(struct Timeout * timeout,
AllocatorCapability heapCapability, struct EventGroup * *
outGroup)
```

Create a new event group, allocated using heapCapability. The event group is returned via outGroup.

This returns zero on success. Otherwise it returns a negative error code. If the timeout expires then this returns -ETIMEDOUT, if memory cannot be allocated it returns -ENOMEM.

Note that, because this allocates memory, it requires an *allocation capability*. See Chapter 7 for more information about what this means.

You can then use eventgroup_set and eventgroup_clear to set and clear some or all of the event flags in this group. Both of these calls return the old values of the bits.

Documentation for the eventgroup_set function

```
int eventgroup_set(Timeout * timeout, struct EventGroup *
group, uint32_t * outBits, uint32_t bitsToSet)
```

Set one or more bits in an event group. The bitsToSet argument contains the bits to set. Any thread waiting with eventgroup_wait will be woken if the bits that it is waiting for are set.

This returns zero on success. If the timeout expires before this returns then it returns -ETIMEDOUT.

Independent of success or failure, outBits will be used to return the set of currently set bits in this event group.

Documentation for the eventgroup_clear function

```
int eventgroup_clear(Timeout * timeout, struct EventGroup *
group, uint32_t * outBits, uint32_t bitsToClear)
```

Clear one or more bits in an event group. The bitsToClear argument contains the set of bits to clear. This does not wake any threads.

This returns zero on success. If the timeout expires before this returns then it returns -ETIMEDOUT.

Independent of success or failure, outBits will be used to return the set of currently set bits in this event group.

You can then subsequently wait for some of the events to be set with the eventgroup_wait function. This takes a set of events to wait for and can wait until either some or all of them are set.

This call can also atomically clear the bits that you've waited on, giving them edge-triggered behaviour.

Documentation for the `eventgroup_wait` function

```
int eventgroup_wait(Timeout * timeout, struct EventGroup *
group, uint32_t * outBits, uint32_t bitsWanted, _Bool
waitForAll, _Bool clearOnExit)
```

Wait for events in an event group. The `bitsWanted` argument must contain at least one bit set in the low 24 bits (and none in the high bits). This indicates the specific events to wait for. If `waitForAll` is true then all of the bits in `bitsWanted` must be set in the event group before this returns. If `waitForAll` is false then any of the bits in `bitsWanted` being set in the event group will cause this to return.

If this returns zero then `outBits` will contain the bits that were set at the time that the condition became true. If this returns `-ETIMEDOUT` then `outBits` will contain the bits that were set at the time that the timeout expired.

Note: `waitForAll` requires all bits to be set *at the same time*. This makes it trivial to introduce race conditions if used with multiple waiters and `clearOnExit`, or if different threads clear different bits in the waited set.

If `clearOnExit` is true and this returns successfully then the bits in `bitsWanted` will be cleared in the event group before this returns.

6.10. Sending messages

A message queue is a FIFO capable of storing a fixed number of fixed-sized entries. There are two distinct use cases for message queues:

- Communicating between two threads in the same compartment.
- Communicating between different compartments.

In the first case, the endpoints are in the same trust domain. The `message_queue_library` library provides a simple message-queue API that is intended for this use case. When the endpoints are in different trust domains, the endpoints must be protected from tampering. The `message_queue` compartment wraps the library in a compartment that exposes an almost identical interface to the library but with the endpoints exposed as (tamper-proof) sealed capabilities.

Queues for use within a single compartment are created with `queue_cre-ate`, which allocates the ring buffer and returns a pointer to the structure. This is a `struct MessageQueue` and callers are at liberty to look inside it directly. There is no expectation that it is protected from the caller. The functions exposed by the library are (by their nature as shared-library functions) shared between any compartments that use the library, but this is a code-size reduction exercise not a security boundary.

Documentation for the `queue_create` function

```
int queue_create(Timeout * timeout, AllocatorCapability
heapCapability, struct MessageQueue * * outQueue, size_t
elementSize, size_t elementCount)
```

Allocates space for a queue using `heapCapability` and stores a handle to it via `outQueue`.

The queue has space for `elementCount` entries. Each entry is a fixed size, `elementSize` bytes.

Returns 0 on success, `-ENOMEM` on allocation failure, and `-EINVAL` if the arguments are invalid (for example, if the requested number of elements multiplied by the element size would overflow).

Queues can be freed simply with `heap_free` but doing so may result in deadlocks. If a thread is blocked trying to send or receive from a queue then it will remain blocking if the queue is freed out from underneath it. The `queue_destroy` function avoids this by waking all threads. Other threads may then trap immediately after they return and try to read from the queue's counters, but at least this is recoverable (see Section 5.11).

Messages are sent with `queue_send` and received with `queue_receive`. These are blocking (if allowed to by a non-zero timeout) calls that send or receive a single message.

You can probe the number of messages in a queue with `queue_items_re-maining`.

Listing 53 shows how to create a message queue. This uses the `non_block-ing` template function. This and `blocking_forever` take advantage of the regularity of CHERIoT APIs (timeouts are always the first parameter) to pass a zero-length and unlimited timeout to a single function. The producer thread

---

Documentation for the `queue_destroy` function

```
int queue_destroy(AllocatorCapability heapCapability, struct
MessageQueue * handle)
```

Destroys a queue. This wakes up all threads waiting to produce or consume, and makes them fail to acquire the lock, before deallocating the underlying allocation.

Returns 0 on success. This can fail only if deallocation would fail and will, in these cases, return the same error codes as `heap_free`.

This function will check the heap capability first and will avoid upgrading the locks if freeing the queue would fail.

Documentation for the `queue_send` function

```
int queue_send(Timeout * timeout, struct MessageQueue *
handle, const void * src)
```

Send a message to the queue specified by `handle`. This expects to be able to copy the number of bytes specified by `elementSize` when the queue was created from `src`.

Returns 0 on success. On failure, returns `-ETIMEOUT` if the timeout was exhausted, `-EINVAL` on invalid arguments.

This expects to be called with a valid queue handle. It does not validate that this is correct.

---

in this example is creating the queue and is then doing a `futex_wake` operation on the global variable where the queue pointer is stored.

```
21  // Allocate the queue
22  non_blocking<queue_create>(
23    MALLOC_CAPABILITY, &queue, sizeof(int), 16);
24  // Wake the consumer thread
25  futex_wake(reinterpret_cast<uint32_t *>(&queue), 1);
```

LISTING 53. Allocating a message queue for use in a single compartment
[from: examples/producer_consumer/queue.cc]

Documentation for the `queue_receive` function

```
int queue_receive(Timeout * timeout, struct MessageQueue *
handle, void * dst)
```

Receive a message over a queue specified by `handle`. This expects to be able to copy the number of bytes specified by `elementSize`. The message is copied to `dst`, which must have sufficient permissions and space to hold the message.

Returns 0 on success, `-ETIMEOUT` if the timeout was exhausted, `-EIN-VAL` on invalid arguments.

The library interfaces to queues are not intended to be robust in the presence of malicious callers. They run in the same security context as the caller, so a caller may abuse them to corrupt its own state. They do aim to be robust with respect to the source or destination buffer for sending and receiving messages being invalid or concurrently deallocated. This robustness is implemented using the scoped error handling and so requires calling compartments to link the relevant error handler, as documented in Section 5.13.

The corresponding `futex_wait` call is in the consumer, in Listing 55. This takes advantage of the fact that the global is initialised to zero and the resulting capability after allocation will be non-zero (in both halves, so the choice to use the first address is arbitrary here). If the consumer thread runs first, the wait call will block then return after the wake call from Listing 53. If the producer thread runs first then the wait call will return immediately.

The producer in this simple example then just sends 200 integers, one at a time, as shown in Listing 54. These will enter the queue until either the scheduler quantum expires or the queue fills up, then the consumer thread will run.

The consumer thread (Listing 55) simply reads each element and prints it. Once every expected message has been received, the consumer destroys the queue.

Documentation for the `queue_items_remaining` function

```
int queue_items_remaining(struct MessageQueue * handle,
size_t * items)
```

Returns the number of items in the queue specified by `handle` via `items`.

Returns 0 on success. This has no failure mechanisms, but is intended to have the same interface as the version that operates on a sealed queue handle.

Note: This interface is inherently racy. The number of items in the queue may change in between the return of this function and the caller acting on the result.

```
29  // Loop, sending some numbers to the other thread.
30  for (int i = 1; i < 200; i++)
31  {
32    Debug::log("Producer sending {} to queue", i);
33    int ret = blocking_forever<queue_send>(queue, &i);
34    // Abort if the queue send errors.
35    Debug::Invariant(ret == 0, "Queue send failed {}", ret);
36  }
```

LISTING 54. Sending messages to a message queue.
[from: examples/producer_consumer/queue.cc]

This is a good general pattern. This example detects the end of the queue because it knows that it will receive 200 messages but a more realistic system would send an end-of-messages marker through the queue. Once this is in the queue, the producer will no longer use the queue and as soon as the receiver reads it the consumer is free to deallocate the queue.

This example prints the number of cycles that elapsed at the end. Try adjusting the queue size and the priorities of the two threads to see how this affects performance.

6.11. Sending messages between compartments

If you are passing messages between compartments, you should use the versions of these functions with the _sealed suffix. These are provided by the

```
47  // Use the queue pointer as a futex.  It is initialised to
48  // 0, if the other thread has stored a valid pointer here
49  // then it will not be zero and so futex_wait will return
50  // immediately.
51  futex_wait(reinterpret_cast<uint32_t *>(&queue), 0);
52  Debug::log("Waiting for messages");
53  // Get a message from the queue and print it.
54  int value = 0;
55  while ((value != 199) && (blocking_forever<queue_receive>(
56                           queue, &value) == 0))
57  {
58    Debug::log("Read {} from queue", value);
59  }
60  Debug::log("Destroying the queue");
61  queue_destroy(MALLOC_CAPABILITY, queue);
```

LISTING 55. Receiving messages from a message queue.

[from: examples/producer_consumer/queue.cc]

compartmentalised version and ensure that the queue's internal state is not mutated by its callers.

The queue_create_sealed function creates a queue in exactly the same way as queue_create (and has the same argument structure) but returns a *sealed* pointer to it. Nowhere outside of the queue compartment can unseal this so the queue is protected against tampering. The queue may still contain malicious or malformed data, but you have guarantees that messages will arrive in order and that they won't be tampered with in flight.

Documentation for the queue_create_sealed function

```
int queue_create_sealed(Timeout * timeout,
AllocatorCapability heapCapability, struct MessageQueue *
__sealed_capability * outQueue, size_t elementSize, size_t
elementCount)
```

Allocate a new message queue that is managed by the message queue compartment. The resulting queue handle (returned in outQueue) is a sealed capability to a queue that can be used for both sending and receiving.

Listing 56 shows how to allocate a queue for sharing between compartments. This is equivalent to the example from Listing 53, but with the producer and consumer separated into different compartments. The queue is protected from both by being managed in the queue compartment, which is provided by the RTOS. In the original, the queue was shared between the producer and consumer by placing it in a (compartment-local) global variable. In this version, it needs to be passed to the consumer explicitly by calling the set_queue function that the consumer exposes.

```
21  // Allocate the queue
22  CHERI_SEALED(MessageQueue *) queue;
23  non_blocking<queue_create_sealed>(
24      MALLOC_CAPABILITY, &queue, sizeof(int), 16);
25  // Pass the queue handle to the consumer.
26  set_queue(queue);
```

LISTING 56. Allocating a message queue for use in a between compartments.
[from: examples/producer_consumer_compartment/producer.cc]

Listing 57 shows the implementation of this function. This explicitly checks that the queue is valid before keeping it by calling queue_items_remaining_sealed. This function returns zero on success or an error code on failure and needs to unseal the queue to succeed, so this works to check that the sealed pointer really is a queue handle. After it has checked that this is a valid queue handle, this function looks much like the code that woke the other thread in the single-compartment case in Listing 53.

```
24  // Check that this is a valid queue
25  size_t items;
26  if (queue_items_remaining_sealed(newQueue, &items) != 0)
27  {
28      return;
29  }
30  // Set it in the global and allow the thread to start.
31  queue = newQueue;
32  Debug::log("Queue set to {}", queue);
33  futex_wake(reinterpret_cast<uint32_t *>(&queue), 1);
```

LISTING 57. Receiving a queue endpoint in the consumer compartment.
[from: examples/producer_consumer_compartment/consumer.cc]

This queue can be destroyed by calling queue_destroy_sealed. You cannot free an object pointed to by a sealed capability unless you also have the capability that authorises unsealing. This means that, unlike the unsealed version, you cannot destroy a queue created with queue_create_sealed except by calling the correct destroy function.

Similarly, you cannot free a sealed object unless you hold the allocation capability that allocated it. In the example, the queue is allocated from the producer's allocation capability. This means that the consumer cannot free it. Instead, the producer waits for the consumer to finish draining the queue and then frees it, in Listing 58.

```
41  size_t itemsRemaining;
42  while ((queue_items_remaining_sealed(
43              queue, &itemsRemaining) == 0) &&
44         (itemsRemaining > 0))
45  {
46    Timeout t{1};
47    thread_sleep(&t);
48  }
49  int ret = blocking_forever<queue_destroy_sealed>(
50    MALLOC_CAPABILITY, queue);
51  Debug::Assert(
52    ret == 0, "Failed to destroy queue: {}", ret);
53  Debug::log("Destroyed queue");
```

LISTING 58. Freeing a message queue once it is empty.

[from: examples/producer_consumer_compartment/producer.cc]

Documentation for the `queue_destroy_sealed` function

```
int queue_destroy_sealed(Timeout * timeout,
AllocatorCapability heapCapability, struct MessageQueue *
__sealed_capability queueHandle)
```

Destroy a queue handle. If this is called on a restricted endpoint (re-turned either from `queue_receive_handle_create_sealed` or from `queue_send_handle_create_sealed`), this frees only the handle. If called with the queue handle returned from `queue_create_sealed`, this will destroy the queue.

The corresponding send and receive functions are identical to their library counterparts, but take sealed queue handles. Sometimes, it's useful to be able to give one compartment the ability to write to a queue and another the ability to read. The queue compartment provides two APIs that let you allocate a handle that is authorised for only sending or receiving, `queue_receive_han-dle_create_sealed` and `queue_send_handle_create_sealed`.

With these APIs, you can have an initial setup compartment that creates a queue and then hands the send and receive endpoints to two others. This

---

Documentation for the `queue_receive_handle_create_sealed` function

```
int queue_receive_handle_create_sealed(struct Timeout *
timeout, AllocatorCapability heapCapability, struct
MessageQueue * __sealed_capability handle, struct
MessageQueue * __sealed_capability * outHandle)
```

Convert a queue handle returned from `queue_create_sealed` into one that can be used *only* for receiving.

Returns 0 on success and writes the resulting restricted handle via `outHandle`. Returns `-ENOMEM` on allocation failure or `-EINVAL` if the handle is not valid.

Documentation for the `queue_send_handle_create_sealed` function

```
int queue_send_handle_create_sealed(struct Timeout *
timeout, AllocatorCapability heapCapability, struct
MessageQueue * __sealed_capability handle, struct
MessageQueue * __sealed_capability * outHandle)
```

Convert a queue handle returned from `queue_create_sealed` into one that can be used *only* for sending.

Returns 0 on success and writes the resulting restricted handle via `outHandle`. Returns `-ENOMEM` on allocation failure or `-EINVAL` if the handle is not valid.

---

provides mutual distrust because neither compartment that holds a send or receive handle can free the queue, nor can they be used for the opposite operation, and the queue compartment protects the integrity of the queue itself.

In many cases, the trust relationship may be asymmetric. For example, a compartment may provide a queue that other untrusted compartments can send messages to, but the senders trust the receiving compartment. The APIs also support this asymmetric use case, where the trusted compartment keeps the original handle but uses `queue_send_handle_create_sealed` to create handles to pass to other compartments.

Try modifying the example to remove the ability from the consumer to send messages. This change should not require restructuring the code, only calling `queue_receive_handle_create_sealed`. Next, try moving queue creation to a separate compartment that sets the endpoint in the consumer and then passes it into the consumer and deallocates it once the producer returns and the queue is empty. The producer should receive a restricted handle that can send but not receive. Try modifying both the producer and consumer to do the operation that they should not be allowed to do and make sure that it fails.

6.12. Waiting for multiple events

The multiwaiter API allows waiting for any of a set of independent events. It is conceptually similar to `select`, `poll`, `epoll`, and `kqueue` in *NIX operating systems or `WaitForMultipleObjects` in Windows. It is designed to bound the amount of time that the scheduler must spend checking multiwaiters and to minimise the amount of memory that multiwaiters consume. Memory is allocated only when a multiwaiter is created, with `multiwaiter_create`. This creates a multiwaiter with space for a fixed number of events.

Documentation for the `multiwaiter_create` function

```
int multiwaiter_create(Timeout * timeout,
AllocatorCapability heapCapability, MultiWaiter * ret,
size_t maxItems)
```

Create a multiwaiter object. This is a stateful object that can wait on at most `maxItems` event sources.

Listing 59 shows how to create a multiwaiter that can wait for two futexes. This example generalises the producer-consumer example from earlier in this chapter to have two producer threads, each of which writes to a different message queue, but a single consumer that reads both. The consumer will use this multiwaiter to block until one or both queues has a message available.

Each `multiwaiter_wait` call is a one-shot operation. The call is passed a set of things to wait for and the associated condition via the `events` array and returns the waited status via the same array. This is typically an on-stack array.

```
84   // Create the multiwaiter object in the scheduler with
85   // space for two event sources.
86   MultiWaiter multiwaiter;
87   blocking_forever<multiwaiter_create>(
88     MALLOC_CAPABILITY, &multiwaiter, 2);
```

LISTING 59. Creating a multiwaiter object. [from: examples/multiwaiter/queue.cc]

Documentation for the `multiwaiter_wait` function

```
int multiwaiter_wait(Timeout * timeout, MultiWaiter waiter,
struct EventWaiterSource * events, size_t newEventsCount)
```

Wait for events. The first argument is the multiwaiter to wait on. New events can optionally be added by providing an array of new-EventsCount elements as the newEvents argument.

Return values:
- On success, this function returns 0.
- If the arguments are invalid, this function returns -EINVAL.
- If the timeout is reached without any events being triggered then this returns -ETIMEOUT.

The multiwaiter can natively wait only for futex notifications but higher-level mechanisms are built out of futexes. For example, if you wish to wait for a message queue (see Section 6.10) to be ready to send, you can call multiwaiter_queue_receive_init to initialise a multiwaiter event with the queue's receive counter and expected value. This event will then fire if the queue becomes non-full. The normal caveats about race conditions apply: the queue may become full again if another thread sends messages in between your receiving the notification and sending a message. For example, consider the following sequence:

1. You try to send buy cannot because the queue is full.
2. You use the multiwaiter to wait for the queue to become non-full.
3. Another thread receives a message from the queue, which makes the queue non-full.
4. Your thread becomes runnable because the futex wake triggered your futex wait to return but does not yet run.

5. Another thread sends a message to the queue, which makes the queue full again.

6. You try to send but the send fails because the queue is now full.

Listing 60 initialises two events, one for each of the queues, and then calls multiwaiter_wait. This will return immediately if an equivalent futex_wait call on either futex would have done so, or will block until one of the queues becomes non-empty. The loop then tries to handle one event from each message queue that has events available.

```
95    // Initialise the events for this wait.
96    std::array<EventWaiterSource, queues.size()> events;
97    multiwaiter_queue_receive_init(&events[0], queues[0]);
98    multiwaiter_queue_receive_init(&events[1], queues[1]);
99    // Block until at least one event fires.
100   int ret = blocking_forever<multiwaiter_wait>(
101     multiwaiter, events.data(), events.size());
102   Debug::Assert(ret == 0, "Multiwaiter failed: {}", ret);
103   // For each message queue, fetch a message if the
104   // multiwaiter indicated that one was available.
105   for (int i = 0; i < queues.size(); i++)
106   {
107     if (events[i].value)
108     {
109       ret = non_blocking<queue_receive>(queues[i],
110                                         &values[i]);
111       Debug::Assert(
112         ret == 0,
113         "Failed to receive message from queue: {}",
114         ret);
115       Debug::log("Received {} on queue {}", values[i], i);
116     }
117   }
```

LISTING 60. Using a multiwaiter to wait for either of two queues.
[from: examples/multiwaiter/queue.cc]

Try modifying this to avoid the multiwaiter_wait call if either of the queues is already non-empty. You can do this either by repeating the non-blocking receive and using the multiwaiter only if it fails, or by checking whether the value field of the event source has been initialised to -1 by multiwaiter_queue_receive_init. Make sure that you don't starve one of the producers by biasing your consumption towards one of the queues.

Remember that the CHERIoT RTOS scheduler also exposes interrupts as futexes. This means that the multiwaiter API can wait for multiple hardware and software events in a single call.

Chapter 7.
Memory management in CHERIoT RTOS

It is common for embedded systems to avoid heap allocation entirely and pre-allocate all memory that they will need. This means that the total amount of memory that a system requires is the sum of the peak memory usage of all components.

The CHERIoT platform is designed to enable safe reuse of memory. The shared heap allows memory to be dynamically allocated for individual uses and then reused. This means that the total memory requirement for a system becomes the peak combined usage of all components. If two components use a lot of memory at different times, they can safely share the same memory.

This chapter covers how to allocate and manage memory. CHERIoT provides spatial and memory safety so there is a complementary aspect to memory allocation: What do you do when you manage memory incorrectly and CHERIoT catches the error? Error handling from CHERI exceptions is covered in detail in Section 5.11.

7.1. Understanding allocation capabilities

The memory allocator uses a capability model. Every caller of a memory allocation or deallocation function must present a capability that authorises allocation. This is a *sealed capability* to an `AllocatorCapabilityState` structure. Sealed capabilities were introduced in Section 1.6.

This uses the static sealing mechanism described in Section 5.6. There is no limit to the number of allocator capabilities that a compartment can hold. Each allocation capability holds an independent quota.

There is no requirement that the sum of all allocation quotas is less than the total available heap space. You can over-commit memory if you know that it will not all be needed at the same time. The quota mechanism gives you a way of limiting the total memory consumption of individual compartments (or groups of compartments) and of cleaning up after failure.

7.2. Creating custom allocation capabilities

A compartment may hold different allocation capabilities for different purposes. The `heap_free_all` function allows you to free all memory allocated with a specified capability, so using multiple allocation quotas can be useful for error recovery.

You can forward-declare an allocator capability with the DECLARE_ALLO-CATOR_CAPABILITY macro. This takes a single argument: the name of the allocator capability. You can then define the allocator capability with the DE-FINE_ALLOCATOR_CAPABILITY macro, which takes the name and the quota size as arguments. These can be combined with the DECLARE_AND_DEFINE_AL-LOCATOR_CAPABILITY macro.

The allocator capabilities are exposed as COMDATs in C++. This allows them to be defined in a header and used in multiple translation units. C does not expose a similar mechanism, so you must use the separate declare and define macros in C if your compartment has multiple compilation units that wish to share an allocator capability and define the capability in a single compilation unit.

In future versions of CHERIoT RTOS, allocator capabilities are likely to gain additional restrictions (for example, separating the ability to allocate from the ability to claim).

7.3. Recalling the memory safety guarantees

Every pointer to a new allocation provided by the memory allocator is derived from a capability to a large heap region and bounded. The *capability monotonicity* guarantees in a CHERI system ensure that a caller cannot expand the bounds of the returned pointer.

The CHERIoT platform provides two additional features for temporal safety. These both depend on a revocation bitmap, a shadow memory space that stores one bit per eight bytes of heap memory. When an object is freed, the allocator paints the bits associated with it.

The *load filter* is part of a CHERIoT core. When a capability is loaded from memory into a register, the load filter checks the revocation bit associated with the base of the capability and clears the tag bit if the capability points to freed memory (filtering out dangling pointers). The load filter ensures that you cannot load, and therefore cannot try to use, any dangling pointers. This gives deterministic use-after-free protection; any attempt to use a pointer to a deallocated object will trap. The object is then placed in *quarantine*.

The *revoker* periodically scans all memory and invalidates any pointers whose base address points to a deallocated object. The monotonicity of bounds ensures that the base of a capability always points either somewhere within the allocation or, if the length is zero, to the word immediately after it.

 The allocator marks the metadata between allocations as freed. This means that a zero-length capability to the end of an object is likely to be untagged.

The load filter ensures that no new pointers to deallocated objects can appear in memory so the revocation sweep can proceed asynchronously. Any object that is in quarantine at the start of a sweep is safe to remove from quarantine at the end.

This combination of features allows the allocator to provide complete spatial and temporal safety for heap objects.

7.4. Allocating with an explicit capability

Documentation for the heap_free function

```
int heap_free(AllocatorCapability heapCapability, void *
ptr)
```

Free a heap allocation.

Returns 0 on success, -EINVAL if ptr is not a valid pointer to the start of a live heap allocation, or -ENOTENOUGHSTACK if the stack size is insufficiently large to safely run the function.

Documentation for the heap_free_all function

```
ssize_t heap_free_all(AllocatorCapability heapCapability)
```

Free all allocations owned by this capability.

Returns the number of bytes freed, -EPERM if this is not a valid heap capability, or -ENOTENOUGHSTACK if the stack size is insufficiently large to safely run the function.

145

Documentation for the `heap_allocate` function

```
void * heap_allocate(Timeout * timeout, AllocatorCapability
heapCapability, size_t size, uint32_t flags)
```

Non-standard allocation API. Allocates size bytes.

The heapCapability quota object must have remaining capacity sufficient for the requested size as well as any padding required by the CHERIoT capability encoding (see its ISA document for details) and any additional space required by the allocator's internal layout, which may be up to CHERIOTHeapMinChunkSize bytes. Not all of these padding bytes may be available for use via the returned capability.

Blocking behaviour is controlled by the flags and the timeout parameters. Specifically, the flags parameter defines on which conditions to wait, and the timeout parameter how long to wait.

The non-blocking mode (AllocateWaitNone, or timeout with no time remaining) will return a successful allocation if one can be created immediately, or nullptr otherwise.

The blocking modes may return nullptr if the condition to wait is not fulfilled, if the timeout has expired, or if the allocation cannot be satisfied under any circumstances (for example if size is larger than the total heap size).

This means that calling this with AllocateWaitAny and Unlimited-Timeout will only ever return nullptr if the allocation cannot be satisfied under any circumstances.

In both blocking and non-blocking cases, -ENOTENOUGHSTACK may be returned if the stack is insufficiently large to safely run the function. This means that the return value of heap_allocate should be checked for the validity of the tag bit *and not* simply compared against nullptr.

Memory returned from this interface is guaranteed to be zeroed.

The heap_allocate and heap_free functions take a capability, as described above, that authorises allocation and deallocation. When an object is allocated with an explicit capability, it may be freed only by presenting the same capability. This means that if you pass a heap-allocated buffer to another compartment, that compartment cannot free it unless you also pass the authorising capability.

> The allocation uses a timeout because the allocation API is able to block if insufficient memory is available. In contrast the deallocation API will always make progress. The allocator uses a priority-inheriting lock, which is dropped while blocking. If a high-priority thread frees memory while a lower-priority thread owns the lock then the lower-priority thread will wake up, complete its allocation or deallocation, release the lock, and allow the higher-priority thread to resume.

If you need to clean up all memory allocated by a particular capability, `heap_free_all` will walk the heap and deallocate everything owned by that capability. This is useful when a compartment has crashed, to reclaim all of its heap memory.

7.5. Using C/C++ default allocators

If you are porting existing C/C++ code then it is likely that it uses `malloc` / `free` or the C++ `new` / `delete` operators. These are implemented as wrappers around `heap_allocate` and `heap_free` that pass `MALLOC_CAPABILITY` as the authorising capability. You can also pass this capability explicitly to allocate things from the same quota as the standard allocation routines.

> `MALLOC_CAPABILITY` is a macro referring to the default allocation capability *in the current compartment*. It refers to a different capability in every compartment.

You can control the amount of memory provided by this capability by defining the `MALLOC_QUOTA` for your compartment. If a compartment is not supposed to allocate memory on its own behalf, you can define `CHERIOT_NO_AMBIENT_MALLOC`. This will disable C's `malloc` and `free` and C++'s global `new` and `delete` operators. Defining `CHERIOT_NO_NEW_DELETE` will disable the global C++ operator `new` and `delete`, but leave `malloc` and `free` available.

Defining these does not prevent memory allocation; you can still define non-default allocator capabilities and use them directly, but it prevents accidental allocation.

7.6. Defining custom allocation capabilities for malloc and free

If you simply wish to change the quota that is available to malloc and free then you can define MALLOC_QUOTA when compiling your compartment. If you require more control, such as controlling the compilation unit that contains the definition of the allocator capability, then you can define CHERIOT_CUS-TOM_DEFAULT_MALLOC_CAPABILITY. This macro will cause stdlib.h to provide a forward declaration of the default allocator capability, but not to define it. You must define it as described in Section 7.2.

This is most useful for C compartments with multiple compilation units. These will need to define the malloc capability in a single compilation unit.

 This limitation will be removed in a future toolchain iteration.

7.7. Allocating on behalf of a caller

Sometimes a compartment needs to be able to allocate memory but that memory is not logically owned by the compartment. This pattern appears even in the core of the RTOS. The compartment that provides message queues, for example, allocates memory on behalf of a caller. It does not hold the right to allocate memory on its own behalf. It does this by taking an allocator capability as an argument and forwarding it to the allocator.

Often, if a compartment is allocating on behalf of a caller, it needs to ensure that the caller doesn't tamper with the object. The token APIs provide a lightweight mechanism for doing this.

When the delegated compartment calls token_sealed_unsealed_alloc, you must provide two capabilities:
- An allocator capability.
- A permit-seal sealing capability.

The first of these authorises memory allocation, the second authorises sealing. The CHERIoT ISA includes only three bits of object type space in the capability encoding so the allocator provides a virtualised sealing mechanism. This allocates an object with a small header containing the sealing type and returns a sealed capability to the entire allocation and an unsealed capability to all except the header.

Documentation for the `token_sealed_unsealed_alloc` function

```
void * __sealed_capability
token_sealed_unsealed_alloc(Timeout * timeout,
AllocatorCapability heapCapability, SKey key, size_t sz,
void * * unsealed)
```

Allocate a new object with size `sz`.

An unsealed pointer to the newly allocated object is returned in `*unsealed`, the sealed pointer is returned as the return value. An invalid unsealed pointer does not constitute an error; the caller will still be given the sealed return value, assuming allocation was otherwise successful.

The key parameter must have both the permit-seal and permit-unseal permissions.

On error, this returns null.

Documentation for the `token_obj_unseal` function

```
void * token_obj_unseal(SKey , void * __sealed_capability )
```

Unseal the object given the key.

The key may be either a static or dynamic key (i.e. one created with the `STATIC_SEALING_TYPE` macro or with `token_key_new`) and the object may be either allocated dynamically (via the token APIs) or statically (via the `DEFINE_STATIC_SEALED_VALUE` macro).

Returns the unsealed object if the key and object are valid and of the correct type, null otherwise.

This function is equivalent to calling both `token_obj_unseal_static` and `token_obj_unseal_dynamic` and returning the result of the first one that succeeds, or null if both fail.

The unsealed capability can be used just like any other pointer to heap memory. The sealed capability can be used with `token_obj_unseal` to retrieve a copy of the unsealed capability. The `token_obj_unseal` function re-

---

Documentation for the `token_obj_destroy` function

```
int token_obj_destroy(AllocatorCapability heapCapability,
SKey , void * __sealed_capability )
```

Destroy the object given its key, freeing memory.

The key must have the permit-unseal permission.

Returns 0 on success. -EINVAL if key or obj are not valid, or they don't match, or if obj has already been destroyed.

---

quires a permit-unseal capability whose value matches the permit-seal capability passed to `token_sealed_unsealed_alloc`.

The virtualised sealing mechanism must be able to derive an accurate capability for the object excluding the header. This is trivial for objects up to a little under 4 KiB. After that, the allocator will create some padding. The padding is placed at the *start* of the allocation, so you can see how much is there by querying the base and address of the returned (sealed) capability.

An object allocated in this way can be deallocated only by presenting *both* the allocator capability and the sealing capability that match the original allocation. This is very convenient for compartments that expose services because the memory cannot go away while they are using it and can be reclaimed only when the same caller (or something acting on its behalf) authorises the deallocation.

7.8. Ensuring that heap objects are not deallocated

If malicious caller passes a compartment a buffer and then frees it, the callee can be induced to trap. There are some situations where this is acceptable. In some cases, compartments exist in a hierarchical trust relationship and it's fine for a more-trusted compartment to be able to crash a less-trusted one. In other cases, the compartment is fault tolerant. For example, the scheduler ensures that its data structures are in a consistent state before performing any operations on user-provided data that may trap. As such, it can unwind to the caller and, at worst, leak memory owned by the caller.

In situations involving mutual distrust, the callee needs to *claim* the memory to prevent its deallocation. The heap_claim function allows you to place a claim on an object. The claim is dropped by calling heap_free.

While you have a claim on an object, that object counts towards your quota. You can claim the same object multiple times. Each time adds a new claim to the object but (if it is already claimed with that quota) does not consume quota.

 You can pass a capability with bounds that do not cover an entire object to heap_claim but your claim will cover the entire object because you cannot free part of an object.

Documentation for the heap_claim function

```
ssize_t heap_claim(AllocatorCapability heapCapability, void
* pointer)
```

Add a claim to an allocation. The object will be counted against the quota provided by the first argument until a corresponding call to heap_free. Note that this can be used with interior pointers.

This will return the size of the allocation claimed on success (which may be larger than the size requested in the original heap_allocate call; see its documentation for more information), 0 on error (if heap-Capability or pointer is not valid, etc.), or -ENOTENOUGHSTACK if the stack is insufficiently large to run the function.

If you need to ensure that an allocation remains valid for a brief, scoped period then heap_claim_ephemeral may be more useful. This function places an ephemeral claim on one or two objects.

Every thread has two *hazard slots* that can hold pointers. The heap_-claim_ephemeral function manages these two slots. These are cleared on every cross-compartment call and can be cleared explicitly by passing NULL to heap_claim_ephemeral.

If a pointer passed to heap_free is present in the allocator, the allocator will defer freeing the object. Writing to the hazard slots is very fast. Unlike heap_claim, this does not require a cross-compartment call.

Documentation for the `heap_claim_ephemeral` function

```
int heap_claim_ephemeral(Timeout * timeout, const void *
ptr, const void * ptr2)
```

Interface to the ephemeral claims mechanism. This claims two pointers using the hazard-pointer-inspired lightweight claims mechanism. If this function returns zero then the heap pointers are guaranteed not to become invalid until either the next cross-compartment call or the next call to this function.

A null pointer can be used as a not-present value. This function will treat operations on null pointers as unconditionally successful. It returns `-ETIMEDOUT` if it failed to claim before the timeout expired, or `-EINVAL` if one or more of the arguments is neither null nor a valid pointer at the end.

In the case of failure, neither pointer will have been claimed.

This function is provided by the `compartment_helpers` library, which must be linked for it to be available.

 Any claim applied with `heap_claim_ephemeral` is lost on *any* cross-compartment call. This includes any blocking operation, which will invoke the scheduler. In general, do not use `heap_claim_ephemeral` for anything other than a local read or write of a single object.

The `heap_claim_ephemeral` API is intended for very brief accesses to objects. You can claim two pointers to support the common pattern of `memcpy` between two caller-provided (i.e. untrusted) buffers. You can claim both and then copy between them.

Chapter 8.
Features for debug builds

CHERIoT provides a small set of APIs for use in debug builds in debug.hh. These include:

- Rich log messages
- Assertions with error messages
- Invariants that are checked in release builds but provide debugging help only in release builds

The message-producing aspects of these APIs use direct access to the UART. This can cause the messages to be interleaved but ensures that they are generated even if part of the system has crashed or deadlocked.

Access to the UART will show up in the linker report. The implementation of the logging functions is in the debug library. You should typically add an audit check that ensures this compartment is not present in release builds.

8.1. Enabling per-component debugging

Debug builds can often be significantly larger than release builds. They contain more code and potentially large strings for debug messages. CHERIoT RTOS is designed to allow debugging features to be controlled on a per-compartment basis to help mitigate this. You can see this in the core components. If you run xmake config --help in a firmware build, you will see this at the end of the output:

```
--debug-allocator=DEBUG-ALLOCATOR Specify verbose output level
(none|information|warning|error|critical) in the allocator
(default: none)
--debug-token_library=[y|n] Enable verbose output and assertions in
the token_library
--debug-loader=[y|n]        Enable verbose output and assertions in
the loader
--debug-scheduler=[y|n]     Enable verbose output and assertions in
the scheduler
```

Each of the core components allows extra debugging modes to be enabled independently, rather than via a global debug-mode switch. Note that most of these are simply binary choices but the allocator allows selecting a level for debugging. We'll return to that difference later.

Adding something similar requires two changes in your xmake.lua file. The first line, at top-level scope, declares the option, as shown in Listing 61.

```
28 debugOption("debug_compartment")
29 -- debug_option#end
30
31 -- use_debug#begin
32 compartment("debug_compartment")
33   add_rules("cheriot.component-debug")
34   add_deps("unwind_error_handler")
35   add_files("example.cc", "example.c")
36 -- use_debug#end
37 -- Explicitly setting the debug option name is not necessary
38 -- here because it matches the compartment name, but if we
39 -- did it explicitly then it would look like this:
40 -- set_debug_option#begin
41   on_load(function (target)
42     target:set('cheriot.debug-name', "debug_compartment")
43   end)
```

LISTING 61. Build system code for defining a debug option.
[from: examples/debug_helpers/xmake.lua]

With this, you will get a message in xmake config --help like the one above, but it won't actually do anything. You can test that this actually works by trying the command:

```
$ xmake config --help
...
      --debug-debug_compartment=[y|n]                    Enable
verbose output and assertions in the debug_compartment
...
```

You must also enable debugging support in your compartment or library by adding the corresponding rule in the description of your compartment or library. This is shown in Listing 62, which adds a debug option to an example compartment.

```
19 compartment("debug_compartment")
20   add_rules("cheriot.component-debug")
21   add_deps("unwind_error_handler")
22   add_files("example.cc", "example.c")
```

LISTING 62. Build system code for using a debug option.
[from: examples/debug_helpers/xmake.lua]

By default, this assumes that the debugOption that you've provided has the same name as the target. Sometimes, it's useful to have a single debug option that enables or disables debugging for multiple components. You can set the cheriot.debug-name target property in your component to the name that you expect in the on_load hook, as shown in Listing 63.

```
28 on_load(function (target)
29   target:set('cheriot.debug-name', "debug_compartment")
30 end)
```

LISTING 63. Build system code for providing the debug option name explicitly.
[from: examples/debug_helpers/xmake.lua]

Now, the compartment will be compiled with a macro that starts with DE-BUG_ and ends with the name of the debug option in all capitals. In the first example above, this would be DEBUG_DEBUG_COMPARTMENT.

This can then be used with the ConditionalDebug class from debug.hh. This is typically used with a using directive as shown in Listing 64 to connect the debug option.

```
81 using Debug = ConditionalDebug<DEBUG_DEBUG_COMPARTMENT,
82                                "Debug compartment">;
```

LISTING 64. Connecting the debug option to a debug type in code
[from: examples/debug_helpers/example.cc]

The first template parameter can be a boolean value that indicates whether this component is being debugged. It can also be a threshold, specified as a DebugLevel enumeration value. Recall that the allocator's output allowed choosing different debugging levels. The allocator uses warnings for API misuse and information for internal consistency checks. If you opt into warnings then you will get debug messages if you use the allocator incorrectly. If you use debugLevelOption instead of debugOption, the build system will provide the level, rather than a simple binary option.

The second is a free-form string literal that will be prepended (in magenta) to any debug line. There are two other template arguments that you can use if you are using debug levels. In the simple case, the boolean parameter controls whether log messages are shown, whether assertions are checked, and whether invariants report a verbose message on failure. By default, the latter two will happen if the threshold is set to warning or lower but the last two template parameters allow users to override this default.

The rest of this chapter will assume that the Debug type has been defined in this way.

8.2. Generating log messages

Printing log messages is the simplest use of the debug APIs. The Debug::log() function takes a format string and then a set of arguments. This is similar to printf or std::format, inserting the arguments into the output, replacing placeholders. The syntax here is modelled on std::format, but does not currently accept any format modifiers. The {} syntax for placeholders makes it possible to add modifiers in the future. This class is designed to avoid needing heap allocation or large amounts of stack space and is intentionally less flexible than a general-purpose formatting library.

Unsigned integers are printed as hex. Signed integers are printed as decimal. Floating point numbers are not supported. Individual characters are printed as characters. Strings (either const char* or std::string_view) are printed as strings.

Enumerated types are converted to strings using the Magic Enum library and printed with their numeric value in brackets. This has some limitations (in particular, by default, it does not work with very large enumeration values). It also requires capability relocations because it generates tables of strings. If you compile a compartment with CHERIOT_AVOID_CAPRELOCS defined then enumerations will be printed as numeric values.

Two other types have rich formatted output. PermissionSet objects (see Section 4.10) are printed using the characters from the tables in Section 1.4. Capabilities (either as raw pointers or instances of the CHERI::Capability class) are printed in full detail.

Listing 65 shows an example of most of these. Note the last two log lines, which print enumeration and capability values.

```
88  Debug::log("Hello world!");
89  Debug::log("Here is a C string {}, A C++ string view {}, "
90             "an int {}, and an unsigned 64-bit value {}",
91             "hello from a C string",
92             std::string_view{"hello from a C++ string"},
93             52,
94             0xabcdULL);
95  auto enumValue = NetworkAddress::AddressKindIPv4;
96  Debug::log("Here is an enum value: {}", enumValue);
97  int x;
98  Debug::log("Here is a pointer: {}", &x);
```

LISTING 65. Printing log messages with the debug log API.
[from: examples/debug_helpers/example.cc]

When you run this, the start of the output should look like this:

```
Debug compartment: Hello world!
Debug compartment: Here is a C string hello from a C string, A C++
string view hello from a C++ string, an int 52, and an unsigned 64-
bit value 0xabcd
Debug compartment: Here is an enum value: AddressKindIPv4(0x2)
Debug compartment: Here is a pointer: 0x80000ef8 (v:1
0x80000ef8-0x80000efc l:0x4 o:0x0 p: - RWcgml -- ---)
```

On the penultimate line, both the name and value of the enumeration are printed. This has some limitations. It will not work for enumerations that have multiple names for the same values or enumerations with very large numbers of elements.

The capability (pointer) format starts with the address and then has the metadata in brackets. The metadata includes the tag (valid) bit, then the range, then the length, object type, and permissions. The letters for the permissions are described in Chapter 1.

The log method takes an optional debug level as a template parameter. If you are using the variant of ConditionalDebug with a DebugLevel template parameter then you disable some log messages based their severity. Try changing the debugOption to debugLevelOption in the build system and modifying this example to print some of the log messages only at higher thresholds. Note that you may need to delete your .xmake and build before doing this to avoid stale caches of the value as a different type causing problems.

8.3. Printing custom types

The standard formatting machinery in C++ can result in large code. The CHERIoT debug logging mechanism is intended to be small and intentionally omits features. It does provide a mechanism for pretty-printing custom types.

Most of the printing is done in the debug library, which contains code for printing different primitive types, including capabilities. The function from this library takes an array of arguments for printing, where each is identified by two uintptr_t variables. One contains the value, the other the discriminator. If the discriminator is untagged, it is treated as an enumeration for the built-in handlers. If it is tagged, it is a pointer to a function that knows how to pretty-print the value. If you want to print a custom type, you first need to define a function that will print it. Listing 66 contains an example of such a function.

This is printing a network address, which is a discriminated union of a 32-bit IPv4 address or a 128-bit IPv6 address.

```
34 void debug_network_address(uintptr_t    value,
35                            DebugWriter &writer)
36 {
37   auto *address = reinterpret_cast<NetworkAddress *>(value);
38   if (address->kind == NetworkAddress::AddressKindIPv6)
39   {
40     for (int i = 0; i < 14; i += 2)
41     {
42       writer.write_hex_byte(address->ipv6[i]);
43       writer.write_hex_byte(address->ipv6[i + 1]);
44       writer.write(':');
45     }
46     writer.write_hex_byte(address->ipv6[14]);
47     writer.write_hex_byte(address->ipv6[15]);
48   }
49   else if (address->kind == NetworkAddress::AddressKindIPv4)
50   {
51     writer.write_decimal((address->ipv4 >> 0) & 0xff);
52     writer.write('.');
53     writer.write_decimal((address->ipv4 >> 8) & 0xff);
54     writer.write('.');
55     writer.write_decimal((address->ipv4 >> 16) & 0xff);
56     writer.write('.');
57     writer.write_decimal((address->ipv4 >> 24) & 0xff);
58   }
59   else
60   {
61     writer.write("<invalid address>");
62   }
63 };
```

LISTING 66. Defining a print function for a custom type.
[from: examples/debug_helpers/example.cc]

This takes two arguments. The first is the value to print, the second is a reference to an object that provides methods for printing individual methods. In this example, the value will be a pointer to the real object and must be explicitly cast. Remember that, although this is not type safe, it *is* memory safe on a CHERIoT system. If the value is not a pointer of the correct size or larger, you will get traps.

The other argument is the writer, which is passed as an abstract class (interface) and provides callbacks into the debug library. This has various overloads of a write method that will print primitive values as if they were passed as arguments to the log function, as well as some with explicit control over formatting.

This function also needs to be accompanied by an adaptor, as shown in Listing 67, that constructs the pair of uintptr_ts that will be passed into the library. This is simply casting the pointer to a uintptr_t for the value and providing the helper function (also cast to uintptr_t) as the type value.

```
67  template<>
68  struct DebugFormatArgumentAdaptor<NetworkAddress>
69  {
70    static DebugFormatArgument
71    construct(NetworkAddress &address)
72    {
73      return {
74        reinterpret_cast<uintptr_t>(&address),
75        reinterpret_cast<uintptr_t>(debug_network_address)};
76    }
77  };
```

LISTING 67. Defining an adaptor for a custom type.
[from: examples/debug_helpers/example.cc]

With those in scope, you can now print network addresses using the same APIs. Listing 68 shows printing an IPv4 and IPv6 address using this API.

```
102  NetworkAddress addr;
103  addr.ipv4 = 0x0100007f;
104  addr.kind = NetworkAddress::AddressKindIPv4;
105  Debug::log("There's no place like {}", addr);
106  memset(addr.ipv6, 0, sizeof(addr.ipv6));
107  addr.ipv6[15] = 1;
108  addr.kind     = NetworkAddress::AddressKindIPv6;
109  Debug::log("There's no place like {}", addr);
```

LISTING 68. Printing a custom type with the debug APIs.
[from: examples/debug_helpers/example.cc]

This should print:

```
Debug compartment: There's no place like 127.0.0.1
Debug compartment: There's no place like 00:00:00:00:00:00:00:01
```

The second line isn't quite perfect IPv6 output (it should be simply :1), but it's good enough to understand what's happening.

8.4. Asserting invariants

Assertions and invariants use the same formatting infrastructure as the log message code. The terms are often used interchangeably. In builds with the debug option enabled, both behave in the same way. They take a condition and a message (including a format string and arguments, as with the logging APIs). If the condition is false, they will print the message and then execute a trap instruction.

If debugging is disabled, assertions do nothing. Invariants still perform the check and trap but do not print the message. Listing 69 shows an example of an assertion and an invariant. These use the scoped error handlers described in Section 5.13 to catch the failure. If they trigger a trap, execution will resume in the CHERIOT_HANDLER block. This uses printf to print a message independent of the debug mode.

```
113  bool someCondition = false;
114  CHERIOT_DURING
115  {
116    Debug::Assert(someCondition,
117                  "Assertion failed, condition is {}",
118                  someCondition);
119  }
120  CHERIOT_HANDLER
121  {
122    printf("Assertion triggered error handler\n");
123  }
124  CHERIOT_END_HANDLER
125
126  CHERIOT_DURING
127  {
128    Debug::Invariant(someCondition,
129                     "Invariant failed, condition is {}",
130                     someCondition);
131  }
132  CHERIOT_HANDLER
133  {
134    printf("Invariant triggered error handler\n");
135  }
136  CHERIOT_END_HANDLER
```

LISTING 69. Assertions and invariants with the debugging APIs.
[from: examples/debug_helpers/example.cc]

If you configure this example with the --debug-debug_compartment=y flag, this section will output something like the following:

```
example.cc:115 Assertion failure in entry
Assertion failed, condition is false
Assertion triggered error handler
example.cc:122 Invariant failure in entry
Invariant failed, condition is false
Invariant triggered error handler
```

The first line of each failure is printed by the assertion or invariant itself, the second is the log message. The next line is the printf. If you build it with --debug-debug_compartment=n then the only line of output from this section should be:

Invariant triggered error handler

The invariant is still checked and is triggering a trap, which leads to an unwind, but no debug APIs are printing messages.

In some cases, you may find that the expression that calculates the assertion condition is expensive and the compiler does not successfully optimise it away in release builds. If the checks call functions in other compilation units, for example, or reads from volatile memory, the compiler cannot remove them even if the result is unused. To avoid this, you can replace the condition with a lambda that takes no arguments and returns a bool. The lambda is never executed in release builds so the compiler will strip it away.

8.5. Using the debug APIs from C

The log APIs are designed to be used from C++ but C11's _Generic keyword made it possible to expose a subset of the functionality into C as well. C++ templates allow users to provide their own specialisations. This is sadly not possible in C and so the logging APIs can print only primitive types. Listing 70 shows the C versions of the C++ APIs from this chapter.

```
 8  CHERIOT_DEBUG_LOG("C example",
 9                    "Printing a number {} and a string {}",
10                    42,
11                    "hello from C");
12  CHERIOT_DURING
13  {
14    CHERIOT_INVARIANT(
15      false, "Invariant check in C failed: {}", 12);
16  }
17  CHERIOT_HANDLER
18  {
19    printf("Invariant triggered unwind in C\n");
20  }
21  CHERIOT_END_HANDLER
```

LISTING 70. Assertions and invariants with the debugging APIs.
[from: examples/debug_helpers/example.c]

Running this will print the following:

```
C example: Printing a number 42 and a string hello from C
example.c:12 Invariant failure in print_from_c
Invariant check in C failed: 12
Invariant triggered unwind in C
```

In C++, these are enabled conditionally based on a template parameter. In C, the macros are defined in such a way that you can wrap them in your own macros, which provide the context parameter and may be conditional.

Chapter 9.
Writing a device driver

CHERIoT aims to be small and easy to customize. It does not have a generic device driver interface but it does have a number of tools that make it possible to write modular device drivers.

9.1. What is a device?

From the perspective of the CPU, a device is something that you communicate with via a memory-mapped I/O (MMIO) interface, which may (optionally) generate interrupts. There are several devices that the core parts of the RTOS interact with:
- The UART, which is used for writing debug output during development.
- The core-local interrupt controller, which is used for managing timer interrupts.
- The platform interrupt controller, which is used for managing external interrupts.
- The revoker, which scans memory for dangling capabilities (pointers) and invalidates them.

Most embedded systems on chip will include additional devices. These range from very simple interfaces, such as general-purpose I/O (GPIO) pins that are mapped to a bit in a register, up to entire wireless network interfaces with rich sets of functionality.

CHERIoT, like most modern systems, makes heavy use of MMIO. Device registers are exposed as if they are memory locations. To read from a device register, you simply execute a load instruction on the CPU. Similarly, to write to a device register, you execute a store instruction.

This model is very convenient for CHERI systems because CHERI capabilities already allow you to restrict access to ranges of memory. This means that we don't need to define a new protection model for device access on CHERIoT. Capabilities can grant access to MMIO ranges just as they do to real memory. You can provide a read-only capability to a device range, or even to a single register.

This abstraction also works at the C level or higher. A device's MMIO region is referred to by a volatile pointer to a structure representing the device's registers. Reading or writing the device's registers then becomes simple field access in C (or C++, or some higher-level language).

A read-only capability to a device's MMIO region may convey more rights than you expect. For example, a device register may be the end of a memory-mapped FIFO, in which case reading it would remove the front entry. More generally, reads of device memory might have side effects. You will generally know this per device, but don't assume that read-only means may-not-affect-device-state when providing capabilities to device memory.

This abstraction is sufficient for *polling*, where you query the device periodically to see if it has anything ready to process. Polling may be sufficient for devices with a simple request-response interface. For example, if you send some plaintext to an AES engine and then read the cyphertext back, you always know that there's data ready (or about to be data ready in a few cycles). In contrast, for something like a UART, Ethernet interface, USB controller, and so on, there will be long periods where the device has no data for you to process. Querying every such device in a loop would be inefficient both in terms of power and performance, so devices can raise *interrupts*. We'll discuss these in more detail in Section 9.5 but, at a high level, they are asynchronous events that come from a device. When a frame is ready on an Ethernet controller, for example, it will send an interrupt letting the CPU know, so that some software can handle the incoming frame.

Between MMIO regions and interrupts, you have the building blocks for interfacing with any CHERIoT device.

9.2. Why do device drivers exist?

Device drivers are software interfaces to devices. In general (not limited to CHERIoT) they exist for two reasons:

Abstraction
A device driver allows software to be written to interface with a *device class* rather than a single device.

Multiplexing
A device driver allows multiple different software components to access the device.

If you want to write a USB protocol stack or a network stack, you need some generic interface to USB controllers or Ethernet interfaces. This code doesn't want to have to be specific to each device, it wants to have an abstract way of talking to any device of the correct class via some *device abstraction*.

Often, the *device multiplexing* is delegated to a higher-level piece of software. For example, a disk interface may provide a generic block device abstraction but then give exclusive access to the next layer up in a storage stack. This may be a volume manager, which presents a set of logical block devices to other things in a kernel. On top of this, you'd often run a filesystem driver, which provides a way of naming variable-sized virtual disks ('files') and allows different users and different programs to store data independently.

The multiplexing and abstraction features may be entangled. On most operating systems, the common interface to the network is a socket, not a time slice in a network device. The TCP/IP stack is responsible for both providing abstractions (TCP and UDP sockets) and for multiplexing (different components can have different sockets and treat them as if they had unique access to a network device).

On a CHERIoT system, the correct structure for any device driver depends on the *trust model*. This determines how (or if) you should build multiplexing on top of abstraction.

For example, if you have a GPIO device that controls some LEDs, you may simply want to delegate direct access to that device to a compartment that wants to control them. Alternatively, you may want to provide an interface that allows individual compartments to have control over a single LED, or allows compartments to monotonically set any of them but requires a different permission for clearing them.

For more complex devices, such as SPI, Ethernet, or USB, you will want a low-level device driver that provides a generic interface to the device. This driver will be wrapped in something that provides a richer interface to other compartments.

In the CHERIoT network stack, described in Chapter 11, the part of the driver that handles abstraction is wrapped in a compartment that provides a firewall. The firewall does more than simply expose the send-packet and receive-packet interfaces of the physical device, it also provides ingress and egress filtering to improve security.

9.3. Specifying a device's locations

Devices are specified in the board description file, which is described in detail in Chapter 12. The two relevant parts are the devices node, which specifies the memory-mapped I/O devices and the interrupts section that describes how external interrupts should be configured. For example, our initial FPGA prototyping platform had sections like this describing its Ethernet device:

```
"devices" : {
    "ethernet" : {
        "start" : 0x98000000,
        "length": 0x204
    },
    ...
},
"interrupts": [
    {
        "name": "Ethernet",
        "number": 16,
        "priority": 3
    }
],
```

The first part says that the ethernet device's MMIO space is 0x204 bytes long and starts at address 0x98000000. The second says that interrupt number 16 is used for the ethernet device.

9.4. Accessing the memory-mapped I/O region

The MMIO_CAPABILITY macro is used to get a pointer to memory-mapped I/O devices. This takes two arguments. The first is the C/C++ type of the pointer, the second is the name from the board configuration file. For example, to get a pointer to the memory-mapped I/O space for the ethernet device above, we might do something like:

```
struct EthernetMMIO
{
    // Control register layout here:
    ...
};

__always_inline volatile struct EthernetMMIO *ethernet_device()
{
    return MMIO_CAPABILITY(struct EthernetMMIO, ethernet);
}
```

This macro must be used in code, it cannot be used for static initialisation. The macro expands to a load from the compartment's import table. Assigning the result of it to a global is an antipattern: you will get smaller code using it directly. The helper shown here will be inlined and expand to a single load capability.

Now that you have a pointer to a `volatile` object representing the device's MMIO region, you can access its control registers directly. Any device can be accessed from any compartment in this way, but that access will appear in the linker audit report.

Any compartment that accesses this device will have an entry in the audit report (see Chapter 10) that looks like this:

```
{
  "kind": "MMIO",
  "length": 516,
  "start": 2550136832
},
```

 There is no generic policy for device access because the right policy depends on the device and the SoC. Consider a device that has two GPIO pins, one connected to an LED used to indicate a fault in the device and the other to trigger the sprinkler system for the building. You would probably write a policy that allows most compartments to indicate a fault, but restricts access to the sprinkler control to a single compartment. From the perspective of both the SoC and the RTOS, the two devices are identical.

You can then audit whether a firmware image enforces whatever policy you want (for example, no compartment other than a device driver may access the device directly). Note that the linker reports will always provide the addresses and lengths in decimal, because they are standard JSON. CHERIoT RTOS supports a small number of extensions to JSON in the files that we consume, to improve usability, but don't use these in files that we produce, to improve interoperability.

There is no requirement to expose a device as a single MMIO region. You may wish to define multiple regions, which can be as small as a single byte, so that you can privilege-separate your device driver.

Some devices have a very large control structure. For example, the platform-local interrupt controller is many KiBs. We don't define a C structure that covers every single field for this and instead just use `uint32_t` as the type for `MMIO_CAPABILITY`, which lets us treat the space as an array of 32-bit control registers.

9.5. Handling interrupts

Interrupts are asynchronous notifications from devices. On most modern systems, including CHERIoT, external interrupts are multiplexed by an *interrupt controller*. The RISC-V *platform-local interrupt controller* (PLIC) handles all interrupts coming from devices and forwards them to the core. When the core is running with interrupts disabled (or, more accurately, *deferred*), interrupts are still received by the PLIC and recorded. Similarly, if two interrupts fire at the same time, the PLIC ensures that they are not lost.

When the PLIC delivers an interrupt to the core, it will trigger the *switcher* to save the current process's state. The switcher will then invoke the *scheduler*, which will query the PLIC to see which interrupts have fired and wake any threads that were waiting for them.

CHERIoT has a unified event model, where the *futexes* are the *only* event source that can block. This means that the same waiting mechanism is used for both hardware- and software-generated events. In both cases, you will wait for a futex (see Section 6.5) and then run code when the scheduler wakes you.

To be able to handle interrupts, you must have a software capability (see Section 5.6) that authorises access to the interrupt. This capability allows you to get a pointer to the futex word associated with the interrupt. Futexes are building blocks for a variety of different synchronisation primitives. For interrupts, the futex word contains a counter that is incremented each time the interrupt fires. Section 9.6 discusses how to wait on this futex.

Before you can wait for interrupts using a futex, you must get the pointer to the futex word. This will be a read-only capability to a 32-bit value. For the Ethernet device that we've been using as an example, you would request the associated interrupt futex with this macro invocation:

```
DECLARE_AND_DEFINE_INTERRUPT_CAPABILITY(ethernetInterruptCapability,
Ethernet, true, true);
```

If you wish to share this between multiple compilation units, you can use the separate DECLARE_ and DEFINE_ forms (see interrupt.h) but the combined form is normally most convenient. This macro takes four arguments:

1. The name that we're going to use to refer to this capability. The name ethernetInterruptCapability is arbitrary, you can use whatever makes sense to you.
2. The name of the interrupt, from the board description file (Ethernet, in this case).

3. Whether this capability authorises waiting for this interrupt (this will almost always be true).

4. Whether this capability authorises acknowledging the interrupt so that it can fire again. This will almost always be true in device drivers but should generally be true for only one compartment (for each interrupt), whereas multiple compartments may wish to observe interrupts for monitoring.

As with the MMIO capabilities, sealed objects appear in compartment reports. For example, the above macro expands to this in the final report:

```
{
  "contents": "10000101",
  "kind": "SealedObject",
  "sealing_type": {
    "compartment": "sched",
    "key": "InterruptKey",
    "provided_by": "build/cheriot/cheriot/release/example-
firmware.scheduler.compartment",
    "symbol": "__export.sealing_type.sched.InterruptKey"
  }
}
```

The sealing type tells you that this is an interrupt capability (it's sealed with the InterruptKey type, provided by the scheduler). The contents lets you audit what this authorises. The first two bytes are a 16-bit (little-endian on all currently supported targets) integer containing the interrupt number, so 1000 means 16 (our Ethernet interrupt number). The next two bytes are boolean values reflecting the last two arguments to the macro, so this authorises both waiting and clearing the macro. Again, this can form part of your firmware auditing.

9.6. Waiting for an interrupt

Now that you're authorised to handle interrupts, you will need something that you can wait on. Most real-time operating systems allow you to register interrupt-service routines (ISRs) directly. CHERIoT RTOS does not allow this because ISRs run with access to the state of the interrupted thread. On Arm M-profile, some registers are banked but the others are visible, on RISC-V all registers of the interrupted thread are visible. This means that an ISR runs with access to the thread and compartment that are interrupted. Not only would this potentially break compartment isolation, it would be difficult to use safely because the ISR would inherit an (untrusted) stack from the interrupted thread and have access to the interrupted compartment's globals instead of its own.

Instead, CHERIoT RTOS maps interrupts onto events that threads can wait on. A single thread with the highest priority that blocks waiting on an interrupt will be run as soon as the switcher and scheduler finish handling the interrupt. The switcher will spill the interrupted thread's state, the scheduler will wake the sleeping thread and note that it is now the highest-priority runnable thread, and then the switcher will resume from that thread. This sequence takes around 1,000 cycles on Ibex, giving an interrupt latency of 50 μS at 20 MHz or 10 μS at 100 MHz.

 A future version of the CHERIoT architecture is expected to include extensions to the interrupt controller to allow direct context switch to a high-priority thread.

Each interrupt is mapped to a futex word, which can be used with scheduler waiting primitives. Futexes are discussed in detail in Section 6.5 but, for the purpose of interrupt handling, you can think of them as counters with a compare-and-wait operation. You can get the word associated with an interrupt by passing the authorising capability to the `interrupt_futex_get` function exported by the scheduler:

```
const uint32_t *ethernetFutex = ethernetFutex =
 interrupt_futex_get(
  STATIC_SEALED_VALUE(ethernetInterruptCapability));
```

The ethernetFutex pointer is now a read-only capability (attempting to store through it will trap) that contains a number that is incremented every time the ethernet interrupt fires. You can now query whether any interrupts have fired since you last checked by comparing it against a previous value and you can wait for an interrupt with `futex_wait`, for example:

```
do
{
    uint32_t last = *ethernetFutex;
    // Handle interrupt here
} while (futex_wait(ethernetFutex, last) == 0);
```

If you want to wait for multiple event sources, you can use the multiwaiter (see Section 6.12) API. This allows sleeping on multiple kinds of event sources so you can, for example, have a single thread that blocks waiting for a message to send from another thread or a message to receive from the device.

9.7. Acknowledging interrupts

If you copy the last example into a real device driver then you might be surprised that the loop runs twice and then stops. It will run once on start, once when the first interrupt is delivered, and then never again. This is because external interrupts are not delivered on a particular channel unless the preceding one has been acknowledged. A more complete version of the loop above looks like this:

```
do
{
    uint32_t last = *ethernetFutex;
    // Handle interrupt here
    interrupt_complete(
        STATIC_SEALED_VALUE(ethernetInterruptCapability));
} while ((last != *ethernetFutex) ||
        (futex_wait(ethernetFutex, last) == 0));
```

This includes two changes. The first is the call to `interrupt_complete` once the interrupt has been handled. This tells the scheduler to mark the interrupt as completed in the interrupt handler. It is possible that the interrupt will then fire immediately, in which case there's no point trying to sleep. The second change checks whether the value of the futex word has changed - if it has, then we skip the `futex_wait` call and handle the next interrupt immediately.

9.8. Exposing device interfaces

CHERIoT device drivers often have two levels of abstraction. The lower level provides an abstraction across different devices that offer similar functionality. The higher level provides a security model atop this.

In most cases, the lower-level abstractions are provided as header-only libraries that can be included in whichever compartments need them. This allows drivers to be incorporated into another compartment that has full access to the device. For example, the scheduler is the only component that has direct access to the interrupt controller, whereas the memory allocator is the only component that has full access to the revoker. In both cases, separating the driver into a compartment would not provide any security benefit because the component that uses the device is allowed to do anything that it wants to the device and does not need to be protected from the device.

If a device has multiple consumers then it may need a compartment to handle multiplexing. For example, our debug APIs use the UART directly, but safe use of the UART would involve locking to avoid interleaved messages. Implementing this model would use the header-only UART driver from a compartment and writing a simple interface for reading and writing (possibly with an authorising capability).

9.9. Using layered platform includes

Each board description contains a set of include paths. For example, our Ibex simulator has this:

```
"driver_includes" : [
    "../include/platform/ibex",
    "../include/platform/generic-riscv"
],
```

These are added *in this order*. The C preprocessor searches files included with #include in this order stopping at the first one found. If a file uses #include_next then the preprocessor will start searching at the place where the current file was found. This lets drivers either completely replace generic versions or include them (via #include_next) with additional code (including macro definitions) before and after the generic version.

For example, the UART device in the generic-riscv directory defines a basic 16550 interface. This is templated with the size of the register because the original 16550 used 8-bit registers, whereas newer versions typically use the low 8 bits of a 32-bit register. This implementation is sufficient for simulated environments but real UARTs with higher-speed cores often require more control over their frequency to get the right baud rate. We can support the Synopsis extended 16550 by creating a platform/synopsis directory containing a platform-uart.hh that uses #include_next <platform-uart.hh> to get the generic version. This can be inserted in the include path before platform/generic-riscv. A specific configuration can use this by not providing anything at a higher level, replace it entirely by providing a custom platform-uart.hh, or provide a modified version of it by using #include_next.

9.10. Conditionally compiling driver code

The DEVICE_EXISTS macro can be used with #if to conditionally compile code depending on whether the current board provides a definition of the device. This is keyed on the existence of an MMIO region in the board description file with the specified name. For example, the ethernet device that we've been using as an example could be protected with:

```
#if DEVICE_EXISTS(ethernet)
// Driver for the ethernet device here.
#endif
```

This highlights why "ethernet" is not a great name for the device: ideally the name should be specific to the hardware interface, not the high-level functionality, so that you can conditionally compile specific drivers. We have used a generic name in this tutorial to avoid introducing device-specific complications.

Chapter 10.
Auditing firmware images

As mentioned in Section 5.6, the CHERIoT link phase emits a linker report at the same time as the final image. This is a JSON document that contains a record of the code identity for every compartment (hashes of every section before and after linking) and every way that a compartment can interact with the world outside of its private state.

 If you're linking with your own build system, rather than CHERIoT RTOS's xmake-based system, you will need to pass `--compartment-report=` to the linker invocation to tell it where to emit the linker report.

The CHERIoT ABI is designed to make this all explicit. A trivial compartment has a code region that is reachable from its pcc and a globals region reachable from its cgp. Any code running in the compartment (unless explicitly constrained) has read-execute access to the former and read-write access to the latter. Any access outside of this region requires an explicit capability to be provided to the compartment's *import table* by the loader. The loader, in turn, will provide such a capability if, and only if, the linker has created metadata instructing it to. This means that the system *fails closed*.

When a security system fails, it will unintentionally enter either a secure or insecure state. If you have a keypad connected to a door lock and the lock receives an invalid message, it can either open or close the door. Should a failure open or close the door? The right choice is very different if the door is to a bank vault or a fire escape. Failing closed means that the failure leaves the system in the secured state (the door closed in this example). This is an important property for a security system. If an attacker wants to break a system that fails open then they simply need to induce a fault of some kind and the failure mode will grant them the access that they require.

The linker creates the audit report and also creates the instructions for the loader. If these instructions are omitted, the loader will not provide the compartment with a capability so, even if the compartment gains knowledge of some address, it does not gain rights to access any memory. If an attacker manages to sneak something into object code that is linked into some firmware and this does not show up in the audit report then it should also not be used in the metadata that the linker generates to instruct the loader to provision capabilities. This approach is intended to ensure that hiding things from the audit report does not result in increased rights (failing closed).

There are a lot of different kinds of capabilities that can end up in a compartment's import table. These include:

- Memory-mapped I/O regions, for direct device access.
- Pre-shared objects.
- Static sealed objects implementing software-defined capabilities (see Section 5.6)
- Local function pointers that change interrupt state.
- Imported functions from other compartments.
- Imported functions from shared libraries.

The audit report contains all of this, along with metadata such as whether functions run with interrupts disabled, whether capabilities to pre-shared objects or memory-mapped I/O regions have write access, and so on.

When you are building a compartmentalised firmware image, you can use this report in two different ways. First, you can introspect over the shape of the compartment to explore what can happen, for example determining which compartments call a specific entry point or have direct access to a device. Second, you can write policies that make sure that you have respected the *principle of least privilege*.

The `cheriot-audit` tool is intended to work with both of these approaches. It runs a *Rego* program over the input. Rego is a language from the OpenPolicyAgent[1] project that is designed for writing policies over JSON documents. It inherits some ideas from JavaScript, Python, and Prolog, but broadly is intended to be a modular language for writing mostly-declarative policies that run over one or more JSON documents.

Rego is a rich language and we'll see in this chapter that it can be used for introspection over firmware in a number of ways. When used for enforcement, a Rego policy is usually a program that evaluates to true if the policy holds. This may be checked automatically on your build infrastructure to ensure that your security goals are met before pushing firmware to the next stage in testing. It may be checked later before signing firmware, to ensure that only firmware images that match your security policy are signed.

Rego programs run by `cheriot-audit` can also produce longer output. Rather than simply telling you that a policy has been matched, they can create a JSON output that describes some properties of a firmware image.

1.   https://www.openpolicyagent.org/docs/latest/policy-language/

In Prolog, predicates are true if they are satisfied (i.e. there is a logical derivation chain that can be used to prove that they are true) or fail if they cannot be proven. Fail does not necessarily mean that a predicate is false, it means that there is insufficient evidence to prove that it is true. Rego inherits this distinction, which can be confusing in some cases. A policy may report true as a JSON value if it passes, but no output (failure) if it does not.

10.1. Running cheriot-audit

The cheriot-audit command takes three mandatory inputs, provided as command-line arguments:

The audit report.
> This is provided with the --firmware-report (or -j) flag. You will find it in the build directory with the same name as the firmware image but a .json extension. This provides all of the information about the linked image.

The board description file.
> This is provided with the --board (or -b) flag and normally found in the boards directory in the SDK, but may alternatively be provided by some other board support package. This describes the memory layout and allows policies to map from the numerical addresses in the audit report to device names.

The query to run.
> This is the Rego query to run, provided with --query (or -q).

Rego is modular. You can provide additional modules with --module (or -m).

To make sure that everything is working, try running a trivial query (true) against the RTOS repository's hello-world example:

```
$ cheriot-audit \
 --board ../../sdk/boards/sail.json \
 --firmware-report build/cheriot/cheriot/release/hello_world.json \
 -q 'true'
true
```

The query true simply evaluates to true as a JSON expression. This is not very interesting, but it checks that the command is working and can find all of the relevant files. You can now try running more complex examples.

It's often convenient to pipe the output of a cheriot-audit to jq, which will pretty-print the resulting JSON.

Most policies will refer to one or more of the inputs, though often indirectly. You can try writing these directly as queries. If the query is input then you should see the entire audit report. If the query is data.board then you should see the board-description file.

In the rest of this chapter, we'll explore how to write more interesting queries.

10.2. Using the default cheriot-audit modules

The cheriot-audit tool has two built-in modules. The compartment module contains helper rules that are common to the compartment model. The rtos module contains helpers that specific to the CHERIoT RTOS.

Rego modules all show up in the data. namespace, like the board-description file. If you want to invoke a rule from the compartment module, it will be written as data.compartment.{rule name}.

10.3. Exploring a firmware image

Now that we can run cheriot-audit on the hello-world example, let's try to learn a bit about it. This example has no compartmentalisation so the UART device is directly accessible in the single user-provided compartment in the example. Try this query, to see what compartments or libraries have access to the UART:

```
data.compartment.compartments_with_mmio_import(data.board.devices.uart)
```
This uses a rule from the compartments package to find any import that matches the address range provided by the board description file's uart device. If everything is built correctly (and, in particular, if you're using the *correct* board description file) then you should see output like this:

```
[
  "debug"
]
```
This tells us that the debug library is directly accessing the UART. Remember that CHERIoT shared libraries do not (unless they are carefully written assembly) protect their state against callers and this means that any compartment that calls any of the entry points in that library should be assumed

to be able to access the UART. Ask `cheriot-audit` which compartments call functions in the debug library with this query:

```
data.compartment.compartments_calling("debug")
```

This should, hopefully, tell you that only the 'hello' compartment can:

```
[
  "hello"
]
```

If you've built the firmware image with allocator or scheduler debugging enabled, the answer will be different. This is the kind of thing that's useful to capture in a policy. You might want to build firmware images where the scheduler has access to a debugging feature for testing, but you wouldn't want to sign those images for widespread deployment.

Now try running the same query against the third example from the RTOS, `03.hello_safe_compartment`. This example moves UART access out to a 'uart' compartment so that the 'hello' compartment can be untrusted and just provide strings to print. You might therefore be surprised that the result of the query looks like this:

```
[
  "hello",
  "uart"
]
```

This tells you that the compartmentalisation objective—removing UART access from the hello compartment—has not been met. The hello compartment still has access to the UART via the debug library.

This is because the example prefers to give useful error messages in case of failure and includes the `fail-simulator-on-error.h` header. This header provides an error handler (see Section 5.12) that logs a message to the UART and exits the simulator if a CHERI exception occurs. If you comment out that header, the example will meet its compartmentalisation objective. Again, this is the kind of thing that's useful to have in a policy. It's useful to include this kind of feature in debug builds, but you want to make sure that you don't leave them enabled in builds that you deploy to end users.

10.4. Decoding software-defined capabilities

CHERIoT builds a software capability model on top of the hardware capability model provided by CHERI. Software capabilities are implemented as objects that are passed around as *sealed capabilities*. Some of these are dynamically allocated, others are baked into the firmware image. Unless you have the sealing capability that permits unsealing a given type, these are just opaque pointers.

Sealed objects that are baked into the firmware are accessible to one compartment as an opaque pointer but can be unsealed by another compartment to access their contents. The compartment that unseals them will trust their contents. You can make them *trustworthy* by auditing their contents at link time.

The RTOS uses software-defined capabilities to authorise memory allocation (which, in turn, is required for creating dynamically allocated sealed objects, among other things). These will show up in the audit report looking something like this:

```
{
  "contents": "00040000 00000000 00000000 00000000 00000000
00000000",
  "kind": "SealedObject",
  "sealing_type": {
    "compartment": "allocator",
    "key": "MallocKey",
    "provided_by": "build/cheriot/cheriot/release/
cheriot.allocator.compartment",
    "symbol": "__export.sealing_type.allocator.MallocKey"
  }
}
```

The contents is a hex string with one block per 32-bit word. The kind identifies them as sealed objects. The sealing_type tells you the compartment and the sealing key that are used to seal the object (i.e. the compartment that can unseal them and the name it gives to the key that it uses).

In the rtos package, there is a Rego rule that matches imports that are sealed with the correct value:

```
11 is_allocator_capability(capability) {
12   capability.kind == "SealedObject"
13   capability.sealing_type.compartment == "allocator"
14   capability.sealing_type.key == "MallocKey"
15 }
```

LISTING 71. The Rego rule for matching objects sealed as allocator capabilities
[from: examples/auditing-rtos/rtos.rego]

This matches every import that refers to a sealed object that is sealed with the correct key, independent of its contents. The contents remain an opaque blob. These capabilities are 24-byte objects, where the first four bytes represent the quota and the remainder is reserved for future use (including internal use by the allocator) and must be initialised to zero. The rtos package uses the following rule to decode them:

```
19 decode_allocator_capability(capability) = decoded {
20   is_allocator_capability(capability)
21   some quota
22   quota = integer_from_hex_string(capability.contents, 0, 4)
23   # Remaining words are all zero
24   integer_from_hex_string(capability.contents, 4, 4) == 0
25   integer_from_hex_string(capability.contents, 8, 4) == 0
26   integer_from_hex_string(capability.contents, 12, 4) == 0
27   integer_from_hex_string(capability.contents, 16, 4) == 0
28   integer_from_hex_string(capability.contents, 20, 4) == 0
29   decoded := { "quota": quota }
30 }
```

LISTING 72. The Rego rule for decoding allocator capabilities
[from: examples/auditing-rtos/rtos.rego]

This uses the earlier rule to check the sealing kind. If the argument is not a sealed object of the correct kind, this fails and so will any rule that tries to use the result. The quota is decoded with a built-in function provided by cheriot-audit called integer_from_hex_string. This takes the contents string, a start offset, and a width as arguments. The rule uses this to get the first word and assign it to the quota variable and then make sure that all of the others are zero.

Rego rules written like this are *conjunctions*. Every statement in the rule must be true. If any statement is not true, the rule fails. This means that by the time we reach the end where decoded is set, the rule has checked that this is a valid allocator capability and returns a JSON object with a single field called quota containing the extracted quota. If any of the rules are false, this is not a valid allocator capability. You can use this later in policies to make sure that everything that is a sealed allocator capability is a *valid* allocator capability.

Most of the time, you'll use this kind of rule with a *Rego comprehension*. Comprehensions take some input array, filter it based on a predicate, and then use the filtered versions to construct a new array or set. For example, the following comprehension starts with every import for every compartment. For each import, the import is assigned to c and the owner of the import to owner. It then uses the is_allocator_capability predicate to filter out imports that are not allocator capabilities. Finally, for each entry that is valid it will construct a new JSON object capturing the name of the compartment that owns this capability and the decoded capability.

```
[
  {
    "owner": owner,
    "capability": data.rtos.decode_allocator_capability(c)
  } |
  c = input.compartments[owner].imports[_] ;
  data.rtos.is_allocator_capability(c)
]
```

Try running this query (on the command line, you will need to remove line breaks) on a firmware image. Here's the output of running it on one of the network stack examples:

```
[
  {
    "capability": {
      "quota": 4096
    },
    "owner": "Firewall"
  },
  {
    "capability": {
      "quota": 16384
    },
    "owner": "SNTP"
  },
  {
    "capability": {
      "quota": 65536
    },
    "owner": "TCPIP"
  }
]
```

This shows that (in this specific build) the TCP/IP compartment can allocate 64 KiB of heap memory, the Firewall compartment 4 KiB and the SNTP compartment 16 KiB. Importantly, nothing else can allocate memory. You might care about determining the maximum amount of heap space that all compartments are able to allocate. A similar comprehension can extract the quota field from the decoded capabilities and then the built-in sum function can add all of these together:

```
sum([ data.rtos.decode_allocator_capability(c).quota |
    c = input.compartments[_].imports[_] ;
    data.rtos.is_allocator_capability(c) ])
```

In many cases, you'll be happy with quotas adding up to more than 100% of heap space. In other cases, you may want to make sure that a particular set of compartments can't allocate more than a fixed amount of heap space, to ensure that a certain amount is available for other uses.

10.5. Writing a policy

Rego policies for cheriot-audit will combine a lot of the building blocks that we've seen so far, as well as some helpers. The compartment module includes some helpers for defining allow lists. These are built using comprehensions, similar to the ones that we looked at earlier, to collect the set of compartments that can do something and then ensure that this is a subset of a provided set.

The rtos module exposes a rule called valid that performs a set of integrity checks on the RTOS. This can be used in a firmware-specific image, or parts of it can be reused. It's also a good reference for the kinds of things that may appear in policies.

The RTOS policy starts with a check that all of the allocator capabilities are valid:

```
62 all_sealed_allocator_capabilities_are_valid
63
```

LISTING 73. The Rego expression checking that all sealed allocator capabilities are valid [from: examples/auditing-rtos/rtos.rego]

This uses a helper that looks similar to some of the introspection code that we've already looked at:

```
34 all_sealed_allocator_capabilities_are_valid {
35   some allocatorCapabilities
36   allocatorCapabilities = [ c |
37     c = input.compartments[_].imports[_] ;
38     is_allocator_capability(c)
39   ]
40   every c in allocatorCapabilities {
41     decode_allocator_capability(c)
42   }
43 }
```

LISTING 74. The Rego rule implementing the check that all sealed allocator capabilities are valid [from: examples/auditing-rtos/rtos.rego]

This uses a list comprehension to collect everything that claims to be an allocator capability (i.e. everything sealed with the correct type). It then asserts that everything in this list must be a valid allocator capability by using the fact that the decode_allocator_capability rule fails if given an invalid allocator capability. If anything is sealed as an allocator capability but is not a 24-byte object where the last 20 bytes are zero, this will fail.

Next, the policy uses some allow lists to make sure that certain devices are reserved for core components:

```
65
66   # Only the allocator may access the revoker.
67   data.compartment.mmio_allow_list("revoker",
68                                    {"allocator"})
69   # Only the scheduler may access the
70   # interrupt controllers.
71   data.compartment.mmio_allow_list("clint",
72                                    {"scheduler"})
73   data.compartment.mmio_allow_list("plic",
74                                    {"scheduler"})
75
```

LISTING 75. The compartment allow lists in the RTOS policy
[from: examples/auditing-rtos/rtos.rego]

The interface to the revoker (the hardware component that invalidates capabilities to freed memory, allowing reuse) is reserved for the allocator. The core-local and platform-level interrupt controllers (CLIC and PLIC) are both reserved for the scheduler: nothing else should directly handle interrupts, the scheduler exposes APIs for other compartments to wait for or acknowledge interrupts.

Finally, it checks the access to some pre-shared objects:

The hazard-pointer list is used to implement the ephemeral claims mechanism described in Section 7.8. The allocator is the only thing that should have access to it (the switcher also exposes a write-only view of a part of it for the current thread).

Concurrent access to this is mediated via a 32-bit epoch variable that is incremented when the allocator starts and finishes reading the list. This means that it is safe to write to if the value is even, and that value is safely stored if the epoch is unchanged before and after writing. This is safe for anything to read, but only the allocator should write to it.

Finally, the rule checks that these are the expected size.

Together, this provides a policy that checks that the properties that the core RTOS expects hold true. There are some omissions here. For example, in a release version, this policy may add checks to ensure that the core RTOS components are the code expected as part of a reproducible build chain. This is not part of the core policy because it would be violated every time the toolchain changed.

184

```
76
77  # Only the allocator may access the
78  # hazard list (the switcher can
79  # as well via another mechanism)
80  data.compartment.shared_object_allow_list(
81    "allocator_hazard_pointers",
82    {"allocator"})
83  # Only the allocator may write to the epoch.
84  # Currently, only the compartment-helpers library
85  # reads the epoch, but it isn't a security problem
86  # if anything else does.
87  data.compartment.shared_object_writeable_allow_list(
88    "allocator_epoch",
89    {"allocator"})
90  # Size of hazard list and allocator epoch.
91  some hazardList
92  hazardList = data.compartment.shared_object(
93    "allocator_hazard_pointers")
94  # Two hazard pointers per thread.
95  hazardList.end - hazardList.start =
96    count( input.threads) * 2 * 8
97  some epoch
98  epoch = data.compartment.shared_object(
99    "allocator_epoch")
100 # 32-bit epoch
101 epoch.end - epoch.start = 4
102
```

LISTING 76. The RTOS policy for access to pre-shared objects
[from: examples/auditing-rtos/rtos.rego]

Chapter 11.
Networking

The CHERIoT network stack is intended to serve three purposes:
- An example of a compartmentalized structure incorporating large amounts of existing code.
- An off-the-shelf solution for common IoT device networking needs.
- An example for building more specialised networking systems.

The current stack contains code from several third-party projects: the FreeR-TOS TCP/IP stack, along with their SNTP and MQTT libraries, and the BearSSL TLS implementation. These are wrapped in rich capability interfaces and deployed in several compartments.

 Currently, none of the simulators provide a network connection. The examples in this chapter will default to using Sonata, but should also work on the Arty A7 and future hardware.

11.1. Understanding the structure of the network stack

The core compartments in the network stack are shown in Figure 6. These do not include the SNTP and MQTT compartments, which we'll see later.

The TCP/IP and TLS stacks are largely existing code, from the FreeR-TOS+TCP and BearSSL projects, respectively. The BearSSL code has no platform dependencies and is simply recompiled. The FreeRTOS+TCP code, unsurprisingly, assumes that it is running on FreeRTOS and is ported using the compatibility layer described in Chapter 14.

In the initial port, the FreeRTOS+TCP code required only one change. It normally expects to create threads during early initialisation. The file that did this was wrapped in something that instead triggered a barrier to allow the statically created threads to start running. Later changes for network-stack reset required some additional steps, though none of these modified any of the FreeRTOS+TCP code.

Each box in the diagram is a compartment (the User Code box is a placeholder for at least one compartment). The compartments have different goals and requirements.

The firewall does both ingress and egress filtering and is the only component in the system that has access to the memory-mapped I/O range for

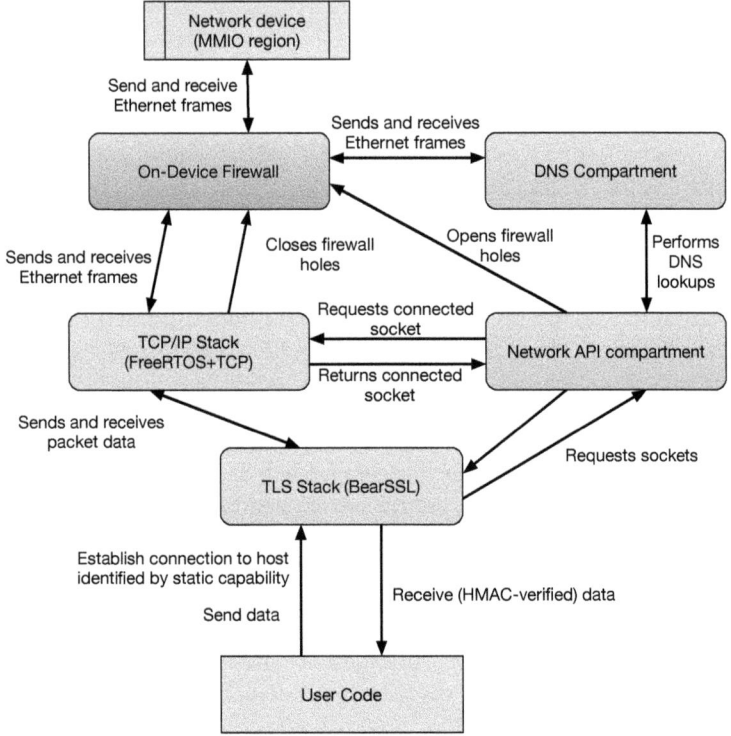

FIGURE 6. The core compartments in the network stack.

the Ethernet device. Ingress filtering reduces the attack surface of the TCP/IP layer. If there are no listening TCP sockets or unrestricted UDP ones, the firewall will drop all packets that do not come from an approved peer. Typically, an attacker on the local network segment can forge origin addresses but that gets harder across the Internet. Egress filtering is less common on embedded devices, which is unfortunate. The Mirai botnet launched large distributed denial of service (DDoS) attacks by compromising large numbers of embedded systems and using them to each generate relatively small amounts of traffic. With the CHERIoT network stack, this is much harder because the firewall compartment will not usually allow other compartments to send packets to arbitrary targets.

The Network API compartment is new code and implements the control plane. When you want to create a socket or authorise a remote endpoint, you must call this compartment. It uses a software capability model to determine whether callers are allowed to talk to remote endpoints and then opens holes in the firewall to authorise this. When you want to create a connected socket, you present this compartment with a software capability that authorises you to talk to a remote host on a specific port. It briefly opens a firewall hole for DNS requests and instructs the DNS compartment to perform the lookup, then it closes that firewall hole and opens one for the connection. The socket that it returns is created by the TCP/IP compartment so you can then send and receive data by calling the TCP/IP compartment directly.

11.2. Synchronising time with SNTP

The *Network Time Protocol* (NTP) is a complex protocol for synchronising time with a remote server. It is designed to build a tree of clock sources where each *stratum* is synchronised with a more authoritative one. Clients send messages to an NTP server and receive the current time back. The full protocol uses some complex statistical techniques to dynamically calculate the time taken for the response to arrive across the network and minimise clock drift. The *Simple Network Time Protocol* (SNTP) is a subset of NTP intended for simple embedded devices. It will not give the same level of accuracy but can run on very resource-constrained devices.

Using SNTP doesn't require writing any code that talks directly to the network but it does require building and linking the network stack, so that is a good place to start. First, you need to find the network-stack code. Listing 77 shows one way to do this, which is similar to how we find the SDK. This provides a hard-coded relative location and allows it to be overridden with an environment variable.

```
10 networkstackdir = os.getenv("CHERIOT_NETWORK") or
11     "../../network-stack/"
12 includes(path.join(networkstackdir,"lib"))
```

LISTING 77. Build system code for including the network stack.
[from: examples/sntp/xmake.lua]

Next, you need to make sure that code using the network stack finds the headers by adding the include directory (Listing 78). You must also explicitly add the SNTP compartment as a dependency in the compartment target, though this is somewhat redundant because we'll also add it globally later.

Finally, the network stack provides an option to users to decide whether they want IPv6 support. This affects some of the definitions in headers so you must define the same flag in your compartment to avoid linker errors.

```
22 compartment("sntp_example")
23   add_includedirs(path.join(networkstackdir,"include"))
24   add_deps("freestanding", "SNTP")
25   add_files("sntp.cc")
26   on_load(function(target)
27     target:add('options', "IPv6")
28     local IPv6 = get_config("IPv6")
29     target:add("defines",
30         "CHERIOT_RTOS_OPTION_IPv6=" .. tostring(IPv6))
31   end)
```

LISTING 78. Build system code for building a compartment that uses the network stack. [from: examples/sntp/xmake.lua]

Next, the firmware definition needs to contain two things. First, it must add dependencies on the components of the network stack, as shown in Listing 79. The first four are ones that we've already discussed. The SNTP compartment is (hopefully) obvious. The time helpers library is not something that we've looked at so far and you'll see what it does when we start using the SNTP APIs.

```
38 add_deps("DNS", "TCPIP", "Firewall", "NetAPI",
39            "SNTP", "time_helpers")
```

LISTING 79. Build system code for adding dependencies on the network stack. [from: examples/sntp/xmake.lua]

Finally, you need to create the threads that the network stack uses. The thread that starts in the Firewall compartment handles incoming packets. This calls into the TCP/IP compartment for each packet, to enqueue it for handling. The other thread handles TCP retransmissions, keep-alive packets, and so on. TCP provides a reliable transport over an unreliable network and so has to buffer each outgoing packet until the receiver acknowledges receipt. Dropped packets are retransmitted until the acknowledgement arrives.

With the build system logic done, you can start using the network stack. Anything that uses the network stack will need to call network_start early on, as shown in Listing 81. This brings up the network stack, gets the DHCP lease, and so on. This is a blocking call and will return once the network is initialised.

```
53  {
54        -- TCP/IP stack thread.
55        compartment = "TCPIP",
56        priority = 1,
57        entry_point = "ip_thread_entry",
58        stack_size = 0xe00,
59        trusted_stack_frames = 5
60    },
61    {
62        -- Firewall thread, handles incoming packets as they
63        -- arrive.
64        compartment = "Firewall",
65        -- Higher priority, this will be back-pressured by
66        -- the message queue if the network stack can't keep
67        -- up, but we want packets to arrive immediately.
68        priority = 2,
69        entry_point = "ethernet_run_driver",
70        stack_size = 0x1000,
71        trusted_stack_frames = 5
72    }
```

LISTING 80. Build system code for defining the network stack's threads.
[from: examples/sntp/xmake.lua]

```
13  Debug::log("Starting network stack");
14  network_start();
```

LISTING 81. Initialisation for the network stack. [from: examples/sntp/sntp.cc]

Next, you must ask the SNTP compartment to update the time. The sntp_update function, shown in Listing 82, is a blocking call that will attempt to update the time and return failure if it does not manage within the timeout. In this example, we simply keep trying in a loop. In a real system, you would probably want to handle the case where the network is unavailable more gracefully.

```
18  Timeout t{MS_TO_TICKS(1000)};
19  Debug::log("Trying to fetch SNTP time");
20  while (sntp_update(&t) != 0)
21  {
22    Debug::log("Failed to update NTP time");
23    t = Timeout{MS_TO_TICKS(1000)};
24  }
```

LISTING 82. Updating the time from the SNTP server. [from: examples/sntp/sntp.cc]

A lot of things happen behind the scenes for this to work. The SNTP compartment holds a capability that authorises it to talk to the remote NTP server. It presents this capability to the network API compartment, which opens the firewall hole for DNS lookups and then instructs the DNS compartment to perform the lookup. The DNS compartment then sends a DNS lookup to the firewall, which forwards it to the Ethernet device and forwards the response back. Next, the network API compartment opens a firewall hole for the local UDP port to the remote host on port 123 (the NTP port) and returns the socket to the SNTP compartment. The SNTP compartment then passes this socket to the TCP/IP compartment to send and receive NTP packets. Finally, it asks the TCP/IP compartment to close the socket and the TCP/IP compartment asks the firewall compartment to close the firewall hole. When the SNTP compartment receives the response and knows the time, it sets some state in a pre-shared object for detecting the time.

Once the current time has been fetched, you can get the current time of day. Listing 83 shows a loop that runs roughly every 50 ms and prints the time (as a UNIX epoch timestamp) if the number of seconds has changed since last time. The gettimeofday function called here is from the time helpers library that was mentioned earlier.

```
28  time_t lastTime = 0;
29  while (true)
30  {
31    timeval tv;
32    int     ret = gettimeofday(&tv, nullptr);
33    if (ret != 0)
34    {
35      Debug::log("Failed to get time of day: {}", ret);
36    }
37    else if (lastTime != tv.tv_sec)
38    {
39      lastTime = tv.tv_sec;
40      // Truncate the epoch time to 32 bits for printing.
41      Debug::log("Current UNIX epoch time: {}", tv.tv_sec);
42    }
43    Timeout shortSleep{MS_TO_TICKS(50)};
44    thread_sleep(&shortSleep);
45  }
```

LISTING 83. Printing the current UNIX epoch time. [from: examples/sntp/sntp.cc]

The SNTP compartment and the time helpers library share a pre-shared object (see Section 5.7) which contains the UNIX timestamp at the time of the last NTP update, the cycle time of the last update, and the current epoch. The

SNTP compartment has a read-write view of this, the time helpers library a read-only view. When the SNTP compartment updates this, it increments the epoch once, writes the new value, and then increments the epoch again. The time library can therefore get a consistent snapshot of the values by reading the epoch, reading the other values, and then reading the epoch again to make sure that it hasn't changed. If the epoch value is odd, the time helpers library does a futex wait operation to block until the value has changed. The SNTP compartment does a futex-wake operation after the update to wake any waiters.

This means that, most of the time, calling gettimeofday does not require any cross-compartment calls.

When you run this example, you should see the time printed once per second, something like this:

```
Network test: Starting network stack
Network test: Trying to fetch SNTP time
Network test: Current UNIX epoch time: 1735563080
Network test: Current UNIX epoch time: 1735563081
Network test: Current UNIX epoch time: 1735563082
Network test: Current UNIX epoch time: 1735563083
Network test: Current UNIX epoch time: 1735563084
```

 At the time of writing, there is a problem with the Sonata network interface's ability to receive IPv6 packets. If you try this example on Sonata and it does not work, try adding --IPv6=n to the end of your xmake line during the config stage.

If you leave this running for a while, the clock will eventually drift. Try modifying this example to update the time from the NTP server once per minute.

11.3. Creating a connected socket

In the traditional Berkeley Sockets model, creating a connected socket is a multi-step operation. First, you must create the socket. Next, you may (optionally) bind it to a specific local port, though this step is usually omitted. Finally, you connect it. The CHERIoT network stack combines these into a single network_socket_connect_tcp call.

As you might expect from CHERIoT, this is a capability-based API. It requires a capability to authorise connecting to a specific host, along with a capability to allocate memory for the socket state. The latter ensures that all

---

Documentation for the `network_socket_connect_tcp` function

```
Socket network_socket_connect_tcp(Timeout * timeout,
AllocatorCapability mallocCapability, ConnectionCapability
hostCapability)
```

Create a connected TCP socket.

This function will block until the connection is established or the timeout is reached.

The `mallocCapability` argument is used to allocate memory for the socket and must have sufficient quota remaining for the socket.

The `hostCapability` argument is a capability authorising the connection to a specific host.

This returns a valid sealed capability to a socket on success, or an untagged value on failure.

---

memory used for a network connection is accounted to the compartment that created it.

You need to define a connection capability before you can use one. Listing 84 shows an example that allows connecting with TCP to the `towel.blinkenlights.nl` host, on port 23, the well-known telnet port. This capability will show up in the auditing report for the firmware image (as discussed in Chapter 10), so you can ensure that specific compartments in your firmware image are permitted to connect only to remote hosts that you authorised.

```
16 DECLARE_AND_DEFINE_CONNECTION_CAPABILITY(
17    Server,
18    "towel.blinkenlights.nl",
19    23,
20    ConnectionTypeTCP);
```

LISTING 84. A static capability that authorises connecting to a remote server.
[from: examples/tcp/tcp.cc]

The connect call is shown in Listing 85. This passes the capability for the server along with this compartment's default `malloc` capability. You can separate the quota that your compartment uses for network-related things and provide a different capability. This is useful if, for example, you wish to call heap_free_all on your default malloc capability but not affect any network state

```
30  Timeout unlimited{UnlimitedTimeout};
31  auto    socket =
32    network_socket_connect_tcp(&unlimited,
33                               MALLOC_CAPABILITY,
34                               STATIC_SEALED_VALUE(Server));
35  if (!CHERI::Capability{socket}.is_valid())
36  {
37    Debug::log("Failed to connect");
38    return;
39  }
```

LISTING 85. Connecting to a remote server. [from: examples/tcp/tcp.cc]

The result of this call is a valid *sealed capability* to the socket. All of the state required for the socket will be allocated with the allocator capability that you passed (and counted against your quota), but is not directly accessible to you. On a POSIX system, the result of a socket call is a file descriptor. On Windows, it is a HANDLE. These are both opaque types that reference some internal data structure that the kernel associates with your process. In contrast, a sealed capability is just a pointer, but a type-safe tamper-proof one. You can pass it between compartments (allowing multiple compartments to use the same socket) but only the TCP/IP compartment can unseal it to access the internal state. If the connection fails, you will get back an untagged capability.

 Currently, network_socket_connect_tcp does not report the reason for a failure. A future version will likely use negative error codes in the address of untagged capabilities, so it's important to check whether the returned value is a valid capability, rather than comparing it against NULL or nullptr.

Assuming that the connection succeeded, you are now ready to start trying to receive data, as shown in Listing 86. The network_socket_receive call is quite different from a conventional socket receive. On most operating systems, a system call cannot allocate userspace memory and must take a buffer for the kernel to write into. This is unfortunate because the kernel knows the amount of data available, but the caller does not. If the caller provides too small a buffer, they must then do another call to get the rest of the data. If they provide too large a buffer, they have wasted memory. In contrast, the `network_socket_receive` API allows the TCP/IP compartment to allocate a buffer large enough for the available data.

```
43   while (true)
44   {
45     auto [received, buffer] = network_socket_receive(
46       &unlimited, MALLOC_CAPABILITY, socket);
47     if (received < 0)
48     {
49       Debug::log("Error: {}", received);
50       return;
51     }
52     for (size_t i = 0; i < received; i++)
53     {
54       MMIO_CAPABILITY(Uart, uart)
55         ->blocking_write(buffer[i]);
56     }
57     free(buffer);
58   }
```

LISTING 86. Receiving data from a remote server. [from: examples/tcp/tcp.cc]

The `network_socket_receive` interface is convenient but it does not guarantee that the TCP/IP stack has not kept a pointer to the returned buffer. The TCP/IP compartment will not do this in normal operation but if an attacker manages to gain arbitrary-code execution in the TCP/IP compartment then they may be able to exploit time-of-check-to-time-of-use (TOCTOU) bugs in your code. This is not a problem for this example, which reads each byte in the returned buffer exactly once.

The result of the `network_socket_receive` is a struct `NetworkReceiveResult`, which contains two fields. The first field, `bytesReceived`, is the number of bytes received, or a negative error code. The second, `buffer` is the buffer (which will be null in error cases). This example uses C++ structured binding to decompose the structure and make it appear as if the function returned two values.

In this example, we are assuming that the TCP/IP stack is trusted. The TCP/IP compartment could attack this example by providing a received size that is greater than the claimed size, or one that lacks read permission. This example has no secrets and, if the network stack is compromised, can do nothing, and so does not worry about these potential problems. If you have such concerns, then you should put the code that uses the result in an error-handling block, or use `network_socket_receive_preallocated` instead.

This example is simply writing the result to the UART directly. The server that it connects to will provide you with an ASCII-art rendering of Star Wars: A New Hope. After the initial banner and the scrolling text, you should see something like this:

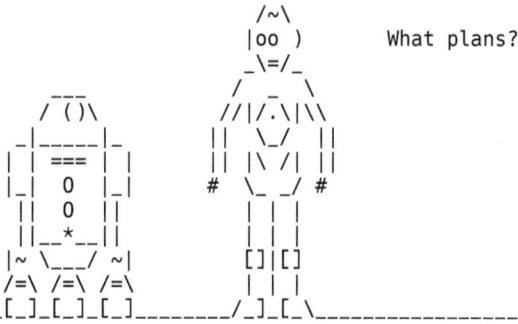

Documentation for the `network_socket_receive_preallocated` function

```
int network_socket_receive_preallocated(Timeout * timeout,
Socket socket, void * buffer, size_t length)
```

Receive data from a socket into a preallocated buffer. This will block until data are received or the timeout expires. If data are received, they will be stored in the provided buffer.

NOTE: Callers should remove global and load permissions from `buffer` before passing it to this function if they are worried about a potentially compromised network stack.

The return value is either the number of bytes received, or a negative error code.

The negative values will be errno values:
- `-EPERM`: `buffer` and/or `length` are invalid.
- `-EINVAL`: The socket is not valid.
- `-ETIMEDOUT`: The timeout was reached before data could be received.
- `-ENOTCONN`: The socket is not connected.

11.4. Creating a listening socket

Listening sockets, like connected ones, require an authorising capability. This is shown in Listing 87 and includes the local port number that you can bind to along with the number of pending connections that are allowed. The second is important for limiting the amount of the TCP/IP compartment's memory you can consume. Each unaccepted socket requires some state in the TCP/IP stack so allowing an unbounded number would consume an unlimited amount of memory. For most embedded uses, one or two is adequate.

```
60 DECLARE_AND_DEFINE_BIND_CAPABILITY(
61    /* Name */ ServerPort,
62    /* Bind on IPv6? */ UseIPv6,
63    /* Port number */ 1234,
64    /* Concurrent connection limit */ 1);
```

LISTING 87. A static capability that authorises binding to a local port.
[from: examples/tcp_echo_server/tcp.cc]

As with the connect operation, the authorising capability is not the only place that the CHERIoT network stack's APIs differ from the traditional Berkeley Sockets APIs. As shown in Listing 88, the socket, bind and listen operations are combined. The network_socket_listen_tcp call creates the socket, binds it to the local port associated with the authorising capability, and makes it ready to accept.

```
75 Timeout unlimited{UnlimitedTimeout};
76 auto    socket = network_socket_listen_tcp(
77    &unlimited,
78    MALLOC_CAPABILITY,
79    STATIC_SEALED_VALUE(ServerPort));
80 if (!CHERI::Capability{socket}.is_valid())
81 {
82   Debug::log("Failed to bind to local port");
83   return;
84 }
```

LISTING 88. Listening for TCP connections to a local port.
[from: examples/tcp_echo_server/tcp.cc]

A listening socket is simply a placeholder for a local endpoint. You cannot send or receive with it, all that you can do is accept new connections. The network_socket_accept_tcp call, shown in Listing 89, creates a new socket for the accepted connection and, optionally, returns the remote IP address and port. If you do not care about the address of the connecting host, you can pass null to the last two arguments.

```
88   while (true)
89   {
90     Debug::log("Listening for connections...");
91     NetworkAddress address;
92     uint16_t       port;
93     auto           accepted =
94       network_socket_accept_tcp(&unlimited,
95                                 MALLOC_CAPABILITY,
96                                 socket,
97                                 &address,
98                                 &port);
99     if (!CHERI::Capability{accepted}.is_valid())
100    {
101      continue;
102    }
103    Debug::log("Received connection from {} on port {}",
104               address,
105               int32_t(port));
106    char byte;
107    while (network_socket_receive_preallocated(
108             &unlimited, accepted, &byte, 1) == 1)
109    {
110      network_socket_send(&unlimited, accepted, &byte, 1);
111      MMIO_CAPABILITY(Uart, uart)->blocking_write(byte);
112    }
113    network_socket_close(
114      &unlimited, MALLOC_CAPABILITY, accepted);
115  }
```

LISTING 89. Accepting TCP connections and running a simple echo-server loop.
[from: examples/tcp_echo_server/tcp.cc]

After accepting a connection, this example simply sits in a loop reading one byte at a time and sending it back. It also writes the received byte to the UART. The send function is very similar to the receive. It takes a pointer to a buffer and a length. The network stack's interface is written defensively. If the length is smaller than the bounds of the buffer, or if the buffer has the wrong permissions, this call will fail.

Note here that the on-stack buffer (the single byte local variable) is derived from our stack pointer and so is automatically local. This ensures that the TCP/IP compartment cannot capture it.

Documentation for the `network_socket_send` function

```
ssize_t network_socket_send(Timeout * timeout, Socket
socket, void * buffer, size_t length)
```

Send data over a TCP socket. This will block until the data have been sent or the timeout expires.

The inner loop is waiting for the receive call to return a value other than 1, indicating that it has failed to receive. This should happen when the connection is dropped.

The inner loop uses an unlimited timeout, so that the demo doesn't fail if you get distracted in the middle of running it. A more realistic example would use a shorter timeout on the receive call. Short timeouts are useful to prevent denial of service issues. This simple example, like many embedded network servers, is single threaded and handles one connection at a time. Without the timeout, a single client failing to gracefully disconnect could prevent any future access until the device is restarted.

If you connect to this example with `netcat`, you can try sending it some text, which it should echo back. Here, my Sonata board has joined my local network with a DHCP-assigned address of 192.168.1.154:

```
$ nc 192.168.1.154 1234
Hello world!
Hello world!
```

On the UART console, you can see the debugging messages, along with the echoed text:

```
TCP Server Example: Starting network stack
TCP Server Example: Creating listening socket
TCP Server Example: Listening for connections...
TCP Server Example: Received connection from 192.168.1.86 on port
62599
Hello world!
```

11.5. Securing connections with TLS

In general, the kind of unencrypted communication that we've seen so far is inappropriate for the modern Internet. Anyone who has control of any node on the network between the device and the remote server can tamper with messages. Such malicious messages may attack software on the device, attempting to exploit vulnerabilities.

This is the threat model for a lot of the network stack work on CHERIoT: a remote attacker is trying to compromise the device. The firewall makes this class of attack somewhat harder, by ensuring that an attacker must spoof packets for a valid connection. This defence is weakened if your device uses a server socket because, by design, these must allow packets from unknown remote hosts.

An attacker who sneaks a packet past the firewall can attack the TCP/IP compartment. This is a fairly complex piece of code, which does dangerous things like packet parsing. It is written in MISRA C and is more likely to be correct and secure than most C code, but it may still contain bugs. The simple act of compiling it for a CHERIoT target mitigates a large number of possible bugs, as does the memory management strategy. Every incoming packet (and every outgoing packet) is a fresh heap allocation, which ensures that dangling references to processed packets will trap, as will bounds errors. Any such bugs will cause the network stack to gracefully reset, as described in Section 11.8.

Without encryption, the TCP/IP stack is not the limit of the attack surface. An attacker can push data through the network stack and into the next compartment. Using *authenticated encryption*, such as TLS, mitigates this.

With authenticated encryption, you can ensure that only messages from a trusted endpoint, such as your cloud server, reach your code. The TLS stack checks each incoming message for cryptographic integrity and forwards the plaintext to you only after it has been decrypted.

Using the TLS stack makes it a critical part of the attack surface. Fortunately, it has a very narrow interface with the TCP/IP stack. Internally, BearSSL uses a ring buffer for messages that are ready to be sent and those awaiting decryption. Before calling the send or receive functions in the TCP/ IP stack, the TLS compartment removes all permissions except load or store (for send and receive, respectively) and sets the bounds to exactly the required amount. Removing the global permission protects the TLS stack from time-of-check-to-time-of-use (TOCTOU) attacks by guaranteeing that the TCP/IP compartment cannot capture the buffer for longer than the duration of the call. Similarly, removing permissions and bounding the pointers to the buffers ensures that no data can leak to the TCP/IP compartment and it cannot overwrite anything.

Beyond this, the TLS compartment has no global state. All state associated with a TLS connection is stored in the connection object, exposed as a sealed capability. This means that two concurrent calls into the TLS compartment for different TLS connections have no shared state, giving *flow isolation*. An attacker who compromises one TLS connection cannot use this to attack another.

When you communicate with a remote server via TLS, you have to identify the server in two ways. As with unencrypted connections, you must provide a host name that can be mapped to a network address. Additionally, you need to provide a *TLS certificate* to identify the remote host.

A TLS certificate is public key along with some metadata describing what it can be used for and when it is valid. Each TLS certificate also has an associated private key, which is (or, at least, should be) kept secret. If you sign something with the private key, someone else can use the certificate to validate that it really was signed by you.

In the simplest case, TLS can use a single certificate. You generate the pair of this certificate and its private key and embed the certificate on your device. This is a dangerous practice because there is no possible way of revoking the certificate if the key is compromised. The key must be in memory on the server that the device connects to and so is vulnerable to attack.

TLS certificates can also be arranged in *certificate chains*, where each certificate is signed by the private key associated with the next certificate in the chain. The root of a certificate chain is usually signed by a *certificate authority* (CA).

With a certificate chain, you can store a certificate on the device that does not correspond to the private key on the server, but which can still be used to verify that key. It is quite common for the server to have a very short-lived certificate, generated every week, so that if the key is compromised the associated certificate expires after a short amount of time and an attacker has a narrow window to use it. This requires your device to hold a certificate that it trusts will appear somewhere further up the chain. The set of trusted certificates is referred to as your *trust anchors*. Any certificate signed with the key corresponding to one of your trust anchors is considered valid. This property is transitive, so any number of certificates can exist between the one corresponding to the server's private key and the one that you hold. This provides a lot of flexibility, at the cost of computational power. Verifying a certificate chain is very fast on a multi-gigahertz machine with wide vector units but can be slow (a second or longer of CPU time) on an embedded device.

If you control the remote server then you already have the .pem file that contains the certificate. If you are connecting to a server that someone else controls then you need to extract it first, or include a large set of trusted anchors. Modern web browsers do the latter, but the certificate bundle is

Most of the network stack APIs are intended to hide the exact implementations that we use. For example, we may wish to replace the FreeRTOS TCP/IP compartment's code with something designed for CHERIoT, perhaps written in a safe language. The TLS compartment currently leaks the fact that it uses BearSSL at the API level, by exposing trust anchors in BearSSL's internal format. This will be addressed in a future version.

larger than most embedded platforms would like. Fortunately, you can use the openssl command to connect to a server and report the certificate chain. Try this for example.com on the HTTPS port:

```
$ openssl s_client -connect example.com:443 -showcerts </dev/null
Connecting to 2606:2800:21f:cb07:6820:80da:af6b:8b2c
CONNECTED(00000005)
depth=2 C=US, O=DigiCert Inc, OU=www.digicert.com, CN=DigiCert
Global Root G2
verify return:1
depth=1 C=US, O=DigiCert Inc, CN=DigiCert Global G2 TLS RSA SHA256
2020 CA1
verify return:1
depth=0 C=US, ST=California, L=Los Angeles,
O=Internet Corporation for
   Assigned Names and Numbers, CN=www.example.org
verify return:1
```

The first bit of the output shows the certificate chain. The first certificate is the DigitCert Global Root G2, a certificate that the DigitCert CA uses to sign their own signing certificates. This certificate is the root that you are expected to deliver out of band. Typically, your openssl install will have some system-provided root certificates that include this one. This certificate is valid from August 2013 to January 2038. It is *probably* safe to use with your device.

The lifetime is longer than most embedded devices last. The CA claims (and their auditors support the claim) that this certificate is stored securely and is used only to sign the intermediate certificates that are used to sign keys for clients. Information about the intermediate certificate, DigiCert Global G2 TLS RSA SHA256 2020 CA1, shows up later in the output:

```
 1 s:C=US, O=DigiCert Inc, CN=DigiCert Global G2 TLS RSA SHA256
2020 CA1
   i:C=US, O=DigiCert Inc, OU=www.digicert.com, CN=DigiCert Global
Root G2
   a:PKEY: rsaEncryption, 2048 (bit); sigalg: RSA-SHA256
   v:NotBefore: Mar 30 00:00:00 2021 GMT; NotAfter: Mar 29 23:59:59
2031 GMT
```

This expires in six years at the time of writing this book, so it might seem safe to use as a trust anchor (for now). Unfortunately, this is not the case. Although this certificate is valid for another six years, there's no guarantee that this intermediate certificate will be the one used to sign the certificate for example.com next time. The certificate that the site operator created is the first to be displayed in the output:

```
Certificate chain
 0 s:C=US, ST=California, L=Los Angeles, O=Internet Corporation for
       Assigned Names and Numbers, CN=www.example.org
   i:C=US, O=DigiCert Inc, CN=DigiCert Global G2 TLS RSA SHA256
2020 CA1
   a:PKEY: rsaEncryption, 2048 (bit); sigalg: RSA-SHA256
   v:NotBefore: Jan 30 00:00:00 2024 GMT; NotAfter: Mar  1 23:59:59
2025 GMT
```

This is valid for one year and will probably have expired by the time that you read this. Note that the lifetime of the *certificate* is not the same as the lifetime of the *key pair*. You can easily generate a new certificate signing request for the same key and have a newly signed certificate valid for another year (or just for a week) using the same key.

If we wanted to use either of the certificates that are directly sent by the server then we could simply copy the bit between BEGIN CERTIFICATE and END CERTIFICATE lines into a file. Unfortunately, we don't so we have to go to the DigiCert web site[1] and download the correct certificate.

Once you have the certificate, BearSSL's command-line tool can convert it into a form that the library expects. The command-line tools are not built by the CHERIoT network stack, so you will need to either build them from the copy of BearSSL in network-stack/third_party/BearSSL or install them from your operating system's package manager. You can then convert the certificate file into a header that contains the trust anchor that you need:

```
$ brssl ta DigiCertGlobalRootG2.crt.pem > DigiCertGlobalRootG2.h
Reading file 'DigiCertGlobalRootG2.crt.pem': 1 trust anchor
```

Once you have the trust anchors and the hostname and port, you have everything that you need to be able to create a TLS connection. The current implementation of TLS in the CHERIoT network stack uses BearSSL, which avoids heap allocation. Unfortunately, this includes all of the big-number arithmetic, which causes it to require very large stacks. Listing 90 shows the stack for this example: it is just under 8 KiB.

---

1. https://www.digicert.com/kb/digicert-root-certificates.htm

```
42 {
43         compartment = "https_example",
44         priority = 1,
45         entry_point = "example",
46         -- TLS requires *huge* stacks!
47         stack_size = 6144,
48         trusted_stack_frames = 6
49     },
```

LISTING 90. Build system code for a thread that will use TLS.
[from: examples/tls/xmake.lua]

This thread is now able to connect to a TLS server without running out of stack space. Recall from the certificates earlier that each has a period when it is valid. The TLS stack will check that the certificate is currently valid, which requires that the TLS stack has access to the current time. This means that you need some code that is similar to the SNTP example at the start. After initialising the network stack, you need to synchronise the clock, as shown in Listing 91.

```
32 network_start();
33 Timeout t{MS_TO_TICKS(1000)};
34 // SNTP must be run for the TLS stack to be able to check
35 // certificate dates.
36 while (sntp_update(&t) != 0)
37 {
38   Debug::log("Failed to update NTP time");
39   t = Timeout{MS_TO_TICKS(1000)};
40 }
```

LISTING 91. Setup required before a TLS connection is possible.
[from: examples/tls/https.cc]

Connecting to a TLS server is very much like connecting to a TCP server. Compare Listing 85, which established an unencrypted connection, to Listing 92, which creates an encrypted connection. Aside from the connect function name, the only difference is that the TLS connect function requires the trust anchors. This is an intentional API choice: CHERIoT aims to be secure by default, so it should be as easy to create secured connections as it is to create insecure ones.

The return value from the tls_connection_create call is either a valid sealed capability, or null. In the future, it will use a negated error code in the untagged capability to report failure. Currently, the only failure that will be reported as a non-null capability is -ECOMPARTMENTFAIL, which will occur if

```
45   Timeout unlimited{UnlimitedTimeout};
46   auto    tlsSocket = tls_connection_create(
47     &unlimited,
48     TEST_MALLOC,
49     STATIC_SEALED_VALUE(ExampleComTLS),
50     TAs,
51     TAs_NUM);
52   if (!CHERI::Capability{tlsSocket}.is_valid())
53   {
54     Debug::log("Failed to connect.  Error: {}",
55                 -static_cast<int32_t>(
56                   reinterpret_cast<intptr_t>(tlsSocket)));
57   }
```

LISTING 92. Connecting to a remote server with TLS. [from: examples/tls/https.cc]

there is a crash in the TLS compartment. If you did not provide a large stack
(as in Listing 90) then you may see this result. Try reducing the stack size to
4 KiB and you will see failure like this in the output:

```
HTTPS Client: Failed to connect.  Error: 1
HTTPS Client: TLS socket: 0xffffffff (v:0 0xfffffe00-0xfffffe00
l:0x0 o:0x0 p: - ------ -- ---)
```

Note that the returned capability for this does *not* expose the socket. The
TLS compartment owns the socket on behalf of the caller. This demonstrates
the value of *capability delegation*. The TLS compartment takes the caller's malloc capability as an argument and can subsequently forward it to the TCP/IP
compartment to allocate the socket. This encapsulation means that it is impossible for the caller to accidentally send data over the socket unencrypted.

This example implements a minimal HTTP client to demonstrate sending
and receiving data over TLS. Do not use this HTTP client in production, it does
no error checking and ignores most HTTP headers. The send code is shown in
Listing 93. As with the underlying TCP send call, the TLS send call may send
less than the requested amount of data. This code is therefore called in a loop,
which will try to send more of the buffer if only some is sent successfully. The
echo server did not need to handle this case because it only ever sent individual bytes and provided an unlimited timeout, so either the byte entered the
TCP socket's send queue or the caller blocked.

This is unnecessary for the example because the amount of sent data is
smaller than the TLS socket's internal buffer size so the loop will never execute, but you can force it to by adding additional headers. Internally, the TLS
stack needs to assemble a complete message and then send it. The message
may need to contain padding if it is too small, so the underlying APIs provide

an explicit flush. CHERIoT's wrapper aims to be easy for the common case and so automatically flushes after a send. If this is not what you want, you are free to extend the source code.

```
69  while (sent < toSend)
70  {
71   size_t remaining = toSend - sent;
72
73   ssize_t sentThisCall =
74     tls_connection_send(&unlimited,
75                         tlsSocket,
76                         &(message[sent]),
77                         remaining,
78                         0);
79   Debug::log("Sent {} bytes", sentThisCall);
80
81   if (sentThisCall >= 0)
82   {
83    sent += sentThisCall;
84   }
85   else
86   {
87    Debug::log("Send failed: {}", sentThisCall);
88    break;
89   }
90  }
```

LISTING 93. Sending data over a TLS connection. [from: examples/tls/https.cc]

Receiving the response data is almost identical to receiving unencrypted data. The call shown in Listing 94 directly mirrors the TCP API from Listing 86. The only difference is that you can trust that the data has not been tampered with in-flight (unless the TLS compartment is compromised).

```
101  auto [received, buffer] =
102    tls_connection_receive(&unlimited, tlsSocket);
```

LISTING 94. Receiving data over a TLS connection. [from: examples/tls/https.cc]

11.6. Communicating with an MQTT server

A lot of IoT applications use MQTT (which doesn't stand for anything and isn't a message queue) as a publish-subscribe protocol for messaging. MQTT exposes an abstraction of a tree of topics, where clients can subscribe to topics and publish new values to that topic. When a client publishes a message on

The threat model for the TLS compartment is directed towards the TCP/IP stack as the main adversary. It implicitly trusts the caller for availability. You can almost certainly crash the TLS compartment if you call it with insufficient stack, insufficient trusted stack, and so on. If you do, you will not impact other TLS flows and the flow that you will impact is allocated from your own heap quota, so you can only attack yourself doing this.

a topic, a copy is sent to every client that has subscribed to that topic. The protocol supports multiple levels of *quality of service* (QoS):

At most once
The server will attempt to deliver the message. If delivery fails, neither the client nor the server will do any additional steps.

At least once
The server will attempt to deliver the message and wait for an acknowledgement. If delivery fails, the server will try again until the message is acknowledged.

Exactly once
The server will attempt to deliver the message and use a two-way handshake to ensure that the message arrives exactly once.

The QoS levels are intended to work even if the network breaks. Clients connect with a unique 23-character identifier. If a client is already connected with the same identifier, new clients may not connect with the same identifier but they may *reconnect*. A reconnecting client will disconnect the original and take ownership of the ID and any messages with higher QoS levels that were destined for the original will be sent to the new owner. The CHERIoT MQTT library contains a helper for creating random client IDs, shown in Listing 95.

```
96   Debug::log("Generating client ID...");
97   constexpr std::string_view clientIDPrefix{"cheriotMQTT"};
98   // Prefix with something recognizable, for convenience.
99   memcpy(clientID.data(),
100         clientIDPrefix.data(),
101         clientIDPrefix.size());
102  // Suffix with random character chain.
103  mqtt_generate_client_id(
104    clientID.data() + clientIDPrefix.size(),
105    clientID.size() - clientIDPrefix.size());
```

LISTING 95. Creating a client ID to use with MQTT. [from: examples/mqtt/mqtt.cc]

The CHERIoT MQTT interface doesn't support unencrypted connections. Connecting to a server requires everything that you needed for a TLS connection. This example is using the Mosquitto public MQTT test server. This server is intended for demos and is not always reliable. If the demo doesn't work, check their web interface[2] to see if it is down.

The mqtt_connect call to connect to the server is shown in Listing 96. This API takes quite a lot of arguments. The first few are familiar from previous connection APIs: they provide the timeout, the allocation capability, and the connection capability. The next two are callbacks for publish messages (someone has published to a node that you subscribed to) and acknowledgement messages (a message that you sent has been acknowledged by the server). Next come the trust anchors, as we saw in Listing 92. The function then takes the sizes for some internal buffers and finally the client ID.

This example omits the last parameter, which has a default value of false in C++. Setting this to true will cause the library to reconnect, rather than connecting, to the MQTT server.

```
109   Debug::log("Connecting to MQTT broker...");
110   auto handle =
111     mqtt_connect(&t,
112                         STATIC_SEALED_VALUE(mqttTestMalloc),
113                         CONNECTION_CAPABILITY(MosquittoOrgMQTT),
114                         publishCallback,
115                         ackCallback,
116                         TAs,
117                         TAs_NUM,
118                         networkBufferSize,
119                         incomingPublishCount,
120                         outgoingPublishCount,
121                         clientID.data(),
122                         clientID.size());
123
124   if (!Capability{handle}.is_valid())
125   {
126     Debug::log("Failed to connect.");
127     return;
128   }
```

LISTING 96. Connecting to an MQTT broker. [from: examples/mqtt/mqtt.cc]

As with other networking APIs, all of the state associated with this connection is allocated from the caller's quota. This includes the TLS and TCP/IP state that is allocated indirectly. Similarly, the result is a sealed capability

2.   https://test.mosquitto.org/sys/ssl.html

that encapsulates the state of the connection. This includes a sealed capability to the TLS state, which includes a sealed capability to the TCP socket state. The MQTT, TLS, and TCP states are visible only to the compartment that owns each of them.

Once you have connected to an MQTT broker, you can send publish and subscribe messages and invoke the run loop to process incoming messages. This example first subscribes to a topic, in Listing 97.

```
136  ret = mqtt_subscribe(&t,
137                       handle,
138                       1, // QoS 1 = delivered at least once
139                       testTopic.data(),
140                       testTopic.size());
141  Debug::Assert(
142    ret >= 0, "Failed to subscribe, error {}.", ret);
```

LISTING 97. Subscribing to an MQTT topic. [from: examples/mqtt/mqtt.cc]

The return value will be either a negative error code or a non-negative packet ID. We don't care about the packet ID in this example, so simply assert that we didn't see an error.

The server will send a reply message to acknowledge the subscription. When you call mqtt_run, it will process incoming messages and invoke the relevant callbacks. The call is shown in Listing 98.

```
148  while (ackReceived == 0)
149  {
150    t   = Timeout{MS_TO_TICKS(1000)};
151    ret = mqtt_run(&t, handle);
152    Debug::Assert(
153      ret >= 0,
154      "Failed to wait for the SUBACK, error {}.",
155      ret);
156  }
```

LISTING 98. Waiting for acknowledgement after subscribing to an MQTT topic.
[from: examples/mqtt/mqtt.cc]

The callbacks that mqtt_run invokes are the ones that were passed in Listing 96. These are CHERIoT cross-compartment callbacks. The one for acknowledgements is shown in Listing 99. This will run in the compartment that defined it, invisible to the MQTT compartment, and on a new *trusted stack* activation record. This example callback is not written defensively. A buggy (or malicious) MQTT compartment could pass invalid pointers that would cause

---

Documentation for the `mqtt_run` **function**

```
int mqtt_run(Timeout * t, MQTTConnection mqttHandle)
```

Fetch ACK and PUBLISH notifications on a given MQTT connection, and keep the connection alive.

This function will invoke the callbacks passed to `mqtt_connect`. The connection object is protected by a recursive mutex, so these callbacks can call additional publish and subscribe functions. If doing so, care must be taken to ensure that the buffer is not exhausted. Calling `mqtt_run` from a callback is not supported.

The return value is zero if notifications were successfully fetched, or a negative error code.

The negative values will be errno values:
- `-EINVAL`: A parameter is not valid.
- `-ETIMEDOUT`: The timeout was reached before notifications could be fetched.
- `-ECONNABORTED`: The connection to the broker was lost. The client should now call `mqtt_disconnect` to free resources associated with this handle.
- `-EAGAIN`: An unspecified error happened in the underlying coreMQTT library. Try again.

---

a trap. If this happens, the switcher will unwind the trusted stack out of the callback, as if the callback simply returned early.

Running the example to this point should give output like this:

```
MQTT example: Generating client ID...
MQTT example: Connecting to MQTT broker...
MQTT example: Connected to MQTT broker!
MQTT example: Subscribing to test topic 'cheriot-book-example'.
MQTT example: Now fetching the SUBACK.
MQTT example: Got an ACK for packet 0x1
```

Next, the example will publish a message on the same topic and make sure that it is received. The publish part is shown in Listing 100. As with the subscribe call, this returns a negative error code or a non-negative packet number.

```
65 void __cheriot_callback ackCallback(uint16_t packetID,
66                                     bool      isReject)
67 {
68   Debug::log("Got an ACK for packet {}", packetID);
69   if (isReject)
70   {
71     Debug::log(
72       "However the ACK is a SUBSCRIBE REJECT notification");
73   }
74   ackReceived++;
75 }
```

LISTING 99. Callback for acknowledging MQTT messages.
[from: examples/mqtt/mqtt.cc]

```
164   ret = mqtt_publish(
165     &t,
166     handle,
167     1, // QoS 1 = delivered at least once
168     testTopic.data(),
169     testTopic.size(),
170     static_cast<const void *>(testPayload.data()),
171     testPayload.size());
172   Debug::Assert(
173     ret >= 0, "Failed to publish, error {}.", ret);
```

LISTING 100. Publishing to an MQTT topic. [from: examples/mqtt/mqtt.cc]

Publishing the message will trigger two messages from the server. There will be an acknowledgement of the publish and, because the example is subscribed to this topic, it will also receive the publish notification. The latter will be sent to the callback in Listing 101, which logs the received message.

Running to this point should give you output like the following:

```
MQTT example: Publishing a value to test topic 'cheriot-book-
example'.
MQTT example: Now fetching the PUBACK and waiting for the publish
notification.
MQTT example: Got a PUBLISH for topic cheriot-book-example:
Cheriots of fire!
MQTT example: Got an ACK for packet 0x2
```

The demo will then wait for four more messages on the same topic. If you happen to run this demo at the same time as other people, you might see them. Alternatively, if you install the command-line tools that come with Mosquitto, you can send a message from the command line:

```
49 void __cheriot_callback
50 publishCallback(const char *topicName,
51                 size_t       topicNameLength,
52                 const void *payload,
53                 size_t       payloadLength)
54 {
55   Debug::log(
56     "Got a PUBLISH for topic {}: {}",
57     std::string_view{topicName, topicNameLength},
58     std::string_view{static_cast<const char *>(payload),
59                      payloadLength});
60   publishReceived++;
61 }
```

LISTING 101. Callback for receiving published MQTT messages.
[from: examples/mqtt/mqtt.cc]

```
$ mosquitto_pub -h test.mosquitto.org
-t cheriot-book-example
-m 'My name is David'
```
This will then show up as:

MQTT example: Got a PUBLISH for topic cheriot-book-example: My name
is David

Don't put anything secret in the message, it will go to anyone running this
demo or anyone observing the public test server.

Finally, the demo disconnects. This is often unnecessary. Most IoT devices
will simply remain connected for their entire operation. They will explicitly
reconnect if the connection drops but never disconnect explicitly.

```
226   ret = mqtt_disconnect(
227     &t, STATIC_SEALED_VALUE(mqttTestMalloc), handle);
228   Debug::Assert(
229     ret == 0, "Failed to disconnect, error {}.", ret);
```

LISTING 102. Gracefully disconnecting from an MQTT server.
[from: examples/mqtt/mqtt.cc]

This function gracefully disconnects, allowing the server to clean up all
state associated with the current connection. It can fail, for example by running out of memory to hold the disconnection messages.

11.7. Enforcing network access policies

The network stack comes with a network_stack.rego file that provides
helpers for inspecting the state of the network stack. You pass this as an
argument to the --module (or -m) flag for cheriot-audit. For the rest of this

section, we'll use cheriot-audit to inspect and audit the Section 11.6 example. From the examples/mqtt directory, you will need to run a command like this:

```
$ cheriot-audit -m path/to/network-stack/network_stack.rego \
 -b path/to/sdk/boards/sonata.json \
 -j build/cheriot/cheriot/release/mqtt.json \
 -q {query}
```

This assumes that cheriot-audit is in your path. If it is not, provide the full path, for example /cheriot-tools/bin/cheriot-audit in the dev container. The first two arguments need to be paths to wherever the network stack and CHERIoT RTOS sources are located. The -j flag should be copied as-is, this finds the JSON file that the linker created with the audit report for the firmware image. Finally, you will provide a query for the -q, which will be different as you work through the examples.

If you want to actually read the JSON output, you will find that piping it to jq is helpful, which will pretty-print (and colour) the output.

 If you're copying the Rego queries to the command line, make sure that you quote them. Placing the query text in single quotes should work for all of the examples in this section.

Let's start with a query that invokes one of the more complex rules. This will find every software-defined capability in the firmware image that is sealed with the type for connection capabilities, and then decodes them into JSON objects. Try this query:

```
data.network_stack.all_connection_capabilities
```

You should see the following JSON as the result:

```
[
  {
    "capability": {
      "connection_type": "UDP",
      "host": "pool.ntp.org",
      "port": 123
    },
    "owner": "SNTP"
  },
  {
    "capability": {
      "connection_type": "TCP",
      "host": "test.mosquitto.org",
      "port": 8883
    },
    "owner": "mqtt_example"
  }
]
```

This tells you that there are two compartments that can make sockets. The MQTT example compartment can make a TCP connection to the Mosquitto test server on port 8883. The SNTP compartment can create a UDP socket and open a firewall rule that allows it to communicate with the public NTP pool on the well-known NTP port. TCP is connection-oriented so the network stack implicitly opens firewall rules on connection. UDP is connectionless so there are explicit APIs for opening firewall rules that allow a UDP host to communicate with explicit peers. The connection capabilities are similar in both cases but their use is different.

Remember that capabilities can be delegated. The MQTT example compartment does not open a socket directly, it is passing this capability to the MQTT compartment, which passes it to the TLS compartment, which then passes it to the network API compartment to access the socket. You can validate this with another query:

```
data.compartment.compartments_calling_export_matching("NetAPI",
`network_socket_connect_tcp(.*`)
```

Rego uses double quotes for normal strings. These follow similar escaping rules to C so, for example, "\t" is a string containing a tab character. You can avoid this processing by using backticks to designate a *raw string*. The Rego raw `\t` is a string containing a backslash and the letter 't'. It's common to use raw strings when constructing regular expressions to avoid needing to escape backslashes.

The report contains the mangled name of the export, which includes the types. This query uses a regular expression to match anything with the function name followed by an open bracket, so will catch any overload of the function (this function has no overloads but specifying all of the arguments is tedious). The output should look like this:

```
[
  "TLS"
]
```

The only compartment that creates TCP connections is the TLS compartment. This is interesting but not very useful.

The policy that we actually want is that no unencrypted data leaves the device. The way to express that is that nothing sends data over a socket except via the TLS compartment. This query is very similar to the last one:

```
data.compartment.compartments_calling_export_matching(
 "TCPIP",
 `network_socket_send(.*`)
```
And, again, tells you that only the TLS compartment is sending data:
```
[
  "TLS"
]
```
If you remember the result of the first query, this might be a surprise. Didn't the SNTP compartment also have a capability that allows it to connect to the network? SNTP doesn't run over TLS, so what's happening here?

You don't send UDP data with network_socket_send, you send it with network_socket_send_to. This requires another variant of the same query:
```
data.compartment.compartments_calling_export_matching(
 "TCPIP",
 "network_socket_send_to.*")
```
And now that we see that the only compartment sending data over UDP is the SNTP compartment:
```
[
  "SNTP"
]
```
Now we can think about ways that a compartment might be able to exfiltrate data with this. First, let's see what this compartment exports:

```
input.compartments.SNTP.exports
```
This compartment exports a single symbol, which takes a single Timeout argument:
```
[
  {
    "export_symbol": "__export_SNTP__Z11sntp_updateP7Timeout",
    "exported": false,
    "interrupt_status": "enabled",
    "kind": "Function",
    "register_arguments": 1,
    "start_offset": 208
  }
]
```
This could potentially leak data via the timeout. If you are concerned about this, you can wrap the calls to this function in another compartment and audit the source of that.

There's another way that you might leak data to the SNTP compartment: via pre-shared objects. You can ask if the SNTP compartment has access to any pre-shared objects with the following query:
```
data.compartment.shared_object_imports_for_compartment(
 input.compartments.SNTP)
```
This tells you that, yes, it does:

```
[
  {
    "kind": "SharedObject",
    "length": 24,
    "permits_load": true,
    "permits_load_mutable": false,
    "permits_load_store_capabilities": false,
    "permits_store": true,
    "shared_object": "sntp_time_at_last_sync",
    "start": 1237648
  }
]
```

This can't contain capabilities, but it is readable so if another compartment has write access to this object then it could communicate data to the SNTP compartment. We can check that with an allow-list query:

```
data.compartment.shared_object_writeable_allow_list(
  "sntp_time_at_last_sync",
  {"SNTP"})
```

This takes the name of a shared object as the first argument and a set of compartments that may hold writeable capabilities to it as the second. Unlike the prior queries, this does not expand to a complex JSON response, it is a single JSON value: true.

This is one of the checks performed by the valid rule in the network_stack package. This takes the network interface as its argument. On Sonata, the Ethernet device is accessed via the second SPI channel. You can check the integrity of the network stack with the following query:

```
data.network_stack.valid(spi2)
```

Again, this should simply evaluate to true. You can use this, along with the other things that you've seen in this section, to build a policy for this example. The start is shown in Listing 103. This is the head of a Rego rule that is parameterised on the device name and forwards to the network stack's validity rule. The network stack checks access for the shared object.

```
8 # Rule for defining
9 valid(ethernetDevice) {
10   # Check the integrity of the network stack
11   data.network_stack.valid(ethernetDevice)
12
```

LISTING 103. The start of the Rego policy for the MQTT example.
[from: examples/mqtt/mqtt.rego]

Next, the policy checks that there are exactly two connection capabilities and that they are the two that we expect. This is shown in Listing 104. The first

check uses the count operator to ensure that the length of the array containing all capabilities is two. The next two checks are more interesting because
they use the fact that Rego expressions include JSON. Each of these starts with
a JSON object literal for the capability that we expect to find (the one that
we saw earlier using cheriot-audit for introspection) and then uses the in
operator to check that this object is part of the array.

JSON is tree-structured data with a small number of primitive types so it is
easy to do exact equality comparisons on arbitrary JSON data. The in operator
uses this to operate over a collection (set, array, or object) and return whether
the collection contains the requested value. This is not string comparison.
The indentation in this example is purely for readability.

```
15
16   # Check that only the authorised set of remote hosts are
17   # allowed
18   count(data.network_stack.all_connection_capabilities) == 2
19
20   {
21     "capability": {
22       "connection_type": "UDP",
23       "host": "pool.ntp.org",
24       "port": 123
25     },
26     "owner": "SNTP"
27   } in data.network_stack.all_connection_capabilities
28
29   {
30     "capability": {
31       "connection_type": "TCP",
32       "host": "test.mosquitto.org",
33       "port": 8883
34     },
35     "owner": "mqtt_example"
36   } in data.network_stack.all_connection_capabilities
37
```

LISTING 104. Rego rules for restricting output in the MQTT example.
[from: examples/mqtt/mqtt.rego]

Finally, in Listing 105 the rule contains checks for the property that you
saw earlier: no unencrypted data can leave the device. This is implemented
with two allow-list rules, which pass only if the set of allowed compartments
contains every compartment that can call the specified set of entry points.

These are all in the mqtt.rego file in the example so you can add -m mqt-
t.rego to your cheriot-audit command line to use them. Now, you can sim-

```
39
40   # Restrict which compartments can send data
41   data.compartment.compartment_call_allow_list(
42     "TCPIP",
43     `network_socket_send\(.*`,
44     { "TLS" })
45   data.compartment.compartment_call_allow_list(
46     "TCPIP",
47     `network_socket_send_to\(.*`,
48     { "SNTP" })
49
```

LISTING 105. Rego rules to ensure that no data leaves the device unencrypted for the MQTT example. [from: examples/mqtt/mqtt.rego]

ply run `data.mqtt.valid(spi2)` (or `data.mqtt.valid(kunyan_ethernet)`, if you're using the Arty A7 builds) to check that the firmware image that you've built from this example complies with the policy.

If you write a similar policy for your real firmware and incorporate it into your code-signing flow then you can ensure that everything running on your device has the properties that we've described. If a developer accidentally leaves an unencrypted debug channel enabled in a release build, for example, then the policy check will fail. Similarly, if someone adds integration with another cloud service, you will see the checks fail and need to update the policy to make sure that it matches your new security goals.

11.8. Understanding TCP/IP-stack reset

CHERIoT provides a lot of out-of-the-box security guarantees simply by re-compiling code. The FreeRTOS+TCP codebase was audited in 2019 and the auditors found ten vulnerabilities. Of these, eight were memory-safety bugs that could either allow arbitrary-code execution or information disclosure. One was a division by zero, which could cause a trap. The remaining one was a failure to properly implement DNS, which could allow DNS cache poisoning.

All of these are mitigated by the compartmentalisation model in the CHERIoT network stack. The DNS attack may still be possible, but very hard to exploit. The vulnerability was that DNS responses were processed even if they did not accompany a query so sending a DNS response to the device would cause it to add the entry to its cache and then not do the DNS query when it was requested. The CHERIoT firewall drops in-bound DNS packets except when a DNS request is known to be in flight, so attempting to send the response to the device early would simply be ignored. An attacker would have needed to time the attack for when a DNS response was in flight. An attacker who can observe DNS requests leave the device and send packets in response can simply lie in the DNS response (unless DNSSEC is being used) and could achieve the same result on any system even without the bug. Alternatively, an attacker could flood the device with responses and hope that theirs arrived first. This would be likely to succeed but would show up as unusual traffic on any network with some monitoring.

The memory-safety bugs would all have the same impact as the division-by-zero error. They would cause the hardware to raise a trap, which would then crash the TCP/IP compartment.

Crashing is usually better than allowing an attacker to gain control of a device, but it's far from ideal. Crashing a compartment is somewhat better because it allows other functionality to keep working. For an IoT device, the Internet bit may be a core part of the functionality. Fortunately, CHERIoT compartmentalisation provides two benefits:

- The fault happens before anything can corrupt memory outside objects that it has access to.
- The blast radius is limited to the compartment boundary and things that are explicitly shared.

This combination means that it's possible to handle the error and gracefully recover. Recovery is complicated in a TCP/IP stack because it is multi-threaded. A crash may happen in the thread where the firewall provides the network stack with new packets. It may happen in the thread that handles TCP/IP retransmissions. It may also happen in any thread that another compartment uses to call network-stack functions. When a crash occurs, the first thing that the error handler needs to do is ensure that all of the threads rendezvous.

The socket structures that the TCP/IP compartment allocates and exposes via sealed capabilities are added to a linked list when they're created. When a crash occurs, the error handler walks this list and places the locks in destruction mode. In destruction mode, all threads waiting on a lock will wake and fail to acquire the lock. This forces any threads that were waiting for the socket lock to return failure.

Next, the error handler does the same to global locks and begins freeing memory. This can cause other threads to crash. That's fine because they will just enter their error handlers as well. The error handlers will check a global variable that tracks the reset state machine to determine whether they need to do anything or just exit.

When a user calls into the TCP/IP compartment, the API functions increment a counter of the number of threads that are present. This is then decremented in the error handler, or if they gracefully exit. When it reaches zero, the error handler knows that reset is finished.

Other threads may allocate memory during the shutdown process, so the error handler will call `heap_free_all` several times during the shutdown process.

Once everything is deallocated, the error handler increments an epoch counter. This is a 64-bit counter (so it will never overflow in the plausible lifetime of the device).

Every socket structure contains a copy of the epoch counter from when it was created. If a socket is not currently being used, it will have been removed from the list, but the memory won't have been freed because memory is allocated with the caller's quota and not the network stack's. The next time the socket is used, the send or receive function will compare the epoch of the socket to the current epoch of the TCP/IP stack. If they differ then the socket belonged to a previous incarnation of the TCP/IP stack. The function will simply report that the connection dropped. This can happen asynchronously, after reset.

Shutting down the TCP/IP stack is the difficult part, but not the part that is useful to users. The next step is to restart it. First, the error handler resets all of the global variables to their initial states (except the epoch). Next, it resumes the IP thread from its initial state and reruns initialisation. Most of the time is spent waiting for a DHCP lease, the rest of the reset happens very quickly.

If you want to test this, you can use the `network_inject_fault` function. This is not compiled in by default, you must add `--network-inject-faults=y` to your xmake `config` line. When you call this function, it sets a flag so that the next incoming packet will have incorrect bounds applied. This will cause the TCP/IP stack to crash somewhere.

From your perspective, you should simply see a connection-dropped error. If you've written robust networking code, you're handling this anyway. Networks are intrinsically unreliable and will sometimes fail for reasons beyond your control. When this happens, you need to reconnect.

The TCP/IP compartment crashing is no different; it will appear as if the connection dropped. If DHCP is taking its usual amount of time, attempting to reconnect may fail for a second or two, and will then succeed.

Documentation for the `network_inject_fault` function

```
void network_inject_fault( )
```

Inject a memory-safety bug into the network stack.

This is disabled unless compiled with the `network-inject-faults` option.

The failure will be propagated through any of the other compartments that you're using from the network stack. For example, if you're using MQTT, the TLS compartment will have a send or receive fail. It will then report that the TLS session has been disconnected to the MQTT compartment. This, in turn, will report to you that the MQTT connection has dropped the next time you call publish, subscribe, or run functions.

Try modifying the MQTT example to handle reconnection if any of the later functions report disconnection. Remember that MQTT supports reconnection (as opposed to connection) to resume an existing connection if the network went away. Change the timeout for one of the `mqtt_run` calls and read a switch or UART to determine when to call `network_inject_fault`.

You should be able to make the network stack crash repeatedly without more than intermittent disconnection.

For a more complete example, look at the Hugh the Lightbulb[3] demo. This is a demo that runs on Sonata and uses an Android app to control the multi-colour LED on the Sonata board via MQTT. It also uses the monochrome LEDs to show the network connection state, so you can see each of the stages in the system:

1. The system has started.
2. The network stack is initialised.
3. The clock is synchronised with NTP time.
4. The connection to the MQTT server is established.
5. The MQTT subscription to the topic for the controller is registered.

If you flip the rightmost DIP switch, it will trigger a crash. The LCD shows a CPU usage graph at the top and a heap-memory usage graph at the bottom, as you see in Figure 7. You'll see a sharp drop in heap usage as all of the TCP/IP state is freed (and then TLS and MQTT state is freed as their respective

3. https://github.com/CHERIoT-Platform/cheriot-demos/tree/main/HughTheLightbulb

compartments see the failure). Then you'll see a short pause as the TCP/IP stack recovers its DHCP lease. Next, you'll see a burst of 100% CPU usage as the TLS session is reestablished.

The whole reset process takes a few seconds, most of which is either waiting for DHCP or reestablishing the TLS connection. During this time, all of the other demo functionality (updating the LCD display and the other LEDs) works fine. The failure is contained to the compartment with the bug and the reset means that other code can continue to be oblivious to this failure.

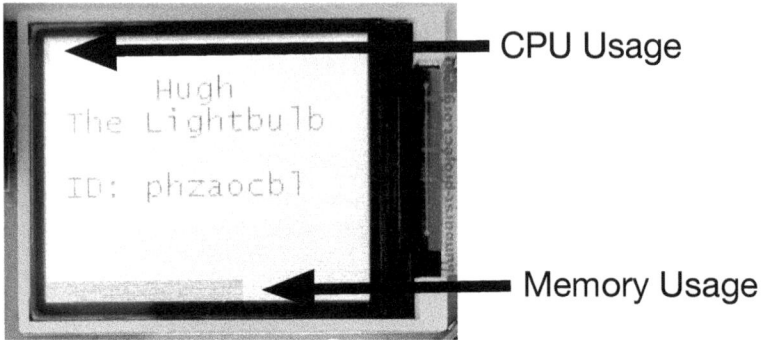

CPU Usage

Memory Usage

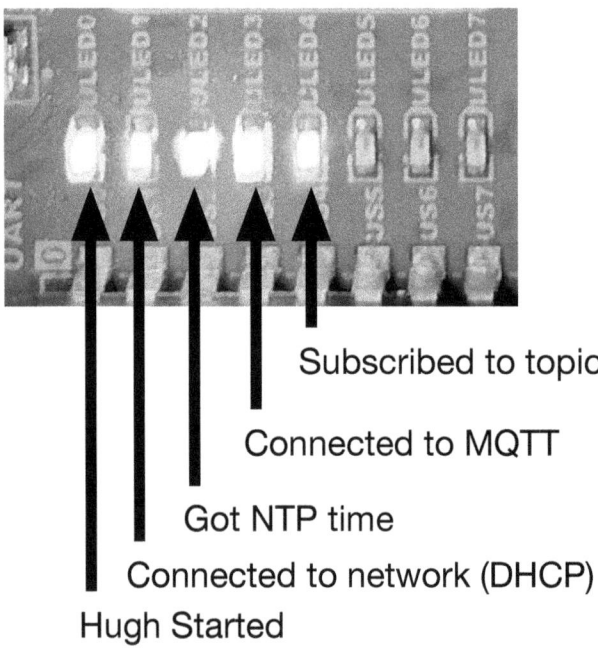

Subscribed to topic

Connected to MQTT

Got NTP time

Connected to network (DHCP)

Hugh Started

FIGURE 7. The Sonata LEDs and LCD display running the Hugh the Lightbuld demo.

Chapter 12.
Adding a new board

CHERIoT RTOS uses a JSON file to describe the target. At first glance, this looks similar to a flattened device tree (FDT) source file. Both contain a layout of memory and locations of devices but the CHERIoT RTOS board description file also contains a lot of information that is useful only at build time, such as the locations of header files and preprocessor definitions for the platform.

When you want to create a board support package (BSP) for a new CHERIoT configuration, this is the first place to start. The CHERIoT RTOS build system allows board description files to be specified either as names in the sdk/boards directory or as file paths. Anything that has been contributed to the CHERIoT RTOS repository will use the former mechanism, anything distributed separately will use the latter.

12.1. Specifying memory layout

CHERIoT RTOS has to differentiate between three kinds of memory in the configuration:

- Code and read-only global data, which cannot contain pointers to revokable heap memory.
- Globals and stacks, which may contain pointers to revokable heap memory.
- The heap, which may contain pointers to revokable heap memory and may itself be revoked.

The allocator is given a capability to the revocation bitmap covering the last range. The revoker must be configured to include (at least) the latter two in its scans. The first category is safe to ignore.

 A future version of CHERIoT RTOS may differentiate between code (and non-capability read-only data) and read-only data so that the former can be run from memory that does not support tags and the latter from tag-carrying memory.

The memory layout will put code then globals into memory and then the heap afterwards. In most systems, there is more code than heap and so, to reduce costs, not all memory needs to support tags.

Our security guarantees for the shared heap depend on the mechanism that allows the allocator to mark memory as quarantined. Any pointer to memory in this region is subject to a check (by the hardware) on load: if it points to deallocated memory, it will be invalidated on load. This mechanism is necessary only for memory that can be reused by different trust domains during a single boot. Memory used to hold globals and code does not require it so an implementation may save some hardware and power costs by supporting these temporal safety features for only a subset of memory. As such, we require a range of memory that is used for static code and data ('instruction memory') that is not required to support this mechanism and an additional range that *must* support this for use as the shared heap ('heap memory'). Implementations may choose not to make this separation and provide a single memory region. At some point, we expect to further separate the mutable and immutable portions of instruction memory so that we can support execute in place (XIP).

Instruction memory is described by the `instruction_memory` property. This must be an object with a `start` and `end` property, each of which is an address.

The region available for the heap is described in the `heap` property. This must describe the region over which the load filter is defined. If its `start` property is omitted, then it is assumed to start in the same place as instruction memory.

The Sail board description has a simple layout:

```
"instruction_memory": {
    "start": 0x80000000,
    "end": 0x80040000
},
"heap": {
    "end": 0x80040000
},
```

This starts instruction memory at the default RISC-V memory address and has a single 256 KiB region that is used for both kinds of memory.

12.2. Exposing MMIO Devices

Each memory-mapped I/O device is listed as an object within the `devices` field. The name of the field is the name of the device and must be an object that contains a `start` and either a `length` or `end` property that, between them, describe the memory range for the device. Software can then use the `MMIO_CAPABILITY` macro with the name of the device to get a capability to that device's MMIO range and can use `#if DEVICE_EXISTS(device_name)` to conditionally compile code if that device exists.

The Sail model is very simple and provides only three devices:

```
"devices": {
    "clint": {
        "start": 0x2000000,
        "length": 0x10000
    },
    "uart": {
        "start": 0x10000000,
        "end":   0x10000100
    },
    "shadow" : {
        "start" : 0x83000000,
        "end"   : 0x83001000
    }
},
```

This describes the core-local interrupt controller (clint), a UART, and the shadow memory used for the temporal safety mechanism (shadow). The UART, for example, is referred to in source using MMIO_CAPABILITY(struct Uart, uart), which evaluates to a volatile struct Uart *, giving a capability to this device.

12.3. Defining interrupts

External interrupts should be defined in an array in the interrupts property. Each element has a name, a number and a priority. The name is used to refer to this in software and must be a valid C identifier. The number is the interrupt number. The priority is the priority with which this interrupt will be configured in the interrupt controller.

Interrupts may optionally have an edge_triggered property (if this is omitted, it is assumed to be false). If this exists and is set to true then the interrupt is assumed to fire when a condition first holds, rather than to remain raised as long as a condition holds. Interrupts that are edge triggered are automatically completed by the scheduler; they do not require a call to interrupt_complete.

12.4. Controlling hardware features

Some properties define base parts of hardware support. The revoker property is either absent (no temporal safety support), "software" (revocation is implemented via a software sweep) or "hardware" (there is a hardware revoker). We expect this to be "hardware" on all real implementations. The software revoker exists primarily for the Sail model and the no temporal safety mode only for benchmarking the overhead of revocation.

If the stack_high_water_mark property is set to true, then we assume the CPU provides CSRs for tracking stack usage. This property is primarily present for benchmarking as all of our targets currently implement this feature.

12.5. Specifying clock speeds

The clock rate is configured by two properties. The timer_hz field is the number of timer increments per second, typically the clock speed of the chip (the RISC-V timer is defined in terms of cycles). The tickrate_hz specifies how many scheduler ticks should happen per second. Ticks were discussed in Section 6.3, they are the minimum unit of scheduling. Threads sleep integer numbers of ticks. A larger duration here means that a short sleep becomes longer, a smaller duration means that the scheduler will be invoked more often. If you have two threads at the same priority then they will be preempted at this frequency, so a 1,000 Hz tick rate will mean that each runs for 1ms. That means that the scheduler will run (at least) once every 100,000 cycles on a 100 MHz core. With a 100 Hz tick rate, the scheduler will run once every million cycles.

Higher tick rates will (usually) give lower latency, lower tick rates will (usually) give higher throughput.

 It is possible to set the tickrate_hz to such a high value that ticks are shorter than the context-switch time. This will cause the timer to fire as soon as a new thread starts running, which will prevent forward progress. This is easy to spot because multithreaded firmware images will fail to run on the board. If you see no output from multithreaded firmwares, try reducing this number. For most uses, 100 is a sensible number. This will make one tick take 10 ms. If you require higher precision for sleeping (or have high clock speeds) you may want something a bit higher.

12.6. Supporting conditional compilation

The defines property specifies any pre-defined macros that should be set when building for this board. The driver_includes property contains an array (in priority order) of include directories that should be added for this target. Each of the paths in driver_includes is, by default, relative to the location of the board file (which allows the board file and drivers to be distributed together). Optionally, it may include the string $(sdk), which will be replaced by the full path of the SDK directory. For example, `"$(sdk)/in-clude/platform/generic-riscv"` will expand to the generic RISC-V directory in the SDK.

The driver headers use `#include_next` to include more generic files so it is important to list the directories containing your overrides first.

12.7. Enabling simulation support

The RTOS has some special behaviour for simulation platforms. If you implement a simulation-exit driver (or rely on the generic RISC-V one) in a `platform-simulation_exit.hh` file, the RTOS will exit the simulator after the last thread has exited.

The short-spin APIs also behave differently in simulation, where time may not be real. These treat short sleeps as elapsing immediately.

The `fail-simulator-on-error.h` header includes an error handler that is useful for debugging. It logs an error and will exit the simulator (if run in a simulator) when a CHERI trap occurs. This is useful for trying to determine where code is failing if you do not have access to a debugger.

These behaviours are all controlled by the `simulation` property. If `simulation` is set to `true` then this board is assumed to be a simulation platform, opting into these behaviours.

12.8. Running with xmake run

Most of the examples in this book were run with the `xmake run` command. This command needs to know how to invoke the simulator or deploy to the device.

In addition, the `run_command` property can be the name of a program (or script) that can either simulate the firmware image or deploy it to a real target. This will be run from the build directory and will be passed the absolute path of the firmware image when `xmake run` is used. The build system will look for the simulator in the SDK directory and, failing that, in the path. Exact paths can be provided by using `$sdk` or `$board` in the name of the simulator. These will be expanded to the full path of the SDK or the directory containing the board description file, respectively.

12.9. Creating board variants

Some boards are minor variations on others. For example, the Sonata simulator is identical to the Sonata FPGA platform, but has a different run command.

Copying the original board file and creating a variation works, but incurs a maintenance burden (unless both are generated by some external system). The build system provides built-in support for this use case. Rather than providing a .json file for the board, you provide a .patch file. This is a JSON document that uses JSON Patch[1] to describe a set of changes.

This file must have two top-level nodes. The base node contains the board to modify. This can be another patch file or a .json file. The patch node contains an array of JSON Patch directives that are executed in sequence.

This is the entirety of the patch file for the Sonata simulator:

```
{
  "base": "sonata-prerelease",
  "patch": [
    {
      "op": "replace",
      "path": "/simulation",
      "value": true
    },
    {
      "op": "replace",
      "path": "/run_command",
      "value": "${sdk}/../scripts/run-sonata-sim.sh"
    }
  ]
}
```

This starts with the Sonata pre-release board file (which tracks the current in-development version of the Sonata FPGA design) and applies two changes. The first sets the simulation property to true, the second replaces the run command with one that invokes the simulator instead of copying the code to the FPGA.

---

1. https://jsonpatch.com

Chapter 13.
Porting from bare metal

If you have existing code that runs happily on bare metal, you may consider CHERIoT for a variety of reasons, for example:

- You want to add network connectivity and need to isolate network communication.
- You are consolidating multiple functions from different microcontrollers onto a single device.
- You really love memory safety.

These reasons are often some variation on needing to do two or more things in different security contexts on a single device. This means that your workloads are now going to run with their privileges reduced enough that they cannot interfere (beyond permitted amounts) with each other.

13.1. Replacing a real-time control loop

Control systems often run with a single loop that polls for some input, manages a (potentially very complex) state machine, and sets some output state. You can get precisely this model by running code in CHERIoT RTOS with interrupts disabled.

A function that has the [[cheriot::interrupt_state(disabled)]] attribute will run with interrupts disabled and has exclusive use of the core until it yields. You can add this attribute to the entry point for the thread running your control loop to start with interrupts disabled.

The scheduler will always schedule the highest-priority runnable thread (or round-robin schedule threads if more than one is runnable at the same priority). If your thread is the highest priority, it won't be preempted, but interrupts may still fire and cause the scheduler to perform some bookkeeping work. Disabling interrupts and running with the highest priority ensures that a thread is scheduled first and continues to run for as long as it wants to.

This is a direct replacement of a real-time control loop, but somewhat misses the point of running an RTOS: no other threads will run.

13.2. Yielding

If it makes sense for a control loop to run on a multitasking operating system, there will be times when it is able to safely yield. Just yielding from a high-priority thread is not normally sufficient because it remains the highest-priority thread and so will be the next to run.

Chapter 6 discusses the various ways for a thread to block. This can be as simple as sleeping. If a realtime thread sleeps for one tick then another thread can run, but the next timer interrupt will return control to the real-time thread (unless another thread is running with interrupts disabled - this can be prevented via a policy on the linker report).

More commonly, a realtime control loop will want to block until some external event occurs and triggers an interrupt. Section 9.6 describes how to wait for an interrupt to fire.

When an interrupt fires, the thread waiting for it will become runnable and, if it is higher priority than any other thread, will be scheduled immediately. If the code that yielded had interrupts disabled then interrupts will be disabled once again on return.

13.3. Replacing direct device access

In bare-metal code for non-CHERI systems, it is common to construct pointers to memory-mapped devices by either casting an integer to a pointer or by creating a global that is placed in the correct location via a linker script.

Neither of these works in the CHERIoT model. Instead, you must use the macros described in Section 9.4 to construct valid capabilities to devices. This mechanism allows auditing, with a link-time record of which compartments can access each device.

If your code is using volatile pointers to access device memory then you should be able to port your code to CHERIoT RTOS by simply changing how you first construct those pointers.

13.4. Replacing interrupt service routines

Some bare-metal environments have special attributes for declaring inter-rupt-service routines and associating them with different channels. As discussed in Section 9.6, this kind of mechanism would violate the CHERIoT security model and is not provided. You can implement your own dispatcher in a CHERIoT environment by waiting on multiple interrupts with the multi-waiter APIs (see Section 6.12) and then calling the interrupt routines yourself.

If interrupts are marked as edge-triggered in the board description then they are implicitly acknowledged in the interrupt controller by the scheduler. If not, then you must explicitly acknowledge them before they can fire again. This model is closer to the implicit masking during an ISR.

Simply waiting for multiple interrupts and handling them as they arrive does not allow interrupt handlers to be preempted. You can wait for different-priority interrupts on different-priority threads, but the threads that handle the lower-priority interrupts must run with interrupts enabled to allow preemption.

Chapter 14.
Porting from FreeRTOS

FreeRTOS is an established real-time operating system with a large deployed base. It runs on tiny microcontrollers up to large systems with MMU-based isolation. The CHERIoT platform aims to provide, on small microcontrollers, stronger security guarantees than FreeRTOS is able to provide on large systems.

This chapter describes how several concepts in FreeRTOS map to equivalents in CHERIoT RTOS.

The FreeRTOS-Compat directory in include contains a set of headers (including FreeRTOS.h) that expose FreeRTOS-compatible wrappers around various CHERIoT RTOS services. These allow you to port existing FreeRTOS code to CHERIoT RTOS with minimal changes. These are not complete, but are expected to evolve over time.

14.1. Contrasting design philosophies

FreeRTOS is primarily designed around a model with a single trust domain. The initial targets did not provide any memory protection. You, the author of an embedded system, were assumed to have control over all components that you're integrating. Later, MPU support was added, building on top of the task model. When using an MPU, some tasks can be marked as unprivileged. These have access to their own stack and up to three memory regions, which must be configured explicitly.

Even when an MPU exists, the trust model is limited to hierarchical trust. The system integrator may mark certain tasks as unprivileged, but individual tasks cannot define more complex trust relationships. Memory safety is limited to the granularity of an MPU region. For example, the scheduler can expose message queues as privileged functions, which protects the queue's internal state from being tampered with by untrusted tasks, but may still overwrite the bounds of an object in an untrusted task if passed a pointer to an object that is not large enough to store a complete message.

As a fundamental design principle, FreeRTOS aims to run on many different platforms and provide portable abstractions. This limits the security abstractions that are possible to implement.

In contrast, the CHERIoT platform was created as a whole-system hardware-software co-design project. The hardware is required to provide properties that the software stack can use to build security policies. The core design of CHERIoT is motivated by a world in which a developer of an embedded system may not have full control over components provided by third parties, yet must integrate them. It is intended to provide auditing support that allows the integrator to make security claims even when integrating binary-only components.

This difference manifests most obviously in the fact that FreeRTOS provides imperative APIs for a number of things that CHERIoT RTOS prefers to create via declarative descriptions. Auditing a declarative description is easier than auditing arbitrary Turing-complete imperative code calling privileged APIs.

FreeRTOS starts from a position of sharing by default and has added MPU support to provide isolation. CHERIoT RTOS starts from a default position of isolation and provides object-granularity sharing.

FreeRTOS was designed to support adding features to systems that did not originally use any kind of OS. This is apparent, for example, in how the programmer interacts with the scheduler. The scheduler is just another service that the system integrator may choose to use. User code chooses when the scheduler starts and may choose to stop it for arbitrary periods.

In contrast, CHERIoT RTOS provides a model more familiar to users of desktop or server systems. The core parts of the RTOS are always available and provide strong isolation guarantees.

14.2. Replacing tasks with threads and compartments

The FreeRTOS task abstraction is similar to the traditional UNIX process abstraction. A task owns a thread and is independently scheduled. It is intended to be isolated from the rest of the system, though on systems without memory protection it has access to everything in the address space.

A task in FreeRTOS is roughly the equivalent of a combination of a thread and a compartment in CHERIoT RTOS. The compartment defines the code and global data associated with the task. The thread provides the stack and allows the task to be created.

CHERIoT RTOS threads have one key limitation in comparison to FreeR-TOS tasks: They cannot be dynamically created. The security model requires a static guarantee that no memory moves between being stack memory (which is permitted to hold non-global capabilities) and non-stack (global or heap) memory. The trusted stack memory and save area memory should never be visible outside of the switcher. Without these static properties, the allocator would be in the TCB for thread and compartment isolation.

As such, there is no equivalent of the FreeRTOS xTaskCreate function. Threads (and their associated stacks and trusted stacks) must be described up front in the build system (see Section 6.1). In some cases, dynamically created threads can be replaced with thread pools, in the same way that coroutines can.

The compatibility layer exposes xTaskCreate and xTaskCreateStatic as macros that generate a warning and evaluate to an invalid thread handle. This is intended to ease porting of code that conditionally uses these APIs.

The best way to replace dynamic thread creation is usually to create the threads declaratively in the build system. If they need to be started only after a certain event, then you can wait on a futex (see Section 6.5) and notify that futex at the point where the original code called xTaskCreate.

14.3. Using thread pools to replace coroutines

The CHERIoT RTOS thread pool (see lib/thread_pool) allows a small number of threads to be reused. This provides a compartment that has two entry points. One is a thread entry point that sits and waits for messages from other threads, the other is exposed for calls by other compartments and sends a message to one of the threads in the pool.

This is most commonly used with C++ lambdas via the async wrapper in thread_pool.h:

```
async([]() {
// This runs in the caller's compartment but in another thread.
})
```

This can be used for cooperatively-scheduled work in a similar manner to stackless coroutines. Each task dispatched to a thread pool will run until completion on one of the threads allocated to the thread pool. When it returns, the thread-pool thread will block until another task is available in the queue.

Some of the use cases for dynamic FreeRTOS task creation can be implemented the same way. On memory-constrained systems, dynamic thread creation can easily exhaust memory for stacks so most systems that depend on dynamic thread creation do so at different phases of computation to allow the stack space to be reused. Pushing these as thread-pool tasks provides similar behaviour, with each task taking ownership of the (safely zeroed) stack after the previous one has finished.

The CHERIOT RTOS-provided thread pool is very simple. You may wish to implement something similar using it as an example, rather than using it as an off-the-shelf component.

14.4. Porting code that uses message buffers

The CHERIoT RTOS message queue APIs (see Section 6.10) are modelled after the FreeRTOS message queue. In most cases, there is a direct mapping between the FreeRTOS APIs and the CHERIoT RTOS ones, as shown in Table 4

FreeRTOS API	CHERIoT RTOS API
xQueueCreate	queue_create
vQueueDelete	free
xQueueReceive	queue_receive
xQueueSendToBack	queue_send
uxQueueMessagesWaiting	queue_items_remaining

TABLE 4. CHERIoT equivalents of FreeRTOS queue operations

The FreeRTOS-Compat/queue.h header provides wrappers that respect this mapping. The CHERIoT RTOS APIs provide some additional functionality that is not present in FreeRTOS so code that does not need to be maintained in both environments may benefit from being moved to the native APIs.

This mapping uses the *queue library*, which is intended for communication between threads in the same compartment. FreeRTOS code typically assumes a single trust domain so this is usually what you want when porting. In some cases, you will split multiple FreeRTOS components into separate compartments. In this case, you will most likely want to use the *queue compartment* (see Section 6.10), which isolates the queue state from callers.

For C++ code, the ring buffer in ring_buffer.hh may be more interesting. This provides a generic ring buffer that can be specialised with different locks on the producer and consumer end.

14.5. Porting code that uses event groups

As with message queues, the CHERIoT RTOS event queue API was modelled on that of FreeRTOS. As such, there is direct correspondence between the FreeRTOS APIs and the equivalent CHERIoT RTOS versions, shown in Table 5.

FreeRTOS API	CHERIoT RTOS API
xEventGroupCreate	eventgroup_create
vEventGroupDelete	eventgroup_destroy
xEventGroupWaitBits	eventgroup_wait
xEventGroupClearBits	eventgroup_clear
xEventGroupSetBits	eventgroup_set

TABLE 5. CHERIoT equivalents of FreeRTOS event group operations

The FreeRTOS-Compat/event_groups.h header performs this translation.

The FreeRTOS event queue structure provides a rich set of operations. In contrast, CHERIoT RTOS aims to provide a small set of core abstractions that can be assembled into complex systems. A lot of users of the event groups API could use simpler wrappers around a futex, rather than an event group.

14.6. Adopting CHERIoT RTOS locks

CHERIoT RTOS provides futexes as the building block for most locks. These can be used to build counting semaphores, ticket locks, mutexes, priority-inheriting mutexes, and so on. Several of these are implemented in the locks library and exposed via locks.h (and locks.hh for C++ wrappers).

The FreeRTOS-Compat/semphr.h exposes FreeRTOS-compatible wrappers for counting semaphores. In FreeRTOS, these are implemented as message queues with zero-sized messages. In CHERIoT RTOS, they are simply futexes that store a count. This means semaphore get and put operations are usually simple atomic operations. The scheduler is not involved unless a thread needs to block (the semaphore count is zero and a thread tries to do a semaphore-get operation) or needs to wake waiters (the semaphore value is increased from zero and there were waiting threads).

Unlike FreeRTOS, CHERIoT RTOS exposes different types for different locking primitives if they are incompatible. This catches some API misuse errors at compile time. For example, FreeRTOS uses `SemaphoreHandle_t` to represent semaphores and recursive mutexes. These must be created with different functions and then locked and unlocked with different functions, but creating something as a semaphore and then trying to lock it as a recursive mutex will compile. In contrast, CHERIoT RTOS exposes these as distinct types and will fail to compile if you try to pass a semaphore to, for example, `recursive-mutex_trylock`.

The `FreeRTOS-Compat/semphr.h` header provides wrappers for the various kinds of FreeRTOS semaphores and mutexes. These expose the FreeRTOS APIs and wrap all of the relevant CHERIoT RTOS types in a union with a discriminator. This adds a small amount of overhead for dynamic dispatch. Code that uses only one type of semaphore can avoid this. Each of the underlying types can be exposed by defining one of the following macros before including `FreeRTOS-Compat/semphr.h` (directly, or indirectly via `FreeRTOS.h`):

CHERIOT_FREERTOS_SEMAPHORE
Expose counting and binary semaphores.

CHERIOT_FREERTOS_MUTEX
Expose non-recursive (priority-inheriting) mutexes.

CHERIOT_FREERTOS_RECURSIVE_MUTEX
Expose recursive mutexes.

Enabling only the subset that you use (which can be done on a per-file basis) will reduce code size and improve performance.

14.7. Building software timers

FreeRTOS provides a timer callback API. This is implemented on top of existing functionality in the FreeRTOS kernel. CHERIoT RTOS does not yet provide such an API, but building one is fairly simple.

The structure of such a service is similar to that of the thread pool in `lib/thread_pool`, except that each callback has an associated timer. These should be added to a data structure that keeps them sorted. The thread that runs the callbacks should wait on a message queue, with the timeout set to the shortest time timer. If this wakes with timeout, it should invoke the first `__cheriot_-callback` callback function in its queue. If it wakes receiving a message, it should add the new callback into the set that it has ready.

There is no generic version of this in CHERIoT RTOS because it is impossible to implement securely in the general case for a system with mutual distrust. Callbacks may run for an unbounded amount of time (preventing others from firing) or untrusted code may allocate unbounded numbers of timers and exhaust memory. As such, it is generally better to build a bespoke mechanism for the specific requirements of a given workload.

14.8. Timing out blocking operations

FreeRTOS uses the combination of `vTaskSetTimeOutState` and `xTaskCheck-ForTimeOut` to implement timeouts. These are implemented in the FreeRTOS compatibility layer. In CHERIoT RTOS, these are subsumed by the `Timeout` structure, which contains both the elapsed and remaining number of ticks for a timeout.

The CHERIoT RTOS design is intended to be trivially composed. Most operations simply forward the timeout structure to a blocking operation in the scheduler (a sleep of a futex wait). They can query whether the timeout has expired without needing to query the scheduler, simply by checking whether the `remaining` field of the structure is zero.

14.9. Dynamically allocating memory

FreeRTOS provides a number of different heap implementations, not all of which are thread safe. In contrast, CHERIoT RTOS design assumes a safe, secure, shared heap. Various uses of statically pre-allocated memory in a FreeRTOS system can move to using the heap allocation mechanisms in CHERIoT RTOS, reducing total memory consumption.

FreeRTOS prior to 9.0 allocated kernel objects from a private heap. Later versions allow the user to provide memory. The latter approach has the benefit of accounting these objects to the caller, but the disadvantage of breaking encapsulation.

CHERIoT RTOS has an approach (described in Chapter 7) that combines the advantages of both. Rather than providing memory for creating objects such as message queues, multiwaiters, semaphores, and so on, the caller provides an *allocation capability*. This is a token that permits the callee to allocate memory on behalf of the caller. The scheduler is not able to allocate memory on its own behalf, it can allocate memory only when explicitly passed an allocation capability. It then uses the sealing mechanism to ensure that the caller cannot break encapsulation for scheduler-owned objects.

14.10. Disabling interrupts

FreeRTOS code often uses critical sections to disable interrupts. This may require some source-code modifications. Critical sections in FreeRTOS are used for two things:

- Atomicity
- Mutual exclusion

Disabling interrupts is the simplest way of guaranteeing both on a single-core system. FreeRTOS provides two APIs for critical sections: `taskENTER_CRITICAL` and `taskEXIT_CRITICAL`, which disable interrupts, and `vTaskSuspendAll` and `xTaskResumeAll`, which disable the scheduler. CHERIoT RTOS is designed to provide availability guarantees across mutually distrusting components and so does not permit either unbounded disabling of interrupts or turning the scheduler off. If mutual exclusion is the only requirement then you can implement these function as acquiring and releasing a lock that is private to your component. This is how they are implemented in the compatibility layer. They use distinct locks and these must be defined in your compartment, as shown below:

```
struct RecursiveMutexState __CriticalSectionFlagLock;
struct RecursiveMutexState __SuspendFlagLock;
```

A futex-based lock is very cheap to acquire in the uncontended case; it requires a single atomic compare-and-swap instruction. If the hardware doesn't support atomic operations then the compiler will replace the compare-and-swap instruction with a function call to a library routine that runs with interrupts disabled. If possible, this approach is preferred for two reasons. First, it ensures that your component's critical sections do not impede progress of higher-priority threads. Second, it removes a burden on auditing.

The second use case, atomicity with respect to the rest of the system, requires disabling interrupts. The CHERIoT platform requires a structured-programming model for disabling interrupts. Interrupt control can be done only at a function granularity. Hopefully, the code that runs with interrupts disabled is already a lexically scoped block. In C++, you can simply wrap this in a lambda and pass it to `CHERI::with_interrupts_disabled`. In C, you will need to factor it into a separate function.

For auditing, you may prefer to move the code that runs with interrupts disabled into a separate library. This lets you separately audit the precise code that is allowed to run with interrupts disabled, but modify the rest of your component without constraints.

14.11. Strengthening compartment boundaries for FreeRTOS components

Microsoft did an internal port of the FreeRTOS network stack and MQTT library. This was not part of the open-source release, but involved very little code change. Most of the porting effort was done via a FreeRTOS compatibility header, which provided wrappers around the CHERIoT RTOS inter-thread communication APIs to make them look like the FreeRTOS equivalents.

FreeRTOS assumes, by default, that all code and globals are shared unless explicitly protected by an MPU region. When porting FreeRTOS components, this assumption is broken unless they are in the same compartment. This is not normally a problem for an initial port, because components are cleanly encapsulated and do not directly modify the state of other components.

 This property does not hold on all RTOS implementations. For example, several ThreadX components directly manipulate the internal state of the scheduler, rather than acting via well-defined APIs.

Using compartments gives some defence in depth against accidental errors, but may not provide strong security guarantees. For example, the FreeRTOS TCP/IP stack provides a `FreeRTOS_socket` call that returns a pointer to a heap-allocated socket structure that encapsulates connection state. Simply compiling this in a CHERIoT compartment has a few limitations.

First, the structure is allocated out of the network stack's quota. This means that a caller can perform a denial of service by opening a lot of connections. Fixing this requires an API change to pass an allocation capability (and possibly a timeout) into the network-stack compartment so that it can allocate this space on behalf of the caller.

Second, the structure is unprotected. The caller can load and store via the returned pointer and so can corrupt connection state. This may allow it to leak the state of connections owned by other components or cause arbitrary failures.

Finally, there is no notion of access control. That might be fine: if you're allowing only one compartment to talk to the network stack then you don't need any kind of authorisation. For more complex uses, you may want to allow one component to talk to a command-and-control server and another component to talk to an update server. Neither of these components should be able to connect anywhere else, so you probably want to use the software capability model to define a static authorisation to make DNS lookups of a specific domain and then have that return a dynamic authorisation that allows connection to that host (or place both the lookup and connection behind a single interface).

This is more work than is necessary to simply make FreeRTOS code work in a CHERIoT system, but is desirable if you want to take advantage of the security properties that CHERIoT RTOS provides over and above what is possible in FreeRTOS.

www.ingramcontent.com/pod-product-compliance
Ingram Content Group UK Ltd.
Pitfield, Milton Keynes, MK11 3LW, UK
UKHW021042180425
457598UK00004B/5